Militant Competition

Militant groups often use violence, perversely, to gain attention and resources. In this book, the authors analyze how terrorist and rebel organizations compete with one another to secure funding and supporters. The authors develop a strategic model of competitive violence among militant groups and test the model's implications with statistical analysis and case studies. A series of model extensions allow the authors to incorporate the full range of strategic actors, focusing in particular on government efforts to counter and deter violence. The results indicate that the direct effects of competition are not as clear as they may seem, and interventions to alter competitive incentives may backfire if states are not careful. This is a timely contribution to a growing body of political economy research on militant group fragmentation, rivalry, fratricide and demonstrative violence.

Justin Conrad is Associate Professor of International Affairs at the University of Georgia and Director of the Center for International Trade and Security.

William Spaniel is Assistant Professor of Political Science at the University of Pittsburgh.

Militant Competition

*How Terrorists and Insurgents Advertise with
Violence and How They Can Be Stopped*

JUSTIN CONRAD

University of Georgia

WILLIAM SPANIEL

University of Pittsburgh

CAMBRIDGE
UNIVERSITY PRESS

CAMBRIDGE
UNIVERSITY PRESS

University Printing House, Cambridge CB2 8BS, United Kingdom

One Liberty Plaza, 20th Floor, New York, NY 10006, USA

477 Williamstown Road, Port Melbourne, VIC 3207, Australia

314–321, 3rd Floor, Plot 3, Splendor Forum, Jasola District Centre, New Delhi – 110025, India

103 Penang Road, #05-06/07, Visioncrest Commercial, Singapore 238467

Cambridge University Press is part of the University of Cambridge.

It furthers the University's mission by disseminating knowledge in the pursuit of education, learning, and research at the highest international levels of excellence.

www.cambridge.org
Information on this title: www.cambridge.org/9781108834186
DOI: 10.1017/9781108992275

First published 2021

A catalogue record for this publication is available from the British Library.

ISBN 978-1-108-83418-6 Hardback
ISBN 978-1-108-99453-8 Paperback

Contents

List of Tables		*page* vii
List of Figures		viii
Acknowledgments		ix
1	Introduction	1
	Our Argument in Brief	4
	The Broader Perspective on Outbidding	8
	Competitive Violence in Strategic Context	11
	Book Outline	14
2	A Formal Model of Outbidding	20
	Strategic Dimensions of Competitive Political Violence	22
	Building a Model of Political Violence	31
	Deeper Theoretical Concerns	41
	Conclusion	49
	Appendix	50
3	The Evidence	57
	Hypotheses and Research Design	58
	Analysis: Country Level	67
	Analysis: Group Level	71
	Insurgency in Northeast India	74
	Conclusion	87

4   Outbidding, Capacity, and Government Enforcement   90
    Enforcement and Recruitment   93
    The Model   97
    Hypothesis and Research Design   106
    Empirical Analysis   111
    Additional Evidence   116
    Conclusion   117
    Appendix   119

5   Outbidding as Deterrence: Endogenous Demands in the
    Shadow of Group Competition   125
    The Microfoundations of Grievances   129
    Modeling Endogenous Grievances   133
    Implications of Outbidding-as-Deterrence   145
    Conclusion   154
    Appendix   156

6   Cornering the Market: Counterterrorism in the Shadow of
    Group Formation   162
    Microfoundations of Counterterrorism Policies   168
    Modeling Entry into the Market for Violence   177
    Manipulating the Market   185
    Conclusion   204
    Appendix   206

7   Conclusion   222
    Competition Promotes Political Violence   222
    Interventions Require Careful Thought   224
    Implications for Future Research   226
    Implications for Policymakers   234
    A Final Word   238

Bibliography   239
Index   256

Tables

3.1   Group-level attacks.   *page* 65
3.2   DV: Total number of attacks.   68
4.1   Correlation matrix of key variables.   110
4.2   Competition, enforcement, and terrorist attacks.   112

Figures

1.1 Worldwide terrorist and rebel group distributions.   *page* 5
2.1 Equilibrium total violence and violence per group.   40
3.1 Terrorist groups and terrorist attacks.   62
3.2 Rebel groups and terrorist attacks.   64
3.3 Effects of increasing group numbers on annual attacks by country.   68
3.4 DV: Total number of attacks.   69
3.5 Multivariate results.   70
3.6 DV: Average group attacks.   71
3.7 Effects of increasing group numbers on annual attacks by group.   73
4.1 Distribution of citizen values and their entry decisions.   102
4.2 Equilibrium violence as a function of enforcement capacity.   105
4.3 Marginal effects of competition.   115
4.4 Illustration of the equilibrium implicit function.   121
5.1 Country years with four or more rebel groups and no attacks.   128
5.2 Cumulative probability distribution examples.   135
5.3 Equilibrium violence under Proposition 5.2.   140
6.1 Country-years with one terrorist group and more than twenty-five attacks.   163
6.2 The two-player extensive form game.   178
6.3 Substantive outcome of the game's equilibrium.   182
6.4 Violence as a function of market size.   188
6.5 Violence as a function of entry cost.   191
6.6 Violence as a function of the incumbent's marginal cost.   196
6.7 Violence for two levels of defensive efforts.   201

Acknowledgments

We would like to thank our colleagues whose feedback, collaborations, and insights helped shape this manuscript from the early stages. This includes, but is not limited to, Victor Asal, Peter Bils, Mia Bloom, Martha Crenshaw, Mark Fey, Page Fortna, Kate Cronin-Furman, Hein Goemans, Kevin Greene, Gleason Judd, Morgan Kaplan, Michael Kenney, Colin Krainin, Christine Mele, Terry Peterson, Brian Phillips, Kris Ramsay, Karl Rethemeyer, Burcu Savun, Brad Smith, James Igoe Walsh, and Linyun Yang. We would especially like to extend our gratitude to the following scholars who participated in a book conference at the University of Georgia and provided critical feedback that helped prepare the book for publication: David Carter, Cullen Hendrix, Amanda Murdie, David Siegel, and Joseph Young. We would also like to thank the National Science Foundation for its support of research (award #1658043 and #2001330) that informed this manuscript in many ways.

Justin Conrad would like to thank the School of Public and International Affairs and the Department of International Affairs at the University of Georgia for tremendous professional and personal support. Justin would also like to thank his wife, Alanna, and his family for their unconditional love and encouragement. Neither this book, nor anything else, would be possible without their support.

William Spaniel would like to thank the University of Pittsburgh, the Center for International Security and Cooperation at Stanford University, and the University of Rochester for their institutional support and guidance from the birth of this project to its completion.

1

Introduction

Following the death of Osama bin Laden, al-Qaeda's new leader, Ayman al-Zawahiri, found himself dealing with a long-running challenge for the group. Al-Zawahiri, like Bin Laden before him, was concerned with how to rein in the terrorist organization's most independent and defiant branch: al-Qaeda in Iraq (AQI). Both Bin Laden and Zawahiri had previously admonished the organization and its deceased leader, Abu Musab al-Zarqawi, for a variety of offenses. In particular, the founding leaders of al-Qaeda felt that al-Zarqawi's indiscriminate tactics risked alienating their core audience. But in 2013, al-Zawahiri faced an even more direct challenge when AQI's leadership announced that the group would henceforth be known as the Islamic State in Iraq and al-Sham (ISIS), dropping the "al-Qaeda" moniker altogether.

Worse, the organization's stated intention was to expand its geographic territory by entering Syria. Although Zawahiri did not object to an al-Qaeda affiliate operating in Syria, the move seemed redundant. Jahbat al-Nusra (JN) had already carried the al-Qaeda flag since the early days of the Syrian Civil War. Especially alarming was ISIS leader Abu Bakr al-Baghdadi's announcement that the group would merge with Jahbat al-Nusra into a single organization. In a very public rebuke, Zawahiri warned Baghdadi and ISIS to remain in Iraq and not push the issue of Syrian expansion any further (Al-Zawahiri, 2013). In response, Baghdadi publicly explained why ISIS was disobeying this direct order from Zawahiri: Baghdadi said he had "chosen the command of my Lord over the command in the letter that contradicts it" (McCants, 2013).

This early disagreement between ISIS and al-Qaeda effectively set the stage for a bitter and violent competition between two distinct organizations. In early 2014, Zawahiri officially severed ties with ISIS

1

and formally declared that al-Qaeda "is not the group responsible for [ISIS's] actions" ("Why Al-Qaeda kicked out its deadly Syria franchise," 2014). From that point on, the groups' rivalry in Syria evolved into internecine warfare, with JN and ISIS fighters routinely attacking and killing one another ("Factbox: Syria's rebel groups," 2014). Their competition also extended well beyond Syria, evolving into a global rivalry with wide-ranging implications for political violence in many countries. Shortly after the groups' public rift, for instance, the leaders of Somali terrorist group al-Shabaab heavily debated which of the two groups it should affiliate with. In October 2015, senior leaders of al-Shabaab, including a commander of the group's mujahidin, Abdiqadir Mumin, defected to ISIS while the main group continued to pledge its allegiance to al-Qaeda.

In addition to sowing internal divisions among many terrorist organizations around the world, the al-Qaeda/ISIS struggle allegedly produced "outbidding" violence – violence used to attract attention and resources to one group instead of others. In Syria and Iraq, and in locations around the world, their competition steadily escalated with supporters of both groups signaling their commitment to the cause, often through brutal displays of violence against civilians. In particular, ISIS became recognized around the world for its "brand" of brutality, including mass beheadings, amputations, and even crucifixions of non-combatants. In 2014, the group massacred around 5,000 Yazidi civilians in a particularly gruesome demonstration of its power. Al-Qaeda frequently responded with competitive displays of violence and this competition extended well beyond the battlefields of Syria. In November 2015, al-Qaeda affiliates seized a hotel in Bamako, Mali, where hundreds were held hostage and more than two dozen were killed. The timing of the attack was immediately suspect, however, as it occurred just a week after ISIS's own sensational attacks in Paris, which killed 130 people. Observers noted that al-Qaeda may have intentionally timed the Mali attack to offset ongoing media coverage of the Paris attacks (Goldman, 2015).

Despite signs that the al-Qaeda–ISIS rivalry would continue to escalate and eventually spiral out of control, the dynamics of the relationship changed dramatically in just a few years. Al-Qaeda initially appeared to contest ISIS's rise with its own surge in violence. This was particularly true in Syria, where it targeted civilians and fought against competitors on the battlefield. Some analysts, however, have argued that following this initial escalation, al-Qaeda's use of violence has largely declined (Hamming, 2020). It is possible that Zawahiri and al-Qaeda's leadership concluded that they had been correct when they scolded AQI and

ISIS leaders over the years. By 2017, it appeared that ISIS's public support was slipping, undermined to some extent by continued revelations of how the group treated civilians under its control, how it crushed dissent, and the brutal tactics that it used. As a result, while al-Qaeda initially responded to ISIS's violence by escalating its own violence, the leadership may have considered it easier to differentiate itself by condemning ISIS's behavior rather than duplicating it (Hamming, 2020).

Little evidence exists, however, to support the contention that al-Qaeda deliberately reduced its violence in an effort to distinguish itself. Further, it is difficult to disentangle such strategic choices from the policy interventions that coincided with the evolution of the al-Qaeda–ISIS rivalry. Governments around the world continued to engage in efforts to counter both groups, but it was ISIS's seizure of the city of Mosul in 2014 that led to major interventions that undoubtedly affected both groups' operations. That event, in fact, prompted the largest international coalition in history, which worked in parallel with the governments of Syria and Iraq to take back the territories conquered by both groups (Quanrud, 2017). Massive counteroffensives launched by Syria, Iraq, and their international partners, as well as concerted efforts to undermine the recruitment efforts of both groups, may have contributed to an observable decline in attacks.

With ISIS's resounding defeat in Mosul, Raqqa, and other strongholds, al-Qaeda has now reemerged from the shadow of its rival. As of the writing of this book, observers have suggested that al-Qaeda is once again increasing its use of violence in an effort to reclaim its dominant role in the global jihadist movement (Hoffman, 2018). While it remains to be seen how (or if) ISIS will respond, the competition between the two organizations has clearly been a key determinant of their behavior. There are a number of factors influencing the rise, decline, and rising again of both groups, but their competitive relationship is central to the story.

The purpose of this book is to examine how competition between militant groups influences their behavior, and especially their use of violence. The book also considers how policy interventions by governments and the response of the public, from which supporters and recruits are drawn, influence these competitive dynamics. Ultimately, we seek to improve our understanding of the strategic environment in which organizations operate and how intergroup competition influences their decision-making.

OUR ARGUMENT IN BRIEF

Competition between militant groups for public support is a defining feature of many conflicts. We use the term "militant group" as an umbrella term that captures both rebel groups (we use the terms "rebel" and "insurgent" interchangeably) and terrorist organizations. Both are types of formal, non-state political groups that use armed force or the threat of armed force to challenge the status quo. The most important distinction for a terrorist organization is that it explicitly targets non-combatants in an effort to spread fear. In practice, however, there is much overlap between the two categories, as some (but not all) rebel groups engage in terrorism. From 1970 to 2015, countries around the world witnessed multiple terrorist organizations and/or rebel groups operating simultaneously within their borders, with as many as fifty-four terrorist groups active in a single country at a given time. Similarly, countries around the world hosted up to ten proper insurgent groups. The figures below (Figure 1.1) show the peak number of active terrorist groups and rebel groups for each country during this time period.[1] At the same time, demonstrative displays of political violence increased worldwide (Cordesman, 2017), with clear evidence of groups using such violence to distinguish themselves from their competitors.

Researchers have recognized the importance of militant group competition (e.g., Bloom, 2005; Conrad and Greene, 2015; Findley and Young, 2012). Yet our discipline, political science, has not fully explored the implications of outbidding violence, from microfounding competitive incentives to exploring their empirical implications. We work toward such a treatment in this book. The theoretical framework and empirical results indicate that the direct effects of competition are not as clear as they may seem, and interventions to alter competitive incentives may backfire if target states are not careful.

Our exploration of these competitive incentives consists of two phases. We begin by investigating how groups optimally compete with one another without interference from outsiders. Each group may produce a level of violence to bring that organization to the attention of would-be

[1] The numbers for terrorist groups are based on our data used in this book, which was compiled from information available in the Global Terrorism Database (GTD). The GTD has rather strict criteria for attributing activity to groups (START, 2016). In many cases, such as the war in Syria, the number of groups operating simultaneously was likely much higher. This is also true of the rebel groups, which are drawn from the Uppsala Conflict Data Programme (UCDP) (Themnér and Wallensteen, 2014).

Peak Number of Terrorist Groups by Country (1970-2015)

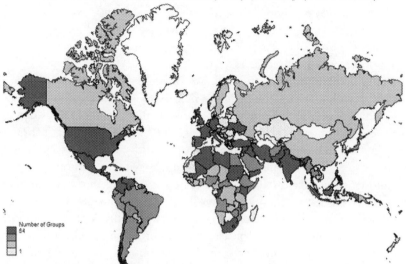

Peak Number of Rebel Groups by Country (1970-2015)

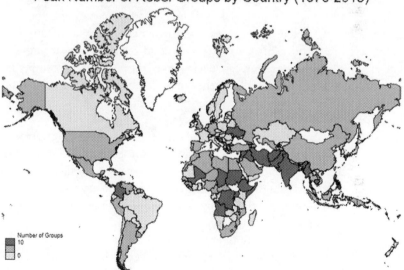

FIGURE 1.1 Worldwide terrorist and rebel group distributions.

supporters. Supporters then use the violence they observe to choose how to divide their resources among the potential recipients.

Under these conditions, introducing another group to the fold generates more violence. The logic is intuitive and falls back on basic principles of firm competition. Imagine, for instance, that only one militant organization exists. It faces no competition now and does not expect to in the future either. Then it has no reason to advertise its brand for the sake of prying attention away from its competitors. After all, it is a monopoly. Supporters have no alternative.

That all changes with the addition of more groups. Consider what happens with a second group in the mix. Now producing little violence is inadvisable. Slacking off in this manner allows the other group to siphon off support by committing a few attacks and increasing its brand recognition. The need to commit some quantity of attacks continues when three, four, or more groups compete with one another. Here, would-be supporters are flush with options. A group that does nothing can easily get lost in the shuffle, thus necessitating some level of violence to remain in the active conversation. Summarizing this logic gives us our first major result, which is consistent with outbidding predictions in the literature: **overall violence increases as the number of competing groups increases**.

But what occurs in the aggregate hides how individual organizations react to additional competition. With another group entering the fray and producing violence of its own, the propaganda value of any one act is less impactful. This leads to our second major result: **an individual group's violence output can decrease as the number of competing groups increases**. The overall increase in violence is therefore the consequence of an additional group outproducing the sum of the remaining organizations' declining output.

Exploring competition between militant groups, including terrorist groups and rebel groups, we find evidence for both of these mechanisms. There is a clear link, for example, between increasing numbers of groups and increasing levels of aggregate violence. An increase from one active group to five active groups can increase the predicted amount of attacks by 87 percent. At the same time, *per-group* violence appears to significantly *decline* as the number of groups increases.

Focusing on competition in isolation, however, leaves our analysis incomplete. The fact that these organizations commit violence compels intervention from targets and peace-promoting international institutions. But the effects of such interventions go beyond their direct intentions. These concerns motivate the second half of our project.

For example, consider police enforcement to intercept contributions to political violence producers. The primary effect is just that. But it also deters some lukewarm individuals from wanting to contribute, knowing that their efforts may go to waste. The groups internalize all of these lost benefits, which disincentivizes them from producing violence in the first place; advertisements are less valuable when there is less revenue to be had. This generates our third major result: **competition drives larger increases in violence in places where police enforcement is weakest.**

We also find evidence for this mechanism. When a state has relatively strong enforcement, adding one or two or three terrorist organizations does not influence the amount of violence that a state experiences to a great degree. But when states face particularly high costs of enforcement, additional terrorist organizations can have dramatic consequences for the amount of violence that a state experiences. We find, for instance, that a state with one active terrorist organization and the weakest level of enforcement has a .31 probability of experiencing at least one terrorist attack. If, instead, that same state has four active organizations, the probability rises to .53.

Whereas policing actions are reactive, governments also have proactive tools at their disposal. Given an emphasis on competition over supporters, an important countermeasure is to change the policy that upsets those who might otherwise donate to an organization. This leads to our fourth major result: **the expectation of outbidding violence can deter a would-be target from implementing an unpopular policy.** An unexpected implication follows from this. The specter of outbidding is more threatening when the number of groups waiting in the wings is larger. Thus, if too many groups will compete, the target thinks better of the unpopular policy and withdraws the issue of contention. With no one left to support the organizations, they forgo costly violence production. As such, more groups may imply *less* violence under these conditions. We must therefore be careful about generalizing the large-n results to all cases.

We underscore that point with our last major finding. Producers sometimes try to go overboard on violence to corner the market and deter potential entrants from forming. Indeed, the violence a single group produces under these circumstances sometimes exceeds what many would produce in a truly competitive market. As a result, **seemingly effective strategies of counterterrorism can be ineffective or backfire.** We show that reducing grievances, increasing the costs of formation, and hardening vulnerable targets can all be counterproductive. The finding is not the result of poor implementation that drives more individuals into the arms of the organizations. Rather, the strategies themselves are flawed under such circumstances. Offensive measures designed to destroy an existing group's infrastructure do not have the same drawback. Surprisingly, however, government success here *requires* that another group enter the competition due to the lead group's enfeebled status. Put differently, the government must play Whac-a-Mole with the organizations.

All told, we urge caution both to researchers and to policymakers interested in the outbidding logic. Competition undoubtedly motivates many organizations to take actions they would not take otherwise, and the broad empirical trends suggest that additional groups lead to more violence. But implementing a policy to manipulate those incentives requires delicate care to ensure that the second-order consequences still align with the overall policy goal.

THE BROADER PERSPECTIVE ON OUTBIDDING

At its core, our book explores three topics: political competition, advertisement, and violence. Each of these has received copious attention in isolation. Some research has explored the intersection of all three. However, competition among militant groups deserves a full-length study to better understand the subtleties of the mechanisms that arise from it.

Rather than think about a militant group's struggle against a target government, the focus of our book is on competition between rival militant groups to capture the pool of scarce resources. Competition, of course, is ubiquitous in life and in existing research. Psychologists have demonstrated how competition influences individual motivation, creativity, and interpersonal relationships (e.g., Amabile, 1982; Deci et al., 1981; Hennessey, 2003). And in economics, competition is one of the fundamental determinants of firm behavior (e.g., Bengtsson and Kock, 1999; Caves and Porter, 1977; Harrigan, 1985; Porter, 1979; Thomas and Venkatraman, 1988).

What makes our work distinct is that militant groups are *political* actors. Political scientists are familiar with the importance of competition. Within American politics and comparative politics, there is a heavy focus on traditional political parties and candidates (e.g., Downs, 1957; Stokes, 1963). But this also permeates into international relations. Waltz (1979) conceives of states as firms, seeking to expand their interests at the expense of others. Theories of interstate rivalry (e.g., Diehl and Goertz, 2001) take this to heart, focusing on cases of intense and long-running competition between states.

However, the focus of our study is a specific consequence of competition: advertisement through violence. In particular, we conceive of violence as a perverse form of advertisement that militant groups use to bring attention and resources to them. Advertisement, of course, is a core component of economic theory of competition between firms. In isolation, marketshare is a zero-sum competition, with firms attempting to obtain larger consumer bases than their rivals (Friedman, 1958; Mills, 1961; Schmalensee, 1976). Running advertisements is one way to shift marketshare in favor of a particular firm (Friedman, 1958; Mills, 1961; Schmalensee, 1976). In the realm of international relations, states may spend money on non-strategic projects for the purposes of advertising the better overall systems they can provide (Musgrave and Nexon, 2018). Nevertheless, we are interested in *competitive violence-as-advertisement*.

Research on the intersection of all three of these concepts is limited, with far more examination of *alliances* among militant organizations (e.g., Bacon, 2018; Christia, 2012; Moghadam, 2017). This line of research finds that cooperation among groups leads to important outcomes, such as higher group survival rates (Phillips, 2014). Specific counterterrorism and counterinsurgency tactics may also be impacted by intergroup cooperation: Milton and Price (2020), for instance, find that leadership decapitation is less likely to be effective against highly networked groups. If cooperation among groups influences their behavior and longevity, then it follows that increased competition should also play an important role.

In the limited existing literature on the subject, "outbidding" has been the key focus. The theory of outbidding is based on the assumption that organizations balance their strategic goals with the need to sustain themselves (Crenshaw, 1985, 1987). Self-preservation is the foremost consideration, however, because the group's broader goals cannot be achieved if the group ceases to exist (Wilson, 1995). The support of the local population is perhaps the most critical resource because it sustains organizations and can simultaneously undermine counterterrorism and counterinsurgency efforts (Walsh and Piazza, 2010). Additionally, organizations draw recruits from the local population. Thus, public support offers both immediate and long-term benefits, and, perhaps, a greater chance of achieving long-term strategic goals (Blomberg, Gaibulloev, and Sandler, 2011; Cronin, 2006, 2009).

In competitive environments, as a result, organizations have greater incentives to exaggerate their strength and commitment in an effort to "stand out from the pack." Violence offers a credible mechanism by which an organization may distinguish itself from others. By engaging in particularly noteworthy violence, groups can signal resolve, creativity, and credibility. Such signaling, in turn, can indicate to the public that their group has the best odds of revising the status quo vis-à-vis the government. This is significant for violent non-state organizations because, while other political organizations might campaign for support based on past victories or accomplishments, groups operating outside the institutional political process must frequently campaign on future achievements (Conrad, 2017). This increases an organization's need to signal that it has a legitimate chance of achieving its goals over time and that it can impose costs on those who stand against it.

The name "outbidding" suggests that the key mechanism is demonstrating an ability to produce political violence. Successful displays of violence offer groups the opportunity to "outbid" one another for the support of the population (Hutchinson, 1972). This central theme in the limited existing research on militant group competition is rather intuitive: more groups should lead to more violence.

Yet despite the intuitiveness of the argument, even a cursory survey of published empirical results points to mixed evidence for the central hypothesis. Some of the earliest empirical assessments of the outbidding effect continue to offer the strongest evidence of a relationship between intergroup competition and subsequent violence. In a series of surveys, Bloom (2004, 2005) finds consistent evidence that outbidding logic appears to have influenced the use of violence by Palestinian groups, especially during the Second Intifada. Much of the violence used by groups during this period, according to Bloom, was intended to undermine the credibility and authority of the incumbent Palestinian leadership, by painting the leadership as weak and ineffective. Simultaneously, terrorist attacks and other forms of political violence launched by these groups were intended to demonstrate a stronger commitment to the "cause" of Palestinian statehood. Hamas and the Palestinian Islamic Jihad (PIJ) were the central purveyors of such competitive violence. Their use of violence, in turn, not only improved the perception of the two groups, but also damaged the perception of the ruling party: "by claiming responsibility for the attacks, Hamas made the PLO look moderate by comparison" (Bloom, 2004, 70).

Bloom's survey evidence suggests that the logic of outbidding violence, at least in the Israel–Palestine case, was largely sound. In other words, the intended outcome of the violence – greater public support – was exactly what occurred for these groups. The results of public opinion polls indicate that as the suicide campaigns of the various groups ratcheted upwards, public support for both Hamas and the PIJ steadily increased. By comparison, public support for Fatah fell precipitously and this trend continued well into 2002. At least anecdotally, then, we have evidence that growing competitive pressures can influence the behavior of militant groups. These pressures can drive their decisions about when to use violence, which can, in turn, influence broader conflict dynamics.

Aside from this limited evidence, does the logic of outbidding appear to be relevant for other conflicts and environments? Since Bloom's analysis, several scholars have attempted to identify evidence of a cross-national link between competition and political violence. When the analysis is applied to additional countries and regions, however, support for the outbidding hypothesis has been mixed. In one of the earliest large-n analyses of outbidding, Chenoweth (2010) finds "preliminary support" linking competition and violence, although her central analysis does not directly measure active competition among non-state actors. Other studies connect to the general outbidding mechanism without testing predictions on violence output.[2]

Additional examinations offer less consistency. Nemeth (2014) only finds conditional support. Nationalist and religious organizations are more likely to use violence in response to increasing political competition, but left-wing groups respond in the opposite way. Meanwhile, Findley and Young (2012) conclude that their wide range of model specifications and measures do not provide evidence for the outbidding effect. Rather, their results indicate "scant support for the idea that the number of insurgent groups increases the likelihood of suicide terror and no support for the notion that outbidding increases terrorism generally" (Findley and Young, 2012, 707).

COMPETITIVE VIOLENCE IN STRATEGIC CONTEXT

In this book, we seek a comprehensive picture of the strategic context in which competing militant groups operate. As such, the book makes a timely contribution to a growing body of research on militant group fragmentation, rivalry, fratricide, and demonstrative violence. This existing research has produced important conclusions on which we will

---

[2] Phillips (2015) finds that increased competition positively influences group longevity. Staniland (2012) finds that competition assists groups' retention of members. Conrad and Greene (2015) find that increased intergroup competition can influence tactical choices, including the selection of targets for terrorist attacks.

eventually build our model. The first and most important conclusion from the existing literature is that we cannot fully understand political violence in many situations without taking into account competition between non-state actors. Put differently, despite mixed evidence on a variety of outcomes, considerable evidence suggests that competition simply *matters*. As such, we cannot understand how conflicts occur, how they unfold, or how they end without taking into account competitive dynamics among the most important actors in those conflicts. Across disciplines, we have seen evidence that intergroup competition significantly influences organizational efficacy and efficiency. In the study of militant groups specifically, an existing theoretical framework and some empirical evidence suggests that competition influences the use and intensity of political violence by groups. This includes group-level decisions about methods and targeting, including the targeting of civilians (Conrad and Greene, 2015).

The second critical conclusion of the literature is that political competition does not occur in isolation. One promising body of literature has focused on the role of the state in militant group fragmentation. Studies have argued that state repression can be an important catalyst in the fragmentation process (McLauchlin and Pearlman, 2012). Viewing state behavior as the dependent variable, Cunningham (2011) finds that the higher the number of groups within a movement, the more likely it is that the state will make concessions. Others have focused on the subsequent likelihood of "spoilers" emerging to oppose negotiations between the government and rebel leaders. Fragmentation of groups and the power distribution among the resulting factions can influence the likelihood that some groups use violence to spoil peace processes (Greenhill and Major, 2007; Pearlman, 2009). Although this literature is limited in quantity, it is among the few to explicitly incorporate actors beyond *n* militant groups.

According to the existing theoretical framework on group competition, the primary reason for a militant group to engage in competitive violence is to build credibility and demonstrate commitment to a cause. Yet we must also understand the actors who observe the violence and respond to it: namely, the public and the government. Both categories of actors have tremendous opportunities to influence competitive violence because it is allegedly conducted *against the government* and *for the benefit of the public*. Ultimately, how these actors respond to group violence influences the subsequent utility of that violence. Changing public support or government efforts to curtail that support should influence the wisdom of outbidding one's opponent through violence.

From these implications arises an important observation about policy interventions: we cannot adequately address political violence without first understanding the nature of competition between militant groups. While many academic treatments often ignore or downplay the role of the government and the public, many policy approaches fail to consider intergroup competition as a key influencer of conflict dynamics. This failure is notable because, like the competitive violence itself, government decisions do not occur in isolation. Rather, they are a critical part of an endogenous process involving the decisions of competing militant groups. In other words, policy interventions may inadvertently lead to changes in the strategic dynamic between militant groups. These changes, in turn, can cause unexpected or unintended consequences. Responsible counterterrorism and counterinsurgency policies therefore cannot ignore the competitive relationships among militant groups. Likewise, when militant groups use violence to compete with one another, they cannot ignore government policy. Both governments and militant groups must consider how their decisions influence the support and behavior of the public. Neither governments nor militant groups nor the public make their decisions without anticipating the decisions of other actors.

We have written this book as a means of addressing these gaps in the literature. We therefore approach the subject of militant group competition with the intention of providing a picture of the full strategic context. This book, and our theoretical approach, is rooted deeply in the existing literature on individual and group-level competition. We draw much of our insight from the study of militant group competition in political science, although we have also incorporated insights from other fields into our understanding of strategic and competitive environments. Our primary goal is to examine the full range of actors and their decision-making processes within these environments.

In particular, we move beyond simple expectations about the effect of intergroup competition on violence and extend the existing models to consider the effects of various policy interventions by governments. How does improved bureaucratic efficiency impact competition among groups? Which kinds of policies have the greatest impacts? These are just some of the questions that we examine throughout the book. Ultimately, the model's implications and empirical evidence suggest that government intervention can dramatically alter the competitive environment and incentives for groups to use violence in an effort to outbid one another.

In one series of empirical tests, for instance, we find strong evidence in favor of the "classic" outbidding hypothesis. The addition of a single terrorist group to an existing conflict can lead to an increase in the expected number of terrorist attacks. But importantly, we also find that when the government has the capacity to police recruitment by militant organizations, additional groups *do not* significantly increase the amount of violence. Findings such as these emphasize that competition and subsequent group behavior depend on the strategic context. By bringing additional actors into the strategic analysis, we can explain the conflicting results from previous studies on militant group competition. In fact, once we account for the other strategic actors in the militant group environment, we even find evidence to support Nemeth's (2014) assertion that, in some cases, "competition may actually lead to less terrorism." In our analysis, however, this negative relationship is not due to characteristics of the group, but rather to strategic considerations between groups and vis-à-vis the target government.

We also derive a great deal of insight from the simple observation that changes in the environment can change the actions of strategic actors. Anticipating government responses or the responses of the broader population, groups may increase or decrease their use of violence as a recruitment tool. This observation leads to counterintuitive findings about how government policy interventions may change the strategic decisions of militant groups. For instance, Chapter 5 details how large numbers of competing groups may have a deterrent effect. Anticipating a great deal of competitive violence, the target government may reduce its policy demands, thereby reducing the quantity of supporters for groups to compete over. More directly, this means that more groups can yield less violence. More subtly, it highlights a problem with connecting the presence of terrorism to the failure of groups to achieve their policy goals. When terrorism would be effective, we do not observe it; the government endogenously takes action to quell the potential violence. When terrorism is less effective, the government views it as the cost of doing business. Thus, observed terrorism correlates with policy failure even though the theoretical relationship is the opposite.

BOOK OUTLINE

We approach the study of competition using a variety of methodological strategies. To develop the core theory and various extensions, we rely on a series of formal models. We do so for a few reasons. First, despite the growing literature on outbidding, researchers have yet to formalize the concept. Although we do not think theories should be formalized for the sake of formalization, models of outbidding show promise. The outbidding literature discusses many facets of competitive behavior. At present, it is unclear whether simple assumptions will yield the rise in violence as group numbers increase. We therefore take a "first principles" approach to modeling outbidding in the next chapter, showing when the relationship holds in a pure contest setting.

Indeed, the variety of approaches, treatments, and predictions of current outbidding theory suggest a need for clarification overall. This is a second reason to formalize the theory. Powell (1999, 29–34) argues that formal models provide "accounting standards" to ensure that arguments are internally valid. Tinkering with assumptions shows us exactly what is necessary for certain results to apply. However, as this research framework highlights, models are mere tools that ensure that one's assumptions imply one's conclusions. As a result, we exert great effort to substantively motivate each model to ensure that the assumptions are reasonable.

Third, formal models allow us to unravel the logic of outbidding progressively. Chapter 2 begins with the central framework of competition over resources. From that first-principles setup, we derive the standard claim that more groups imply more violence. Later chapters add other substantive concerns to the mix, either demonstrating a conditional relationship or certain circumstances that cause the standard claim to flip. The progressive structure of the models shows that the additional circumstances lead to unexpected findings, rather than those unexpected findings just being a general property of competitive behavior.

Fourth, our models give us greater confidence that some of our empirical results are not an artifact of noisy data. One of our main theoretical findings is that increasing the number of militant groups causes a decrease in per-group violence production. We also observe this empirically. Existing outbidding theory suggests this should not be the case (e.g., Nemeth, 2014, 345). Without the model to adjudicate group-level dynamics from aggregate dynamics, it would be tempting to conclude that the evidence we marshal runs contrary to the competition logic.

Finally, terrorist groups operate under secrecy. Researchers cannot easily obtain first-hand perspectives from those organizations and attempts to do so carry enormous physical risks. Formal theory does not solve those problems. But it does clarify the incentives and tradeoffs that terrorists face using a commonly understood framework.

That all said, we do not believe that formal models alone can provide a full accounting of competition and political violence. We also rely on both quantitative and qualitative empirical evidence. On the quantitative front, statistical analysis allows us to demonstrate that the implications of outbidding theory apply broadly. The violence we observe is consistent with a world where competition drives actors' decision-making processes. Indeed, total violence output rises with the number of competing groups. Moreover, the effect is conditional on a government's capability to intercept the contributions that the groups seek. The conditional nature of the relationship fosters greater confidence that competition drives the overall trend and not other mechanisms that might produce similar implications.

Statistical methods can establish broad trends, but they do not establish the mechanisms behind those relationships. Doing that requires the finer-grained nuance that comes with analysis of a specific case. We therefore include substantial discussion of how individual groups thought through their incentives on the ground. There are weaknesses to this approach, of course. Direct accounts are few and far between as we described before. In addition, each case can only establish the mechanism for that particular situation. However, when accompanied with the formal logic and quantitative findings, case studies paint a more complete picture of the theory and its implications.

With that in mind, the book proceeds as follows. Over the next two chapters, we develop and test a strategic model of competitive violence among militant groups. As such, we closely examine the empirical evidence in favor of the classic outbidding approach. The remaining chapters are then devoted to understanding the effect of government policy interventions on incentives for groups to employ competitive violence. A series of model extensions allow us to incorporate the full range of strategic actors, focusing on government efforts to counter violence.

Chapter 2 develops a baseline understanding of competitive violence through a simple contest model. The model departs from some previous treatments on the subject by featuring n militant groups and by explicitly assuming that the use of violence as a mechanism is both costly and provides diminishing returns. Given these considerations, our model produces interesting and counterintuitive implications from the perspective of previous outbidding research. First, the model suggests that the basic premise of outbidding is correct: more groups produce more aggregate violence. As other groups' violent output increases, individual groups have incentives to increase their allotment to keep pace. There are limits to this competition, however. If the other groups collectively plan to spend endless resources on violence, then the marginal value of a single attack from the remaining group is low. Intuitively, if the other groups will commit one thousand attacks, a sole attack from the remaining group is likely to be lost in the shuffle. As a result, the remaining group's optimal level of violence declines as competition increases. Thus, in cases where violence levels were competitive to begin with, adding another group to the mix causes others to decrease their use of violence. Ultimately, even though overall violence increases, the incentives for a single group to use violence may decline. This implication from our model likely explains a great deal about why previous empirical studies of outbidding have reached mixed conclusions.

In Chapter 3, we directly assess the empirical evidence of the propositions derived in the previous chapter. First, we conduct a large-n analysis of terrorist violence in line with the kinds of empirical analyses that have constituted the study of outbidding thus far. We take advantage of the Global Terrorism Database to identify the number of violent attacks that occur in each country each year between 1970 and 2015 (START, 2016). We then examine whether there is a relationship between aggregate violence and the number of active militant groups in a state. We find evidence to support the basic outbidding hypothesis: more militant groups (terrorist groups or insurgent groups) are significantly associated with more violence at the state level. We subsequently analyze the relationship between the number of groups and the average quantity of violence of those groups. In accordance with our model expectations, we find that while increasing competition appears to lead to more violence overall, the per-group average declines. Finally, to more fully explore the causal mechanisms at work in this process, we examine in detail the multi-dimensional insurgency in Northeast India since 2009. We focus on the illustrative cases of the Garo National Liberation Army (GNLA) and the National Socialist Council of Nagaland (NSCN), two organizations among a multitude of militant groups in the region. We find in both cases that as aggregate violence in the country and the region increased, both groups curtailed their own use of violence due to concerns about diminishing returns.

In Chapter 4 we extend our model for the first time beyond the contest among militant groups and begin to analyze other relevant actors. Even existing work that acknowledges the interaction between groups and their audiences typically excludes the government from the analysis. We develop a model of outbidding that includes the government's choice to invest in enforcement to reduce recruitment. Its comparative statics show that enforcement tempers the outbidding effect: more groups imply more violence, but low government enforcement costs make the increase negligible. In our statistical analysis, we find broad empirical support for our mechanism: competitive violence is most pronounced when governments incur higher marginal costs of enforcement. These results increase our confidence that competition drives violence more broadly, as competing explanations do not predict this conditional effect.

In Chapter 5, we further extend the strategic implications of government intervention. The theory of outbidding states that terrorist, insurgent, and rebel groups use violence to capture a greater share of their audience's resources. We argue that opponents of these groups should anticipate this dynamic, which potentially alters their demands. Although a seemingly obvious implication of outbidding is that violence increases as the number of groups (and thus competition) increases, we show that this may not hold if the demand is endogenous. This is because targets, fearing group competition, limit their aims. The results help explain some of the empirical inconsistencies regarding outbidding. Using comparative statics from the model, we then discuss the challenges to making valid empirical inferences regarding the theory.

In Chapter 6, we endogenize entry into the market of competitive political violence. Some interesting implications follow. In equilibrium, an existing group may overproduce violence to corner their market and deter entry by a potential competitor. Contrary to the basic expectation of the outbidding thesis, then, violence can be greater with only a single group than when the second group enters the market. We then investigate four policy interventions by which a target government might mitigate the violence: offensive measures that undermine the lead group's marginal cost of violence, defensive measures that absorb a portion of all violence, deterrent measures that increase the cost of group formation, and concessions to the group's audience to reduce grievances. Of these, only some types of defensive measures are guaranteed to decrease violence. By contrast, increasing the burden of entry and decreasing grievances can counterintuitively increase violence.

Finally, in Chapter 7, we consider the combined lessons of our analysis. We examine the implications of our findings for both academic research and policy decisions. In particular, we argue that the phenomenon of competitive militant violence is a complex and nuanced process. In some strategic contexts, the relationship is straightforward, while in others, actors may behave in ways counterintuitive to expectations regarding outbidding. Effective counterterrorism and counterinsurgency policies therefore require a detailed understanding of the competitive environment and the incentives for specific groups to signal their competency through violence. In these pages, our hope is that both researchers and policymakers gain a more nuanced understanding of militant group competition and its consequences.

2

A Formal Model of Outbidding

This chapter develops our baseline model of competition and political violence. Despite a growing literature on the subject, researchers have yet to formalize the core strategic tradeoffs behind outbidding theory. We rectify that here.

Because this is the first attempt to formalize how competition affects political violence production, we take a "first principles" approach. At its heart, outbidding theory frames violence as an advertising tool for recruitment. Many treatments of the theory then incorporate other facets that can affect that competition. Target governments can influence terrorism patterns by relaxing their substantive policies or strengthening their counterterrorism efforts. Entrepreneurs of political violence must decide whether to form groups to enter the competition.

Using the first principles approach means that we focus on the advertising properties of political violence. We do this for three reasons. First, it is the most basic feature unique to multiple competing groups. All other facets of the theory either operate in the shadow of attention gathering or they make deeper assumptions about how would-be supporters allocate their resources. Government interventions, in turn, operate in the shadow of that competition. Entry into the political violence marketplace must consider the profitability of formation, which competition determines. A strategic decision to forgo support from pacifist supporters to capture market share in the realm of violence presupposes that subsets of the population respond to both tactics.

Second, and as a consequence of the first reason, we need to understand the implications of pure competition in political violence before we can address more complicated issues. For example, consider a setting where groups decide whether to enter before competing with one another.

Competition is a subgame of that entry game. As such, we have to understand the former before we understand the latter. Moreover, suppose that such a model of group entry demonstrated that the quantity of violence increased in the number of groups that formed. It would be unclear if this is (1) a consequence of the competition conditional on entry or (2) a product of more groups entering when the conditions are generally favorable to violence. Using the simple competition game as a baseline gives us a way to answer that question (Paine and Tyson, 2020).

Finally, the implications of pure competition run surprisingly deep. In fact, we focus on just the competition part in the first half of this book. This includes mapping out the theory, investigating whether its properties appear in the data, and supporting the mechanism in action with qualitative evidence. The second half emphasizes the implications for government interventions into outbidding. In the process, we add nuance to the theory and find specific circumstances that yield predictions contrary to those results. We do not omit the other aspects because we think they are unimportant. Indeed, we often reference them in brief when discussing the robustness of the main results. Rather, we view our work as the first step in a broader understanding of competition. With luck, the framework we develop here will be useful for further research on the subject.

To preview the remainder of this chapter, the next section develops the key features of competition and political violence. We motivate eight facets of the strategic environment, ranging from how the production of violence requires effort to how violence outputs from multiple groups map onto support levels. Our goal is to develop the model from the bottom up, thinking about what features a model of outbidding should include. The survey leads us to conclude that we should formalize outbidding using contest models.

The next section develops our baseline contest model. Each group chooses to produce violence and support flows to the organizations in proportion to those decisions. Two central results emerge. First, as the number of competing groups increases, so too does overall violence production. The logic is simple and captures the intuition of existing articulations of outbidding. More groups implies more competition, forcing overall effort to increase and lowering the rents that groups capture.

Second, and this time contrary to existing outbidding theory, we show that each group's individual effort may *decrease* as the number of groups grows. Given the logic of competition, this is counterintuitive. But formalizing the problem clarifies where intuition goes wrong. To illustrate, suppose that two groups are competing over forty units of value. Suppose further that each group would optimally spend ten units and thus split the prize so they both win twenty units. Both are happy to accrue some profits in the process.

Now consider what would happen if two more groups entered the fray. By the traditional logic, each should spend *more* than ten units on violence. But this implies that the groups would collectively spend more than forty units to split less than that amount in benefits. The competition must therefore be unprofitable for at least one group. In turn, those higher violence outputs are unsustainable. We should therefore expect lower average group effort with the addition of more competitors.

In the next section we briefly describe some robustness checks. Our focus is on whether the central logic of violence-as-advertisement holds with other components of competition. Reassuringly, the answer is yes.

This chapter then concludes with a discussion of the path forward. After all, the strategic framework we develop here is a baseline model. It therefore leaves questions unanswered from both empirical and theoretical perspectives. Do organizations actually behave in a manner consistent with the logic we develop? Does their rationale for that behavior follow our causal mechanism? And can a target of the anticipated violence manipulate the competitive incentives? We answer all of these questions and more in the later chapters.

STRATEGIC DIMENSIONS OF COMPETITIVE POLITICAL VIOLENCE

Before developing a model of competitive political violence, we must first understand the incentives and constraints that militant groups face. Once we have a full appreciation of the issues, we can then develop a model structure to analyze the interaction. As such, we highlight eight critical features that any model of outbidding should incorporate.

Strategic groups. First, we need to include a set of multiple strategic groups that choose their violence allocation. This is the minimum criterion necessary to model outbidding behaviors. Game theory is the study of strategic interaction. If groups independently select levels of violence without considering their rivals' decisions, outbidding theory is dead on arrival – it is not possible to consider how additional groups affect violence output decisions if militant groups ignore their competition.

Fortunately, the evidence is conclusive. The intensity and type of competition determines the behavior of militant groups. This competition, in turn, is driven by the availability of resources in a given theater (McCarthy and Zald, 1977). Groups condition their selection of strategies and tactics on the likelihood that they will secure more resources, including public support (Bloom, 2004; Chenoweth and Stephan, 2011). When more than one group pursues the same set of resources, their strategies and tactics are necessarily influenced by strategic expectations of what other groups will do. While the literature provides a mixed view of how groups respond to increasing competition, there is a consensus among all of these studies: militant organizations do not make choices in a vacuum. They are often acutely aware of the operations of other non-state actors and they factor this information into their own decisions about the efficiency and utility of violence. Further, evidence suggests that the behavior of ideologically aligned groups, formal allies, and otherwise "friendly" groups can influence group decisions about violence as much as the behavior of more traditional "rivals" (e.g., Ferguson, 2017; Phillips, 2014, 2015). The choices made by militant groups are therefore heavily influenced by the choices that their competitors make.

A pool of limited resources. Second, for such competition to exist at all, there must be a pool of limited resources that organizations compete over. This pool can take many forms: recruits looking to join an organization, funds from sympathetic donors who wish to remain civilians, money from a state sponsor, or simple prestige. Critical to prior works on outbidding, the pool must be rival – that is, whatever one group captures, another group cannot. The existence of such a zero-sum benefit creates a fundamental incentive for militant groups to compete with one another.

The size of this pool may vary from situation to situation. Sympathy for the cause will be greater among populations with greater grievances against the target. In contrast, better governmental policing can intercept donations and arrest potential recruits before they join up. Basic demographics such as the population of a region and its economic capacity may also impact the pool. Thus, it will be useful to have a parameter that captures the overall value of all resources available to the organizations.

To isolate the effects of competition, we focus on capturing this pool of resources as the militant group's objective. This falls in line with existing research on militant group goals (Cronin, 2009, 40) and the outbidding literature's philosophy that the "success" of a terrorist organization is not necessarily linked to policy concessions. Although some organizations may wish to coerce a target to achieve strategic objectives, competition between groups suggests that many aim to simply maximize the status and grandeur of their own organization.

This approach fits with a broader literature examining the causes and consequences of rebel group fragmentation. According to this literature, two important factors contribute to intra- and intergroup violence. First, ideological similarities and differences among factions help explain why organizations fragment as well as their subsequent interactions. Ideological "distance" between groups has been found to alternatively threaten group cohesion (Hafez, 2020) or bolster it (Gade, Hafez and Gabbay, 2019). Increased competition among factions, in turn, may lead to a feedback loop in which organizations feel pressured to differentiate themselves even further (Ogutcu-Fu et al., 2019). One point of differentiation – and disagreement – frequently occurs over the targeting of non-combatants (Mendelsohn, 2019). Second, power distributions among factions can have significant consequences for intergroup violence. In particular, power asymmetry appears to be correlated with higher levels of violence, as dominant groups may view opportunities to eliminate weaker opponents (Bakke, Cunningham and Seymour, 2012; Gade, Hafez and Gabbay, 2019; Pischedda, 2020). Although we do not examine ideological differences in this book, in Chapters 5 and 6 we consider how a dominant group may drive the marketplace of violence.

Attacking a competing faction does not further a group's ability to achieve its larger strategic goals. But many studies have argued that groups balance their strategic or "outcome" goals with day-to-day "process" goals (Arjona, 2016; Crenshaw, 1985; Wilson, 1995). In other words, there are two central concerns for any organization, including militant political organizations. First, groups have some stated policy objective or set of strategic outcomes they wish to achieve. Although their strategic goals have become somewhat muddled in recent decades, al-Qaeda's initial demands were relatively clear. In his "Declaration of war against the Americans occupying the Land of the Two Holy Places," Osama bin Laden (1996) outlined the organization's primary policy objectives. These included ending the repressive Saudi monarchy and the removal of American troops from the Arabian Peninsula. Al-Qaeda's attacks against the US Navy destroyer *USS Cole* in Yemen, American embassies in East Africa, and US and Saudi targets in Riyadh and Khobar all seemed to demonstrate a laser focus on achieving the group's strategic goals. Perhaps one reason why their attacks seemed so focused is because the group enjoyed a relative lack of political competition during these years. But even with minimal competition, Abrahms (2006) has pointed out that terrorist groups rarely achieve their stated policy goals.

This failure to achieve policy goals may result, in part, from groups placing a disproportionate emphasis on their second central concern: survival. Surviving means having the resources to continue day-to-day operations. Acquiring resources means bringing the pool of available money and labor to one's own group and not to another's. The struggle is particularly important for groups with similar ideologies or goals: "Where competition does exist, it is in part because the two associations are *not* in opposition with respect to their [strategic] objectives and therefore appeal to similar or identical contributors" (Wilson, 1995, 264). Appealing to the same audience means that recruitment in competitive scenarios is sometimes a zero-sum game. Wilson (1995) points out that the degree of competitive behavior is proportional to the "relative amount of resources" available to each group. Because the existence of one or more competing groups diminishes that relative amount, groups necessarily shift their focus from strategic to process goals. In an effort to shore up support and recruitment, militant groups (whose raison d'etre is violent resistance to a government) may increase their public displays of violence to bolster their credibility at the expense of their rivals.

By focusing on acquisition of the pool of resources as the strategic goal of the groups, we capture those incentives for competition.

Resource acquisition increases in violence. Third, the share of resources a group captures increases its violence output. This is a crucial scope condition in the outbidding literature. If violence serves as advertisement, then some audience must be sympathetic to its use – contributors want to see violence and want to reward it. Going back to the previous element, we must therefore define the pool of resources as those available to violent militant organizations. Once again, the pool of individuals with such sympathies may be small or large, but we can account for that in the model by varying the total quantity of resources. Otherwise, violence would be unproductive. We would in turn expect organizations to race toward de-escalation, which then makes explaining outbidding violence difficult.

Chai (1993) has shown that violent organizations tend to attract increasingly violent recruits. Following a spate of Islamic State videos featuring beheadings of abductees, a Virginia man was arrested in 2016 for violently attacking a man and woman with a knife. Investigators argued that the man, Wasil Farooqi, was directly inspired by both the use and style of violence employed by ISIS (Steinbuch, 2016). In fact, the entire phenomenon of foreign fighters streaming into Syria and Iraq to support the group has frequently been blamed on "violence junkies" who are simply attracted by the Islamic State violence on display in those countries (Stern and Berger, 2015). A subset of the population therefore exists that is attracted to displays of violence by default.

Yet group displays of violence are not exclusively targeted at such violent individuals. Broader cultural acceptance of violence – as a means of resistance or political protest – can also strongly influence group decisions to engage in violence (Bloom, 2005; Mullins and Young, 2012). Bloom (2004), for instance, argues that a general acceptance of violence was a prerequisite for popular approval of terrorist tactics during the Second Intifada in Israel. A broad "motivation for political violence within Palestinian society" therefore provided a fertile recruitment ground for organizations like Hamas, who used suicide attacks to win popular support (Bloom, 2004, 65). The pool of potential recruits can therefore range from a handful of hyperviolent individuals to an entire segment of society that legitimizes the use of political violence. Either way, groups can attract more followers and more resources by engaging in violent acts.

This discussion does not preclude the existence of individuals who are not so supportive. These include people who actively dislike violence or are just not radicalized enough to want to help a militant group. However, outbidding does not center on these individuals. We therefore begin by focusing on the size of the audience that wants to lend support. Once we have a grasp of how this logic works, we can then delve into some interesting second-order effects of those who might not want to lend support. These situations will serve as robustness checks in this chapter and extensions in later chapters.

Precisely why contributors reward a group with more contributions as that group increases its violence output can follow two different mechanisms. First, and as most of the above discussion referred to, more attacks keep any one organization's name in the news longer. A naïve contributor is simply more likely to be pulled toward that organization as a result. Alternatively, more sophisticated contributors might read violence as a signal about which group is most committed to the cause. Seeing greater output demonstrates that the group is willing to pay the price to coerce the target or be the more effective group in the long run. The sophisticated contributors then bias their resources in favor of the more productive organizations. In either case, the first-order consequence of one group committing more violence is that it receives more of the benefits.

Diminishing marginal returns on violence. Fourth, a group's violence output has diminishing marginal returns on the pool of goods the group receives. An inactive group that commits no attacks in a year is unlikely to receive support from extremists who share the same ideological sympathies when active competitors exist. Committing a single attack puts the group on the radar. Committing a second attack, or exerting more effort and spending more resources to increase the severity of the single attack, solidifies their position. However, the difference between a tenth and an eleventh attack, or between 1,000 and 1,001 casualties, is less drastic. Groups may still produce such high violence levels, but they need to think carefully about whether the marginal utility of yet more violence is worth the cost.

The diminishing marginal return of violence is especially evident as a militant group's target audience becomes desensitized to such displays. These organizations must continually struggle to stay top-of-mind and grab media attention, and the inherent challenge in doing so helps explain why groups shift tactics when a tactic becomes passé (Conrad and Greene, 2015). The Islamic State's recorded beheadings during the summer of 2014 may have led to widespread media attention, attracted recruits, and inspired copycats like Farooqi. Yet the benefits of this sensational tactic seem to have declined rapidly with each subsequent incident.

The first ISIS beheading that captured the attention of a global audience was that of James Foley, a photojournalist who had been covering the Syrian Civil War. Members of ISIS kidnapped Foley in late 2012 and held him hostage for nearly two years before he appeared in a video made by the group in 2014. In the video, after apparently being forced to read a script denouncing the United States as the "real killer," an ISIS member decapitates Foley with a knife. The video and Foley's death subsequently became the lead news story for major national and international media sources around the world. The Islamic State had allegedly beheaded Syrian soldiers and even some of its own members prior to the killing of Foley. But the graphic murder of a Western non-combatant marked a new phase for the organization and led to a dramatic rise in its level of infamy. US Secretary of Defense Chuck Hagel stated that the violence was "beyond anything we have ever seen" (Friis, 2015). This kind of reaction, prevalent among world leaders at the time, only added further authority to an organization that was largely unknown just a year earlier. In fact, the single incident of James Foley's death is often credited with prompting the formation of the largest counterterrorism coalition in history (Abrahms, 2020).

The events in the video are well-known by now, but an oft-forgotten part of the video serves as a preview of how the public beheadings would soon reap diminishing benefits for the group. Toward the end, another captive journalist is shown and an ISIS member says that his life "hangs in the balance," suggesting that his fate would depend on what the United States chose to do next (Carter, 2014).[1] The man being held captive, another journalist by the name of Steven Sotloff, would be beheaded by ISIS in the same public manner. But even though his death occurred only two weeks after Foley's, Sotloff's name does not conjure the same level of recognition today. The Islamic State would actually continue publishing videos of its members beheading foreign journalists and aid workers well into 2015. But it seemed that with each additional murder, the sensationalism and notoriety of the tactic was declining. A basic search on the NexisUni media database of stories related to James Foley and ISIS, for instance, produced well over 10,000 hits. By comparison, an identical search using the name of the sixth foreign aid worker or journalist killed after Foley – a man by the name of Peter Kassig – returned barely 3,000 hits. In addition to provoking a massive foreign intervention, ISIS's ability to grab headlines with their brutal tactics declined rapidly. Notably, Peter Kassig was murdered less than three months after James Foley.

A subtle implication of the diminishing marginal returns axiom is that the distribution of resources is not extremely sensitive to which group commits the most violence when overall violence is widespread. For example, if one group commits fifty attacks, the distribution of resources will look very similar regardless of whether the other group commits forty-nine, fifty, or fifty-one. This captures the idea that, at such high attack levels, citizens cannot easily identify the more productive of the two groups. Alternatively, even if the citizens could, it does not have a major impact on their decisions. Note that this does not preclude the small differences mattering more at lower levels. For example, if one group commits two attacks, then the distribution ought to have major differences depending on whether the other group commits one, two, or three.

---

[1] The group's stated goal in the video was the termination of US involvement in the Syrian Civil War.

One group's violence output hurts the rest. Fifth, as a competitor increases its violence, other groups receive a smaller share of the resources. This follows from the previous two components. If the pool of resources is fixed and violence increases one group's share of those resources, then it must decrease the share that others capture. This is evident in especially noisy environments, where many groups are competing simultaneously over the same limited set of resources. In chaotic conflicts such as the wars in Iraq and Syria, groups struggle to be seen and heard amid a plethora of similar, otherwise indistinguishable organizations. One analysis suggests that in a single six-month period during the Iraq War, more than 100 named militant groups emerged, seemingly overnight (Filkins, 2009). The vast majority of these groups did not last long. And the ones that did operated in obscurity relative to larger, more established groups. One possible explanation for so many groups' lack of traction in these environments is that they are attempting to break into a market of violence that is already oversaturated. The resources over which they compete – media attention, public support, material resources, etc. – are simply stretched too thin to support so many groups.

Notably, we do not assume that violence is always a substitute or always a complement. In other words, the model we build does not make any universal claims that one group's violence production makes another group want to produce less or produce more. Indeed, a couple of extreme examples indicate that the model we develop should allow for violence to be a complement or a substitute depending on the context. Imagine that a group initially plans on producing no violence at all. Then another group has little incentive to produce much either, as even a small quantity of attacks allows it to dominate the narrative. If the first group decides to increase its efforts, then its opponent may wish to follow to sustain its prominence. Violence is a complement here. In contrast, imagine that the first group produces an overwhelming quantity of violence. Then the second group may see competing as fruitless and scale back its efforts. Violence here is a substitute.

Competition is not winner-takes-all. Sixth, sympathizers do not collectively donate all of their time and money to a single organization. Although groups that commit more violence generally attract larger followings, smaller groups can sustain themselves with lower levels of violence. This can be for a number of reasons. Some sympathizers may have an active preference for keeping less famous groups afloat. Others may find these groups more attractive either for ideological or regional/tribal reasons. Despite al-Qaeda's clear monopolization of the jihadist movement in the early 2000s, for instance, many independent regional groups continued to thrive.

Violence is costly. Seventh, groups must pay a price for the violence they commit. These costs accumulate for a number of reasons. To begin, militant groups face direct financial costs for their operations. Although the allure of indiscriminate violence has often been linked to its relatively low cost (Enders and Sandler, 2006; Kupperman, Van Opstal and Williamson, 1982), even seemingly crude tactics like bombings and armed assaults can require significant financial resources. The 2002 bombing of a Bali nightclub by the terrorist group Jemaah Islamiyah may have cost the organization $50,000, even though the construction of the bomb involved readily available materials (Kaplan, 2006). While smaller attacks may require considerably less financial support, the attacks themselves are often a small part of the overall operational costs for an organization. Such costs include payroll and training expenditures, as well as the costs of maintaining operational security (Vittori, 2011).[2] The costs of a single terrorist attack, therefore, are often much greater than one would initially suspect because it involves more than just bomb-making materials or guns. And this is why one of the most important ways that governments counter extremist groups is by attacking or undermining their finances (e.g., Shapiro and Siegel, 2007; Winer, 2008).

In addition to the financial costs associated with terrorist attacks, groups frequently face considerable costs in terms of maintaining their labor force. Put simply, the risk that terrorist operatives will be captured or killed is extraordinarily high under many circumstances. For suicide bombers, it is a near certainty. This is why a group's decision to use suicide tactics is thought to be correlated with the overall risk of capture for terrorist operatives and associated security risks (Berman and Laitin, 2005; Hafez, 2007). Threatening a group's supply of rank-and-file members, these losses have the potential to seriously disrupt an organization's capabilities.

---

[2] As an example of the costs of operational security, the constant disposal of cell phones can dramatically increase a group's expenditures.

A third source of costs is broad retaliation by the government. It should be evident that the more groups engage in public displays of violence – in other words, the more they "surface" and expose themselves to government countermeasures – the more costly those displays become. Again, policing efforts may crack down on a group's financial resources, or governments may engage in offensive military operations in an effort to wipe out the organization. More active groups may be at a higher risk for assassinations of key leaders (Byman, 2006; Cronin, 2009). As a result, many terrorist attacks go publicly unclaimed because groups may be concerned about inciting additional government countermeasures. This is especially true for large attacks against civilian targets, which increases the risk of backlash. Correspondingly, groups claim attacks on civilians at a lower rate (Abrahms and Conrad, 2017).

The costs of violence are sunk. Finally, the costs to commit violence are sunk once paid. That is, the groups cannot recover the prices they pay in the process of executing an attack regardless of how many resources they acquire afterward. The reason for this is simple. Whether a terrorist organization emerges as the preeminent perpetrator of political violence or becomes completely irrelevant, their prior attacks have already finished. All the money paid cannot be recuperated and each lost foot soldier cannot be resuscitated. This forces organizations to carefully consider their outlays, lest they invest heavily and have nothing to show for it.

Note that these various costs do not imply that violence is unproductive. Indeed, equilibrium analysis below shows that groups always select a level of violence that will result in a gain of resources that offsets the cost. Nevertheless, these costs give militant groups their major constraint. If violence were free, groups would have an incentive to produce unlimited attacks. But militant organizations face resource and labor constraints. Given that the benefits gained from an attack may be small – especially with other groups competing for those same resources – organizations may not want to spend more than they can recuperate.

BUILDING A MODEL OF POLITICAL VIOLENCE

The above elements of competitive political violence all point to using a contest model to analyze the groups' decisions. Indeed, economists commonly use contest models to analyze traditional advertising decisions by firms (Friedman, 1958; Mills, 1961; Schmalensee, 1976).[3] And as Bloom (2005) anticipated, these strategic dimensions are similar:

- Firms and groups compete for a pool of resources, be it revenue from sales or support from ideological partisans.
- More advertising is better for a firm or a group, but additional advertisements from competitors are bad.
- The market can support multiple competitors.
- Advertising is costly and cannot be recovered, whether they are commercials from firms or suicide bombings from terrorist organizations.

Contest success functions fulfill the substantive rules outlined above: Group i's allocation is increasing in its effort, decreasing in all other groups' effort, generates some positive value if Group i exerts positive effort, and comes at an unrecoverable cost. These attractive properties have led the advertisement literature to adopt contest functions. Thus, many of our preliminary findings trace back to that broader subject matter. However, political violence has dimensions that do not arise in traditional advertising. These unique properties are our focus in this chapter's robustness checks and the later chapters' extensions.

To develop a baseline understanding of competitive political violence, consider the following complete information game. Militant groups numbering $n \in \{2, 3, \ldots\}$ simultaneously select a level of violence against a target. We denote Group i's violence allocation decision as $v_i \geq 0$.[4] For now, the target is an unmodeled actor; we incorporate the target in various ways in the later chapters. One could interpret the violence as the number of attacks, the scope of attacks, the number of casualties, or the amount of destruction; all of those should be increasing in the

---

[3] See Konrad (2009) for an extensive analysis of contest functions as well as specific discussions of contests in the advertising literature.

[4] Thus, the theoretical amount of violence a group could produce is unconstrained. One may worry that this does not capture some realistic constraint that militant groups face. However, as we show below, groups naturally constrain themselves due to the negative net payoffs that extensive violence outputs produce. As such, having a constraint would mean that a group would produce the minimum of its theoretical constraint and the quantity we derive below. We do not include an upper limit in the model so as to avoid having to phrase every claim in terms of the minimum of the upper limit and the calculated optimum.

effort the organizations exert. The game ends with a mass of individuals choosing how to divide a share of $\pi > 0$ total resources across the groups.[5]

Each group's payoff utility function contains two parts. We use the simple contest function to generate Group i's share of the goods. That is, given $v_1, \ldots, v_n$, Group i receives $\pi \frac{v_i}{v_1 + \ldots + v_n}$ of benefits.[6] Thus, a group's share of the resources is a ratio of its own violence output compared with the other groups' outputs. This captures all of the key elements from the previous section.

However, violence comes at a cost. Specifically, regardless of the benefit allocation, Group i pays $m_i v_i$ where m_i reflects Group i's marginal cost. As before, we model the marginal costs as exogenous for now and endogenize that part of the utility function in later chapters. It will also be useful to consider the symmetrical case where $m = m_1 = \ldots = m_n$ to establish some baseline results; we explore asymmetries in the robustness checks of this chapter and for a more specific application in Chapter 6. Subtracting $m v_i$ thus captures how each additional unit of violence uses more financial resources and labor and risks sparking retaliation and backlash from moderates.[7]

Combining these elements together, Group i's overall utility equals:

$$u_i(v_i) = \pi \frac{v_i}{v_1 + \ldots + v_n} - m v_i \qquad (2.1)$$

This utility function clarifies that the organizations value market share, which is the cornerstone of the outbidding literature (Nemeth, 2014).

---

[5] We therefore have a one-shot interaction. We do this for a variety of reasons. First, the equilibrium of a one-shot interaction is also an equilibrium of a repeated game, with those actions projected out over each stage. Second, obtaining new equilibria by the folk theorem requires sufficiently large shadow of the future. However, the half life of a terrorist group is relatively short. Depending on the measure, between 68 percent (Young and Dugan, 2014) and 74 percent (Dugan, 2012) survive less than one year. Perhaps more telling for our purposes, groups fail more often in the presence of more competitors. Finally, for risk-neutral actors, one interpretation of a contest function as producing the probability a group becomes the sole-surviving winner rather than the expected share of the resources it receives. In this framing, there is no future to model.

[6] This utility function is undefined when all violence outputs equal 0. How we define payoffs under these circumstances is irrelevant. No matter how we resolve the issue, at least one group will have an infinite marginal gain by deviating to an arbitrarily small amount of violence. Thus, no violence-free equilibria exist.

[7] Choosing a linear loss function simplifies the solution of the contest game. The key assumption to generate a unique optimum is that the loss function is weakly convex. This seems plausible: after accounting for short-term economies of scale, intense effort eventually forces a group to sacrifice basic needs, as time is a fixed resource.

Policy preferences are absent, consistent with Cronin's (2009, 40) argument that policy concessions are a low priority for a vast majority of terrorist groups.

Readers familiar with contest models will recognize this as a Tullock (1980) contest success function. We will be working with variants of this form for the majority of the book. However, many other contest success functions also capture a majority of the requirements from the previous section. As such, it is worth pausing to understand why the Tullock model is a useful representation of the strategic situation – or why Kotler and Bliemel (2009) call it the "fundamental theorem" of market shares.[8]

To begin, Skaperdas (1996) shows that ratio contest success functions are the only form that satisfies independence from irrelevant alternatives for a reasonable set of axioms.[9] In other words, if Group i does not participate in the contest, then each other group's proportional share of the benefits should be equal to the remaining proportion of the benefits that Group i does not capture when it does participate. Less formally, the contest should produce qualitatively similar distributions among n groups regardless of whether group $n + 1$ participates in the contest. This does not preclude that additional group from pulling resources from the others by producing violence. Indeed, violence from group $n + 1$ causes contributors to think about moving away from the original groups and toward group $n + 1$. Rather, independence from irrelevant alternatives means that the additional group's effort will not cause the contributors to reevaluate how Group 1 compares with Group 2, or Group 3, or so forth.

Second, our ratio contest success function has two significant advantages over the logistic function, which is also a popular alternative specification. For one, the difference between one group's effort and another's does not determine their relative shares. This eliminates the strong assumption that two groups' respective shares are the same under

---

[8] The following motivation does not mean that other contest success functions are not worth exploring. Rather, it explains why we place the Tullock model as the central focus and shift other contest success functions to the robustness check section later in this chapter.

[9] Those axioms require that the contest success function produces a valid probability distribution across all players, the allocation increases in one's own contribution but decreases in each other's, and the function is anonymous in the sense that it cares only about contributions and not about each group's identity. In the robustness checks section, we develop a contest function that relaxes that final axiom. See Clark and Riis (1998) for a generalization.

$v_1 = 1$ and $v_2 = 2$ as they are for $v_1 = 10,000$ and $v_2 = 10,001$ (Skaperdas, 1996, 289). It also ensures that the groups do not have increasing marginal returns as their efforts approach parity (Hirshleifer, 1989, 104–105).[10] In addition, the equilibrium of ratio contest success functions also better matches the substantive record on political violence – endogenous efforts from difference-form contest functions entail only one actor producing effort (Baik, 1998).

Finally, the contest in Formula 2.1 is attractive from a design perspective. Groups want a large piece of the pie but also worry about the costs of violence production. As a result, they have an incentive to slack off. Contributors ought to find this worrisome. After all, they may want to see more political violence.[11] To induce that behavior, they might want to allocate their contributions in a manner that elicits the most violent response from the groups. The contest success function we use is exactly that optimal allocation rule (Dasgupta and Nti, 1998).

On the bright side, contest models afford more flexibility than one might initially realize. For instance, our model has complete information. This would seem to stand as a barrier to thinking about how outbidding violence serves as a signal to the audience. After all, signaling in the traditional sense requires a source of incomplete information. What the source of that uncertainty is within the conflict literature is often broad, ranging from resolve and commitment to capability and durability.[12] This is a problem for generating theoretical expectations and empirical predictions because different sources of uncertainty have different implications (Fey and Ramsay, 2011).

Fortunately, a deeper dive into the contest literature allows our model to narrow our focus to one type of uncertainty and gives our model a broader interpretation. Skaperdas and Vaidya (2012) study persuasion as a form of contest. Each actor exerts effort to bring evidence to the forefront that their side is correct. Applying this idea to our model, the evidence the groups present is violence, with the goal of convincing citizens that they are the rightful flagbearers of the cause.

---

[10] The ratio function does not have increasing marginal returns for any opposing effort level as long as the effort level is exponentiated by a value less than or equal to 1 (Hirshleifer, 1989, 103); in the Tullock contest success function the exponent is 1.

[11] We provide microfoundations for this claim in Chapter 5.

[12] See, for example, Kydd and Walter 2006 (76–77), Fortna 2015 (529), and Conrad and Greene 2015 (548–550).

Understanding the Violence Decision

With the contest model described and given the proper motivation, how do the groups respond to these strategic incentives? The appendix to this chapter provides a rigorous explanation for each group's equilibrium strategy. However, there is a straightforward intuition that governs the process. As a group increases its level of violence, two things happen to it. One, its share of the benefits increases. And, two, it pays greater costs of production. These conflicting incentives ultimately cause each group to limit its violence output. This is because units of violence exhibit decreasing marginal returns – substantively, a group's first attack provides a greater jump in publicity than the difference between its 999th attack and its 1,000th attack. In turn, at some point, the cost of an additional attack exceeds its marginal benefit. The group then becomes content with its output.

The above logic treated each group's violence decision as independent of one another. In fact, however, each group needs to simultaneously consider how these incentives impact the remaining groups. This in turn affects the initial group's allocation. To wit, if a group expects the others to commit great resources to the cause, the marginal impact of each unit of its own violence is small. Intuitively, committing one attack has greater impact on the market when the remaining groups collectively commit two attacks than when they collectively commit 100.

All told, each group balances the marginal cost of violence against the relative benefit, conditional on expectations about other groups' outputs. The appendix shows that each group selects $v = \frac{\pi(n-1)}{mn^2}$. This equilibrium violence quantity has two intuitive properties. First, as the overall pool of benefits π increases, so too does each group's violence output. After all, having more resources to gain makes each group more willing to incur greater costs in pursuit of those benefits. It also captures the notion that the audience's receptiveness to terrorism matters (Bloom, 2004; Nemeth, 2014); if the audience is narrow, π is close to 0, and the violence any group produces is correspondingly minimal. In contrast, higher marginal costs m imply less violence. This relationship flips the previous logic; the more costly violence is, the less willing militant groups are to produce it.

Comparative Statics

Our main interest is in how violence production changes as the number of groups fluctuates. Recall that standard outbidding theory predicts that competition encourages militant groups to exert greater effort. Our first proposition corroborates that theory:

Proposition 2.1 *Total violence strictly increases in the number of groups (i.e., $\sum_{i=1}^{n} v_i = \frac{\pi(n-1)}{nm}$ strictly increases in n).*

To make sense of this first result, it helps to recast the situation as multiple firms seeking to capture the profits in a market. If a single firm exists, it need not waste money on advertising for its products; consumers have no other choice. One additional firm brings competition; now they must begin advertising, lest it leave the market open for the other to advertise and capture the pool of revenue. Nevertheless, some profits still remain, as the marginal value of a firm's advertisements is decreasing. Maintaining these levels of profits with three firms proves impossible though, as the third firm would want to produce advertising of its own to capture some of the surplus. The third firm's pressure reduces the surplus for everyone. A similar logic holds as the number of firms continues to increase. As such, advertising goes up as the number of firms increases and the sum of all profits decreases.

In this analogy, the firms are militant groups, the advertisements are political violence, and the revenue is the benefits that supporters give to active organizations. The creation of another group renders the previous level of violence insufficient; the new group would want to add to the fray. Overall violence correspondingly increases. However, because the pool of resources remains fixed, the net utility across groups declines. True to that, as the number of groups approaches infinity, each group's payoff goes to 0.[13] This tracks how all of the rents from a market disappear as that market becomes fully competitive.

A blunter interpretation of what goes on here is a comparison with a prisoner's dilemma. The outcome of the game is inefficient from the perspective of the militant groups. To see this, suppose that each group cut its violence output in half from the equilibrium allotment. Then each group would still receive the same quantity of benefits but spend strictly less in effort to obtain that amount. As a result, all parties are better off. However, no group can credibly commit to those lower levels. Indeed, if a group expected that the others would halve their outputs, it would

---

[13] One can observe this by noting that each group's share from the contest equals $\frac{\pi}{n}$, and each produces $\frac{\pi(n-1)}{mn^2}$ in violence at marginal cost m. Thus, the total cost function goes to $\frac{\pi}{n}$ as n goes to infinity.

want to increase its allotment and obtain a larger share of the prize. As a result, collusion in this manner is unsustainable.

Nevertheless, each group could do worse than the equilibrium outcome. For example, suppose all parties increased their allotments a little bit beyond the equilibrium recommendation. Then they would still split the resources in the same manner as before but pay more to do so. As such, the parties do capture some rents by participating in the contest.[14] But consider how adding an additional group affects each party's ability to capture those rents. The extra competition makes it impossible for the other groups to sustain their previous level of profitability. The extra group adds pressure, forcing total violence to increase. This explains the central finding. It also previews the coercive dynamic that becomes more pressing as the number of groups increases, which is the central tension in Chapter 5's extension.

In any case, Proposition 2.1 conforms to part of traditional outbidding theory's predictions. In particular, competition is supposed to drive violence and Proposition 2.1 says this holds at the *aggregate* level. But what holds across the groups collectively may not hold at the individual level. Put differently, it is possible that total violence increases even as each group's violence output decreases. The following proposition indicates that this unexpected decline holds:

Proposition 2.2 *A group's level of violence strictly decreases in the number of groups (i.e., $\frac{\pi(n-1)}{mn^2}$ strictly decreases in n).*

Combined, Propositions 2.1 and 2.2 add nuance to existing outbidding theory. The conventional wisdom predicts that competition drives groups to exert greater effort to differentiate themselves from the others. Violence therefore increases at the group level, which in turn causes overall violence to rise as well. Yet Proposition 2.2 shows that overall violence increases despite decreasing per-group violence.

What does traditional outbidding theory overlook? The standard explanation correctly identifies how competition drives additional violence. But it fails to recognize that increasing violence levels at the group level makes total effort levels unsustainable. Thinking about the extreme

---

[14] The rents are the value of the good minus the sum total of violence production multiplied by its marginal costs, or $\pi - m\left(\frac{\pi(n-1)}{nm}\right) = \frac{\pi}{n}$. The total rents therefore decline in the number of groups. It also goes to 0 as n approaches infinity, as the above discussion hinted at.

case makes this apparent. Imagine that two groups would produce some positive level of violence in the absence of competitors. Also suppose that, as traditional outbidding theory predicts, adding groups leads each group to produce more violence than they did before. At some point, the overall cost of all this violence must exceed the total benefit the groups can compete for.

But therein lies the contradiction. If total costs exceed total profits, at least one group must receive a negative payoff. Each of those groups could instead guarantee a payoff of 0 by producing no violence at all, paying no cost, and receiving no benefit. Because 0 is better than some negative amount, that group would be unwilling to produce the assumed level of violence.[15]

The above logic demonstrates that individual violence must eventually decrease as the number of groups becomes sufficiently large. However, in this chapter's setup, a related logic also applies when the group numbers are relatively small. To understand why, consider how a group best responds to any opposing amount of violence. If all opposing groups plan to use precious few resources on violence, the remaining group can capture most of the market by only committing a moderate amount of violence. Anything more is overkill that unnecessarily drains that remaining group's resources, so it need not go further than that.

As the opposing levels of violence increase, the remaining group has incentive to increase its allotment to keep pace. But there are limits to that competition. If the other groups plan to spend endless resources on violence, then the marginal value of a single attack to the remaining group is low. Intuitively, if the other groups will commit a thousand attacks, a sole attack from the remaining group is likely to be lost in the shuffle. As a result, the remaining group's optimal level of violence ultimately declines as competition increases. Thus, in cases where violence levels were competitive to begin with, adding another group's violence to the mix causes the others to want to ratchet down their allotments. Overall violence increases, but the per-group quantity *decreases*. Figure 2.1 illustrates this relationship.

---

[15] More rigorously, suppose that each of the two groups produces v in violence. If additional groups cause each group to produce more violence than they would with fewer groups, then for any n, the total quantity of violence must be greater than nv. (It must be greater because each group's level of violence exceeds v. However, we do not need to specify the size of the increase to produce a contradiction.) The total cost to produce all that violence is mnv. Trivially, there exists an n such that $mnv > \pi$. By that point, the cost of violence exceeds the benefit.

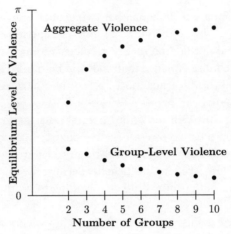

FIGURE 2.1 Equilibrium total violence and violence per group.

To be clear, we do not view Proposition 2.2 as a universal claim. Later chapters will demonstrate special conditions where the number of groups correlates with greater individual output. This can also be the case with various types of asymmetries with the new groups, including different marginal costs for violence or unique ways the contest function weighs each group's violence output. We discuss these further in the robustness checks below. But the central logic is strong across the board in the extreme case. The sum violence efforts cannot exceed the total value of the prize, otherwise at least one group's allocation results in a net loss. If adding a group always (weakly) increased per-group output, the sum violence would eventually cause this contradiction. As a result, adding groups must eventually cause a decrease in per-group violence.

In sum, the point here is not that increasing groups universally decreases a particular group's violence output. Rather, it is that standard outbidding theory overlooks this countervailing incentive. Whether that countervailing incentive predominates across actual forms of group competition is an empirical question, not a theoretical one. Consequently, we empirically investigate per-group violence in the next chapter. For now, the critical takeaway is that we ought to temper our expectations about per-group behavior. A statistical relationship showing a decrease in per-group violence is completely consistent with the competition mechanism that outbidding theory promotes.

Before moving on, it is worth briefly reemphasizing the comparative statics of the other two parameters. Both the total resources available (π)

and marginal cost of attacks (m) function in intuitive ways. Each group's output increases in the pool of resources and decreases in the cost. This is because competition looks more attractive when there is a lot to win and the price to play is low. As a result, total violence levels also increase when π is larger and m is smaller.

Although these points about π and m seem obvious, it is important to establish them now for the game with competition among existing groups. In Chapter 6, we extend the model to feature an incumbent group and a potential challenger. There, we will see that the marginal cost may not decrease violence. In addition, increasing the spoils can *decrease* violence. Establishing these results here allows us to confirm that the aforementioned counterintuitive results are a function of the incumbent group trying to deter entry rather than a general consequence of competition.

DEEPER THEORETICAL CONCERNS

As is common in conflict research, we use our model to explore how particular strategic actors respond to difficult tradeoffs. Proposition 2.1 gave our main result: total violence increases in the number of competing groups. However, our model is a simplification of reality by design, just like all other models. Recognizing this limitation, the important question is not whether our model *is* reality, but whether the central competitive effect holds across alternative ways to model the contest between the groups.

From one perspective, this question is superfluous. Chapters 5 and 6 ask whether other strategic factors dominate the competition incentives. As a result, to conduct a proper "experiment" (Paine and Tyson, 2020), we need to start with a model that generates the standard outbidding effect and then make changes from there. In other words, this chapter's main model gives us a default expectation consistent with standard inter-pretations of outbidding, at least on the overall level. Later chapters can then ask whether the additional incentives – for example, endogenous grievances or incumbent/challenger dynamics – dominate that expected effect.

Nevertheless, we still take the concern about the generality of the contest function to heart. As such, the next few pages explore some alternative modeling assumptions about the contest. The main conclu-sion is that competitive incentives broadly encourage the behavior we have uncovered. However, as other chapters later clarify, we do not view the relationship as absolute. Some specific situations may result in some alternative expectations.

Endogenous group entry. Because our key independent variable is the number of groups, we begin there. In the baseline model, n groups exist and choose how much violence to produce. Yet when the target begins undertaking policies that upset a population, sometimes the groups must choose whether to form first.

This is potentially problematic for our argument. When sympathies run deep, more political violence producers may find entry into the market attractive. After all, a larger available pie offsets the cost of entry. If so, then an empirical observation of many groups and lots of violence may be an artifact of the entry decision. By this alternative explanation, competition does not cause violence; rather, a large market causes both more groups to enter and more violence.

From one perspective, this criticism immediately folds. Proposition 2.1 is a comparative *static*. It shows that violence increases in the number of groups *holding all else equal*. We therefore know that adding groups has a direct theoretical connection to higher violence outputs.[16]

From another perspective, one may wonder what happens when we endogenize group entry. Fortunately, we can observe competition still having the intended effect under these circumstances. Consider an extension where each group begins by simultaneously choosing to enter at cost $c > 0$. Afterward, each group that enters plays the baseline model, choosing $v_i \geq 0$ at marginal cost $m > 0$ and receiving benefits according to the contest success function.

As the above intuition anticipated, the number of entrants increases as the market size increases. To see why, note that a group's entry decision boils down to comparing the entry cost to its utility for the baseline model when competing with a certain number of groups. The market supports organizations until that cost is greater. Thus, the equilibrium in pure strategies consists of n groups entering, where n is the maximum such that the utility for entering exceeds the cost.[17] Larger π values imply that more groups enter, which captures the theoretical confounder.

---

[16] Of course, our model does not guarantee that, within substantive cases, competition causes violence to increase. It is just a theoretical link. We return to this point in Chapter 4, where we develop a hypothesis that is unique to competition and not the alternative theory that large markets cause both more groups and more violence.

[17] Explicitly, the utility for n groups entering is $\frac{\pi}{n^2}$. Thus, the number of groups entering in this equilibrium is the largest integer n such that $n < \sqrt{\frac{\pi}{c}}$.

Nevertheless, competition still has an effect conditional on that entry decision, when holding the market size fixed. Compare two cases, one where the entry costs permit n groups to enter, and another slightly lower cost that permits $n + 1$ to enter. Those costs are sunk. We can therefore attribute any difference in violence outputs to the competition effect. Per Proposition 2.1, equilibrium violence equals $\frac{\pi(n-1)}{nm}$ in the first case and $\frac{\pi n}{m(n+1)}$ in the second. The latter is larger, again because the addition of another group increases the competition effect.

An important caveat to the above argument is that it only holds when the groups must choose whether to enter the market at the same time. Although this makes sense in some cases, at other times a challenger must decide whether to enter the market against an existing incumbent. The corresponding strategic environment is more complicated and has deeper theoretical implications. As such, it deserves a longer discussion than a mere robustness check. We save Chapter 6 for this purpose.

Ideological positioning. Thinking about entry in a similar manner addresses concerns about ideological positioning in the marketplace. Existing outbidding treatments commonly require that would-be contributors view violence in a positive manner (Bloom, 2005). Suppose that a certain portion of the population felt otherwise and only wished to assist pacifist organizations. A simple way to model this is to quantify that subset as $p > 0$ and imagine that each group that forgoes violence receives $\frac{p}{q}$, where q is the number of those groups.

Just like the previous extension, such an addition changes a group's opportunity cost for switching to political violence. The critical difference is that the value for staying out depends on how many other groups plan to do the same. However, the solution for such a game relies on the same principle as before. As more groups enter, less value exists in the corresponding violence subgame and more value remains in staying non-violent. At some point, the next additional entrant finds the competition unprofitable. The same logic operates here as in the previous robustness check. Overall group numbers and violence depend on the opportunity costs of entry, but competition still drives violence conditional on the number of groups that form.

Allowing for groups to have asymmetric support levels for nonviolent resistance also helps explain which groups enter. Suppose that one group would receive only a fraction of the peaceful support that another would receive. Then that first group has greater incentive to turn to violence.

That is, groups that have a hard time getting their message out peacefully are more likely to resort to more aggressive actions.

Public backlash. On a related subject, the public may grow intolerant of a group when it begins to produce too much violence. We do not see that as impacting the contest segment of the groups' utility functions. After all, we define the audience that distributes contributions as the subset of individuals who want organizations to inflict harm on the target. In the words of Cronin (2009, 104–105), such individuals constitute the "active support" that a group can receive. But groups also rely on "passive support" to sustain themselves. This includes (non)actions like overlooking suspicious activities or not cooperating with investigations into a group. Passive supporters may not necessarily agree with a group's methods, but maintaining their tacit compliance is critical for group efficiency.

Nevertheless, those sympathies have limits. As militant groups produce ever more violence, the daily risk to civilians rises. At some level of violence, self-preservation may override any political affinity. And additional violence may tip the scales back in favor of the government, as individuals begin to see the militant groups as the greater threat. Individuals may then begin to actively help target governments crack down on group activities, as occurred in Iraq during the Anbar Awakening. Similarly, the 1997 massacre of civilians in the Egyptian town of Luxor by the extremist group al-Gama'a al-Islamiyya led to a wave of public resentment (Wright, 2006) from which the group never recovered. Weariness and disapproval can happen over a lengthy period of time, as it did for many of the terrorist organizations active in Italy in the 1970s and 1980s – among the most competitive environments of all time according to the GTD database. Public disgust over the cacophony of violence from these groups led, in part, to a slow decline in their activity over the course of two decades (Della Porta and Tarrow, 1986).

Our model can capture passive support incentives through the cost function. Although the most straightforward interpretation of production costs are the financial and labor necessary to commit an attack, it also covers any general disutility for committing attacks. If passive supporters increase social ostracization or assistance to security forces as a group commits greater violence, then the cost term covers the incentive. More attacks still mean a greater share of the active support, but they also mean higher scrutiny and greater capital losses.

Note that individual and total violence both decline in m. Thus, if the subset of individuals who do not support violence are more intolerant of the practice in general, m increases and violence correspondingly decreases.[18]

Endogenous group destruction. A common policy goal to reduce terrorism is to eliminate offending groups (Crelinsten and Schmid, 1992; Crenshaw, 1987; Pillar, 2001). This is true for unilateral actions, military coalitions, and international organizations. Our model provides some insight into the logic of that strategy. Suppose a target state can pay to remove some number of groups before the contest phase of the game. Violence increases in the number of competing groups in our model. As a result, group removal has the intended effect.

That removing groups can reduce terrorism is not surprising. However, the model reveals two less obvious points about this. First, comparative statics from the main model reveal an interesting implication about that target's decision. Recall from Proposition 2.1 that total equilibrium violence equals $\frac{\pi(n-1)}{nm}$. Figure 2.1 illustrates that this increases in n but at a slower rate for each additional group.[19] Thus, if the opposing actor only has the ability to remove one group, it is more likely to take that action when there are *fewer* groups overall – and correspondingly, when the overall rate of violence is relatively low.

Second, suppose that actor has better capacity and can consider destroying multiple groups. The shape of Figure 2.1 implies that paying to remove any one group provides less marginal benefit to the target when the number of groups is large. In turn, the target has an incentive to choose a "go big or go home" reduction strategy. Removing one group at a flat rate might not be worthwhile, but eliminating five groups at five times that flat rate might be.

This is a simple extension, but it is nevertheless important to understand the basic dynamics of eliminating groups now. Chapter 5 develops a model where the target of violence chooses a policy that could agitate the militant groups' audience. Eliminating a group causes the target to increase its policy demands, and the more agitated audience induces the remaining groups to commit more violence overall. Likewise, Chapter 6

---

[18] On a micro-level, public dissatisfaction with a group's output could rise at a faster rate as the group produces greater violence. For example, the public might not begin resisting a group if it commits a single attack, but committing another, and another, and another, has a compounding effect. We could incorporate that into the model by making the groups' cost function convex – for example, mv^2. This would not have any significant impact on our theoretical results. It would, however, discourage higher rates of violence because the marginal cost of an attack is higher at high production levels.

[19] Other values in the figure are set as $\pi = 1$ and $m = 1$.

considers a model where an incumbent group decides whether to deter a potential entrant and how a target state can manipulate those incentives. There, we see that the government might want to promote competition. In turn, having this result here verifies that our later claims are a consequence of more complicated strategic interactions rather than being basic implications of the contest.

Asymmetric audience preferences. Another issue worth exploring is the symmetrical nature of the audience's response to all groups. That is, individuals view all violence in exactly the same manner no matter its source. Thus, if Group 1 and Group 2 both produced ten units of violence, then contributions are equally likely to go to both. One may wonder what would occur absent that assumption.

There are two ways to think about alternative framings. One has a simple implication. Suppose that some subset of contributions will go to specific organizations as long as those organizations remain active. Supporters split the remainder according to the contest function. The first subset represents individuals who have a default allegiance. The remainder are free agents in the marketplace that the baseline model captured.

Such a contest produces identical equilibrium results to those discussed before. Groups still want to produce some quantity of violence. Automatically capturing some portion by doing so is just a bonus. In turn, each group adjusts its expectations and only produces violence according to the size of the free agent pie. Overall violence therefore declines, but it still increases in the number of groups.

A more interesting alternate specification weighs the violence totals by different quantities. In practice, one particular group may hold extra sway or stature over the rest of the organizations. For example, attacks from groups like al-Qaeda and the Tamil Tigers captured the attention of the media better than those of less well-known organizations at the time of their heydays. Alternatively, one particular organization may have a reputation of trust that convinces more supporters to go to that organization despite a comparable amount of violence from competitors. In any case, the formal implication is that an attack from those organizations generates disproportionate sway over the contest function as compared with attacks from other organizations.

To capture this idea, let v_S represent the violence output from the special organization and $\alpha > 1$ be a multiplier that enhances that organization's value of attacks. Greater values of α indicate greater bias for the special group. The other n groups do not receive the multiplier. Thus, the special group's return from the contest equals $\frac{\alpha v_S}{\alpha v_S + v_1 + \ldots + v_n}$, while all other groups receive $\frac{v_i}{\alpha v_S + v_1 + \ldots + v_n}$.[20]

As we show in the appendix, overall violence still increases in the number of groups here.[21] That said, depending on the weightings, a particular group's output might increase following the addition of another group. Nevertheless, average violence must eventually decline, otherwise the groups would pay more in production costs than the total value of the prize at stake.[22]

Asymmetric group capabilities. Another asymmetry may arise when a lead group has mastered the production of violence, such that it faces a lower marginal cost of effort than everyone else. Like the previous extension, we can model this by allowing the special group to have a marginal

---

[20] Nti (2004) and Franke et al. (2013) consider, from a design perspective, a more general setup where each actor can have a unique weighting. Broadly, they show that the optimal allocation rule for the designer (in our case, the citizens) to maximize effort (in our case, violence) handicaps the stronger actor. Doing so encourages weaker actors to exert more effort, which yields an overall increase. Franke et al. (2013) further show that effort always maximizes when there are more than two groups in the designed optimal contest with handicaps.

[21] This refers to the comparative static on n – that is, what happens when another non-special organization enters the competition. The result does always extend in the opposite way – that is, adding a special group to a collection of ordinary organizations. An extreme case helps clarify why. Suppose that α was an arbitrarily large number. Then when the special group enters, it can produce a tiny amount of violence and still outpace all other groups' contributions. Knowing they are outmatched, the other groups may cut their effort and cause an overall decline in violence.

[22] The change in the contest function here may open up a broader question about whether the same general implications apply to other mappings. In fact, we can recover the results under a variety of other conditions. For example, one might imagine that each actor faces differential diminishing marginal returns to their contribution to the contest function. Contributions have diminishing marginal returns in the original contest because the second derivative of $\frac{v_i}{v_1 + \ldots + v_n}$ is negative. In contrast, diminishing marginal returns to the contribution to the contest would include a function like $\frac{\sqrt{v_i}}{\sqrt{v_1} + \ldots + \sqrt{v_n}}$. Here, the first unit of effort puts greater sway on how the contest allocates weights to that actor than the next unit. This reinforces a group's decision to reduce its violence conditional on another group entering. We could also allow for each group's contribution function to maximize at a particular value and see the same general principles. Such a structure is an alternative way to capture the idea that too much violence from one group causes contributors to turn away from that organization.

cost $\underline{m} \in (0, m)$. Thus, its utility function equals $\frac{v_S}{v_S + v_1 + \ldots + v_N} - \underline{m} v_S$.[23] All other groups maintain the same payoff functions.[24]

This extension has a slightly different implication compared with the previous asymmetry. The appendix shows that total violence increases in the number of the ordinary groups, consistent with Proposition 2.1. Per-group violence results show some variation. When an additional ordinary group arises, each ordinary group decreases its output. In contrast, the group with greater capacity may increase its allotment. This is because a low number of competitors gives it incentive to slack off to some degree, as it can still acquire a large amount of support. But adding a competitor dilutes that support level, which sometimes convinces the lead group to abuse its comparative advantage in violence production. Nevertheless, if we sum the total violence across all groups and divide by the number of groups, the rate still decreases. This is consistent with Proposition 2.2's general idea. It also guides how we implement the next chapter's quantitative exploration.

Luck and false claims. We should exercise caution in describing the mechanical generality of Proposition 2.1's result. More groups do not produce more violence for every contest success function. Consider the distribution rule that Dasgupta and Nti (1998) examine and Amegashie (2006) generalizes. Here, Group i receives $\frac{v_1 + \alpha}{v_1 + \ldots + v_n + n\alpha}$ portion of the good. Amegashie (2006) describes α as a "luck" parameter, where each group can earn a portion of the good despite not having exerted any effort at all. One could also interpret α as capturing the audience's inability to track which groups are responsible for attacks. This is consistent with a related literature on false claims, which argues that groups may attempt to take credit for attacks they did not commit (Kearns, Conlon, and Young, 2014; Kearns, 2019). It also helps explain why there are sometimes multiple, competing claims for a single attack.

It is easy to see that total violence can be nonmonotonic in n. The α value behaves like a portion of violence each group automatically

---

[23] Because games are identical across positive affine utility transformations, this is equivalent to the group valuing support at a higher level than other groups.

[24] This is a subtle difference between asymmetric group capabilities and audience preferences. Audience bias for one group has a direct effect on all other groups. In contrast, if lower capacity for one group affects others, it must arise indirectly through the strategies they all select.

allocates. As such, each group offsets its true violence production by that amount. Thus, provided that α is not too large, adding an extra group to a small exiting competition still drives up violence. However, as n becomes large, each of those α values begins to accumulate. Eventually, they consume the marginal return on violence to the point that no group produces any at all. Proposition 2.1's prediction therefore goes away.

Nevertheless, it is worth thinking about the substantive assumptions that underlie this contest success function. It rewards groups for merely declaring their existence. Even in the face of enormous violence from competitors, a silent organization still receives some share of the resources. This runs contrary to the motivating principle behind outbidding – groups need to produce violence to make recruits aware of their existence and lure them to their organization. As such, we have theoretical reason to discount this contest form's assumptions.

CONCLUSION

This chapter serves two purposes. First, we provide a series of micro-foundations that should guide any model of outbidding. A few of these elements are basic: groups are strategic, they compete over a set of resources, and any funds they spend to capture those resources are sunk. The remaining elements describe how violence maps onto the division of those resources. A group's share increases – at a diminishing marginal rate – in its violence output but decreases in other groups' violence outputs. But the competition is not winner-takes-all, so that multiple groups can acquire resources if they try to do so. Together, these points brought us to contest models, which meet all of the assumptions we require.

Second, using a standard contest model to capture outbidding incentives generated two insights. It primarily provided formal confirmation of the common outbidding conjecture in the literature. As the number of groups increase, so too do competitive pressures. Total violence therefore increases in the group numbers. But current understandings of outbidding do not capture the mechanism that explains why. The extra group does not cause all other groups to increase their violence. Indeed, *per-group* violence declines. Total violence instead increases because the extra group adds more than the combined marginal decreases by each other group.

The central theory raises two questions, which we spend the remainder of the book addressing. To begin, do purveyors of political violence behave according to the mechanism? This is both a quantitative and qualitative question. On the quantitative side, one may wonder whether groups indeed produce more violence on average when they have more competitors. On the qualitative side, one may wonder whether groups actually consider these incentives when making their decisions. These issues are the main topics of the next chapter and we touch on them again in Chapter 4.

The other question is how the target of the political violence can alter the incentives of the outbidding market. Contest models have existed for decades, and correspondingly the literature on the subject has enormous depth. However, we are the first to adapt the framework to militant group competition. As such, we have new theoretical ground to explore once we break out of the basic contest structure and start thinking about how target governments can manipulate the market.

Policymakers have many tools at their disposal on this front. They can adopt defensive measures at home, defending against attacks by better fortifying targets and policing to intercept contributions to the groups. Alternatively, they can adopt offensive measures, seeking to reduce an organization's capacity or ability to form. They can also try to sidestep the problem altogether by making policy adjustments intended to reduce grievances among those who might otherwise support the groups.

These policies warrant further investigation. Their direct effects could hide counterintuitive second-order consequences for each group's decision to produce violence. If so, the theoretical consequences, empirical implications, and associated policy recommendations may be different for some special circumstances than what we presented here. We therefore make such extensions the focus of Chapters 4, 5, and 6.

APPENDIX

We now prove the formal claims from this chapter.

Proof of Proposition 2.1

Line 2.1 gives Group i's objective function. The first-order condition of this is:

$$\frac{\partial}{\partial v_i} \left(\pi \frac{v_i}{v_1 + \ldots + v_n} - m v_i \right) = 0$$

$$\pi \frac{v_1 + \ldots + v_n - v_i}{(v_1 + \ldots + v_n)^2} = m \qquad (2.2)$$

To look for a symmetric equilibrium, set $v_i = v$ for all i. Substituting that into Line 2.2 yields:

$$\pi \frac{nv - v}{(nv)^2} = m$$

$$v^* = \frac{\pi(n-1)}{mn^2} \tag{2.3}$$

With n groups, the total violence production is therefore nv^*, or:

$$\frac{\pi}{m}\left(1 - \frac{1}{n}\right)$$

Taking the derivative of this with respect to n gives $\frac{\pi}{mn^2}$. All of these values are strictly positive. Thus, equilibrium violence is strictly increasing in n.

Proof of Proposition 2.2

The proof is as simple as taking a derivative of Line 2.3 with respect to n:

$$\frac{\partial}{\partial n}\left(\frac{\pi(n-1)}{mn^2}\right)$$

$$-\frac{\pi(n-2)}{mn^3}$$

Because $n \geq 2$, per-group production strictly decreases.[25]

Asymmetric Audience Preferences

We now break from the baseline model by having a special group, denoted S, that receives a multiplier $\alpha > 1$ to its contest contribution. The other $n \in \{1, 2, \ldots\}$ groups have the same capabilities as in the original model.

To begin, consider the special group's utility function:

$$\pi \frac{\alpha v_S}{\alpha v_S + v_1 + \ldots + v_n} - m v_S$$

[25] The derivative at $n = 2$ is 0, but we are only interested in how the behavior changes as n increases away from that value.

Taking the first-order condition of this yields:

$$\frac{\partial}{\partial v_S}\left(\pi\frac{\alpha v_S}{\alpha v_S + v_1 + \ldots + v_n} - m v_S\right) = 0$$

$$\frac{\pi\alpha(v_1 + \ldots + v_n)}{(\alpha v_S + v_1 + \ldots + v_n)^2} = m \qquad (2.4)$$

Meanwhile, a generic ordinary group i's utility function is:

$$\pi\frac{v_i}{\alpha v_S + v_1 + \ldots + v_n} - m v_i$$

And taking the first-order condition of this yields:

$$\frac{\partial}{\partial v_i}\left(\pi\frac{v_i}{\alpha v_S + v_1 + \ldots + v_n} - m v_i\right) = 0$$

$$\pi\frac{\alpha v_S + v_1 + \ldots + v_n - v_i}{(\alpha v_S + v_1 + \ldots + v_n)^2} = m \qquad (2.5)$$

We again look for an equilibrium where the ordinary actors play a symmetric strategy. Making the substitution that $v_1 = \ldots = v_n = v$, we can rewrite Line 2.4 as:

$$\frac{\pi\alpha n v}{(\alpha v_S + n v)^2} = m \qquad (2.6)$$

And we can rewrite Line 2.5 as:

$$\frac{\pi(\alpha v_S + (n-1)v)}{(\alpha v_S + n v)^2} = m \qquad (2.7)$$

This generates a system of two equations with two unknowns. Setting the left-hand sides of Lines 2.6 and 2.7 equal to each other and rearranging in terms of v_S generates:

$$\frac{\pi\alpha n v}{(\alpha v_S + n v)^2} = \frac{\pi(\alpha v_S + (n-1)v)}{(\alpha v_S + n v)^2}$$

$$v_S = n v - \frac{(n-1)v}{\alpha} \qquad (2.8)$$

Substituting Line 2.8 into Line 2.6 and solving for v yields:

$$\frac{\pi\alpha n v}{\left(\alpha\left(n v - \frac{(n-1)v}{\alpha}\right) + n v\right)^2} = m$$

$$v^* \equiv \frac{\pi\alpha n}{m(\alpha n + 1)^2}$$

Thus, the n ordinary groups each play v^* in equilibrium. Substituting v^* into Line 2.8 generates:

$$v_S = \frac{\pi \alpha n^2}{m(\alpha n + 1)^2} - \frac{(n-1)\left(\frac{\pi \alpha n}{m(\alpha n + 1)^2}\right)}{\alpha}$$

$$v_S^* \equiv \frac{\pi n}{m(\alpha n + 1)^2}$$

Thus, the special group plays v_S^* in equilibrium.

We can now investigate how total violence increases in the number of ordinary groups. With n ordinary groups and one special group, the sum of violence equals:

$$\frac{n\left(\frac{\pi \alpha n}{m(\alpha n + 1)^2}\right) + \frac{\pi n}{m(\alpha n + 1)^2}}{\frac{\pi n}{m(\alpha n + 1)}} \tag{2.9}$$

Taking the derivative of Line 2.9 with respect to n yields:

$$\frac{\pi}{m(\alpha n + 1)^2}$$

This is strictly positive. Thus, total violence strictly increases in the number of groups.

We can also show that each group's production goes down as n increases. Consider first the special group's production. Taking the derivative of v_S^* with respect to n and showing it is negative gives:

$$\frac{\pi(1 - \alpha n)}{m(\alpha n + 1)^3} < 0$$

$$\alpha n > 1$$

This is true because $\alpha > 1$ and $n \geq 1$. Therefore, the special group's violence output decreases in the number of ordinary groups.

Now consider an ordinary group's production. Taking the derivative of v^* with respect to n and showing it is negative gives:

$$\frac{\alpha \pi(1 - \alpha n)}{m(\alpha n + 1)^3} < 0$$

$$\alpha n > 1$$

As before, this is true.

Taken together, these imply that overall per group production also declines in the number of groups.

Asymmetric Group Capabilities

We now break from the baseline model by having a special group, denoted S, that has a lower marginal cost $\underline{m} \in (0, m)$ than the rest of the groups. The others maintain their original utility functions.

We begin by calculating the special group's first-order condition:

$$\frac{\partial}{\partial v_S}\left(\frac{\pi v_S}{v_S + v_1 + \ldots + v_n} - \underline{m}v_S\right) = 0$$

$$\frac{\pi(v_1 + \ldots + v_n)}{(v_S + v_1 + \ldots + v_n)^2} = \underline{m} \tag{2.10}$$

And likewise for a generic group i's first-order condition:

$$\frac{\partial}{\partial v_i}\left(\frac{\pi v_i}{v_S + v_1 + \ldots + v_n} - mv_i\right) = 0$$

$$\frac{\pi(v_S + v_1 + \ldots + v_n - v_i)}{(v_S + v_1 + \ldots + v_n)^2} = m \tag{2.11}$$

We still look for an equilibrium where the ordinary actors play a symmetric strategy. Making the substitution $v_1 = \ldots = v_n = v$, we can rewrite Line 2.10 as:

$$\frac{\pi n v}{\underline{m}} = (v_S + nv)^2 \tag{2.12}$$

And we can rewrite Line 2.11 as:

$$\frac{\pi(v_S + (n-1)v)}{m} = (v_S + nv)^2 \tag{2.13}$$

This generates a system of two equations with two unknowns. Setting the left-hand sides of Lines 2.12 and 2.13 equal to each other and rearranging in terms of v_S yields:

$$\frac{\pi n v}{\underline{m}} = \frac{\pi(v_S + (n-1)v)}{m}$$

$$v_S = (m - \underline{m})nv + \underline{m}v \tag{2.14}$$

Substituting Line 2.14 into Line 2.12 and solving for v yields:

$$\frac{\pi n v}{\underline{m}} = (((m - \underline{m})nv + \underline{m}v) + nv)^2$$

$$v^* = \frac{\pi n}{\underline{m}\left(\frac{mn}{\underline{m}} + 1\right)^2}$$

Thus, the n ordinary groups each play v^* in equilibrium. Substituting v^* into Line 2.14 generates:

$$v_S = (m - \underline{m})n \left(\frac{\pi n}{\underline{m} \left(\frac{mn}{\underline{m}} + 1 \right)^2} \right) + \underline{m} \left(\frac{\pi n}{\underline{m} \left(\frac{mn}{\underline{m}} + 1 \right)^2} \right)$$

$$v_S^* = \frac{\pi mn^2}{\underline{m}^2 \left(\frac{mn}{\underline{m}} + 1 \right)^2} - \frac{\pi (n^2 - n)}{\underline{m} \left(\frac{mn}{\underline{m}} + 1 \right)^2}$$

Thus, the special group plays v_S^* in equilibrium.

We can now investigate how total violence increases in the number of ordinary groups. With n ordinary groups and one special group, the sum of violence equals:

$$\frac{n \left(\frac{\pi n}{\underline{m} \left(\frac{mn}{\underline{m}} + 1 \right)^2} \right) + \frac{\pi mn^2}{\underline{m}^2 \left(\frac{mn}{\underline{m}} + 1 \right)^2} - \frac{\pi (n^2 - n)}{\underline{m} \left(\frac{mn}{\underline{m}} + 1 \right)^2}}{\frac{\pi mn^2}{\underline{m}^2 \left(\frac{mn}{\underline{m}} + 1 \right)^2} + \frac{\pi n}{\underline{m} \left(\frac{mn}{\underline{m}} + 1 \right)^2}} \tag{2.15}$$

Taking the derivative of Line 2.15 with respect to n yields:

$$\frac{\pi \underline{m}}{(\underline{m} + mn)^2}$$

This is strictly positive. Thus, total violence strictly increases in the number of groups.

We can also show that each ordinary group's violence production decreases by taking the derivative of v^* with respect to n and showing that it is negative:

$$-\frac{\pi \underline{m}(mn - \underline{m})}{(mn + \underline{m})^3} < 0$$

$$mn > \underline{m}$$

Because $m > \underline{m}$ and $n \geq 1$, this is true.

Next, we can examine when the special group's violence production decreases by taking the derivative of v_S^* with respect to n and verifying that it is negative:

$$\frac{\pi \underline{m}(mn - 2\underline{m}n + \underline{m})}{(mn + \underline{s})^3} < 0$$

$$mn - 2\underline{m}n + \underline{m} < 0$$

This may or may not be true depending on the parameters. Moreover, it is possible that the relationship is nonmonotonic, with initial increases to n causing additional violence but further increases to reduce violence.

Nevertheless, we can still show that the aggregate per-group violence – that is, the sum of all violence divided by the total number of groups – strictly decreases in n. To do this, note that the element of interest is Line 2.15 (total violence) divided by $n + 1$ (the total number of groups). Taking the derivative of that value with respect to n and showing that it is negative gives:

$$\frac{\pi(\underline{m} - mn^2)}{(n+1)^2(mn + \underline{m})^2} < 0$$

$$mn^2 > \underline{m}$$

This is true because $m > \underline{m}$ and $n \geq 1$.

3

The Evidence

The previous chapter developed a formal model of outbidding. In it, each militant group commits violence to sway a pool of contributions to its own ranks rather than to opposing organizations. Working through the strategic incentives demonstrated two interesting results. First, competition breeds more violence – as the number of groups increases, so too does the overall rate of destruction. Second, the average amount of violence per group decreases. Thus, the overall gain is a byproduct of the additional group's violence rather than existing groups raising their production to compensate for the new competition.

The theoretical findings raise a couple of empirical questions. To begin, do we observe these trends in the data? An affirmative answer would support the notion that the competition logic is critical for understanding political violence in general. And our evidence indeed suggests this is the case. In this chapter we estimate that an increase from one active group to five active groups can increase the number of violent attacks a country experiences by 87 percent. However, the same increase in active groups can lead to a *decrease* in per-group violence.

Of course, large-n empirical analysis of conflict has limitations. In an ideal research design, we would randomly assign new groups to some regions and randomly maintain the status quo in others. This would allow us to estimate the causal effect of an additional group on overall violence output and group-level violence production. However, creating additional groups like this is as dubious as it is impractical. Meanwhile, any statistical analysis – causally identified or not – cannot speak to the underlying logic of the model. That is, quantitative empirics can only inform us about what happens, not *why* it happens.

Given that a central purpose of formal models is to understand why things happen, our second empirical question is whether groups respond to the incentives in the manner we would predict for the reasons our model outlines. We focus on per-group violence for two reasons. First, the overall increase in violence is not the result of intent by the players in the game. Rather, it occurs as a natural consequence of their individual-level incentives. And second, qualitative discussion of overall increases is already present in the literature (Bloom, 2005). The individual-level result is the novel substantive aspect of the previous chapter's model and so we focus our efforts on that.

We use the Garo National Liberation Army (GNLA) to work through the substantive logic. The GNLA provides a useful case to analyze for a few reasons. Over the course of 2012 and 2013, the GNLA witnessed an evolution in the competitiveness of insurgent groups in Northeast India. This generates variation in our key independent variable. Also during that time, the GNLA's capabilities and opportunities remained relatively static. Thus, key potential confounding variables remain constant. If anything, violence ought to have increased as the central government redeployed its forces away from the conflict zone. Yet the GNLA reduced violence with the spike in competition and its motivations match the model's central prediction. We trace a similar process among the factions of the National Socialist Council of Nagaland (NSCN).

HYPOTHESES AND RESEARCH DESIGN

We begin with the quantitative part of our empirical analysis. The counterintuitive implications derived from the formal model offer one possible explanation for why empirical evidence of the outbidding effect thus far has been mixed. Several studies support the notion that increasing competition can lead to behavioral changes among militant groups, including the *type* of violence they employ (e.g., Conrad and Greene, 2015; Nemeth, 2014; Phillips, 2015). But perhaps the most comprehensive test of the basic outbidding hypothesis – more groups leads to more violence – finds little supporting evidence. Findley and Young (2012) examine the relationship between the number of active organizations in a country and the number of terrorist attacks that occur in a given month. They find that the relationship is not statistically significant in a series of models that use counts of the number of insurgent groups or "veto players" as independent variables. Findley and Young also examine the influence of increasing competition on suicide attacks specifically, and, while they find preliminary support, the relationship does not hold once they control for other factors. Taking all of their findings together, Findley and Young state that "in contrast to arguments in much of the literature, we find scant evidence of an outbidding-terrorism link" (Findley and Young, 2012, 719).

Given that other scholars find evidence of increased competition driving changes at the aggregate (country) level, the absence of support for the simplest outbidding hypothesis is puzzling. One possible explanation is that Findley and Young (2012) was one of the first studies to examine the question using a large-n approach. Chenoweth (2010) examined the question earlier, but her tests were more limited and she used a proxy measure – the competitiveness of a state's political institutions – in place of a direct measure of group competition. But these earlier studies were necessarily working with more limited temporal periods. Findley and Young (2012), for instance, use data on terrorist attacks only through 2004. Using data from more recent years might reveal the evidence they were ultimately searching for. The logic of outbidding, as elaborated by Bloom (2004), was largely based on observations made during the Second Intifada in Israel. The Findley and Young (2012) study therefore only includes a few years of data beyond these central events (and only a few years of data beyond the 9/11 attacks). Perhaps not coincidentally, the small group of studies that find some evidence of outbidding behavior all use more recent data on terrorist violence (e.g., Conrad and Greene, 2015; Nemeth, 2014; Phillips, 2015).[1]

Our goal is to examine, with the most recent data available, whether cross-national evidence exists to support Proposition 2.1. The proposition states that total violence strictly increases in the number of groups and represents the basic implication of the outbidding approach:

Hypothesis 3.1 *States with more active militant groups experience more terrorist attacks than states with fewer groups.*

To examine the evidence, we require data on both the number of groups and the amount of violence occurring within a specific polity. As with the majority of studies on the topic, we take advantage of the Global Terrorism Database (GTD) to identify the number of violent attacks that occur in each country (START, 2016). The GTD is the most

---

[1] The central conclusions presented in this chapter, however, are robust when varying the time period under examination.

comprehensive collection of information on such attacks and the version
of the dataset used here includes details on more than 156,000 attacks
occurring around the world since 1970. To be included in the data, an
incident must be intentional, must be violent, and the perpetrators of the
incident must be non-state actors (START, 2016, 9–10). Additionally,
an incident must be "aimed at attaining a political, economic, religious,
or social goal" and/or the incident is intended to "coerce, intimidate, or
convey some other message to a larger audience (or audiences) than the
immediate victims" (START, 2016, 10). While such incidents are generally considered to be "terrorist" attacks, the database's inclusion criteria
meets our more broad interest in any violence that is demonstrative – the
kind that can be used to send a message to enemies as well as existing
and potential supporters. Additionally, conflation of demonstrative violence against non-combatant targets with intragroup violence is less of a
concern, as the GTD project explicitly considers "Intra/Inter-group conflict" violence to be outside the definition of terrorism (START, 2016).
The data therefore focus exclusively on the kind of violence we have
conceptualized in our model.

Although a wide range of information about individual attacks is
available in the GTD, we only require three pieces of information to test
the propositions derived in the previous chapter. First, we need to know
where each attack occurred – specifically, in which country. Second, we
need information – where available – on rates of attack per group. This
will allow us to determine if group-level violence changes in the manner that we anticipate. We return to discuss the group-level data in more
detail below.

The final puzzle piece is more complicated. We need to know when
each attack occurred. These three characteristics will allow us to group
attacks by country and by year. Although the GTD offers the specific day
and month of attacks, we expect group responses to competitive dynamics to be a more slow-moving process. This is why we examine annual
changes in violence, as short-term changes in violence are likely suscep-
tible to more idiosyncratic processes.[2] It is also more difficult to identify
accurate daily or monthly estimates of when new groups emerge, from
a data collection perspective but also from the perspective of terrorist

---

[2] This could be another possible explanation for the lack of statistically significant findings
by Findley and Young (2012). They use the country-month as the unit of analysis and
therefore may be diluting the effect of longer-term trends driven by the competitive
environment.

groups themselves. Terrorist groups and their leaders may be unaware of such changes at the precise moment that they are occurring – let alone make strategic changes to their use of violence in response. And this is especially true in the most dynamic environments, such as the Syrian Civil War, where so many groups emerged overnight that it would be difficult for an organization to track these changes on a daily basis.[3] Yearly estimates of active groups, on the other hand, are inherently more reliable because they require less specificity. Using the dates and locations of each attack, we produce counts of the number of attacks occurring within a country in a given year, and examine if these counts change, on average, given changes in the number of groups operating in that country. For robustness purposes, we also create an alternative measure that includes extraterritorial attacks committed by active groups in the country. The results when using this alternative measure are comparable to those reported here.

In our largest sample in the models listed later in this chapter, we have data for more than 2,000 country-years between 1970 and 2015. This includes all country-years in which at least one violent attack occurred. The maximum number of attacks, 3,933, occurred in Iraq in 2014. The median number of attacks in the sample is twelve, suggesting that many countries experienced some, but not an overwhelming amount, of attacks during the time period. Additionally, given that the GTD inclusion criteria are somewhat broad, many attacks are not particularly noteworthy in terms of the destruction or fatalities inflicted. So even a country that experienced twelve attacks may not be viewed as particularly conflict-prone if the violence is peripheral. This suggests that each country's experience with violence can vary widely. While many countries in the data experience low-level, isolated events, others experience more sustained and sophisticated kinds of violent campaigns. In the empirical analysis, we control for the presence of a civil conflict, but the basic GTD data provide information about violence committed across a diverse set of environments.

The GTD also offers a relatively simple way to calculate the number of active organizations in each country – the independent variable in all of our analyses. We count the number of groups in each country-year that perpetrated at least one violent attack.

---

[3] See "Guide to the Syrian Rebels" 2013.

In the largest sample in the empirical analysis, the number of groups ranges from one active group to fifty-four active groups. Although Italy in 1977 represents the maximum value of fifty-four, India has many of the highest values in recent years. Around 40 percent of country-years in the sample involve only a single active group according to the GTD, which means that a large majority of observations in the sample involve two or more groups.[4] The median number of groups in the data, in fact, is two. So the central tendency is an observation that provides an ideal baseline to examine the role that increasing competition plays in the amount of violence a country experiences.

Figure 3.1 offers a preliminary look at the relationship between the number of active terrorist groups and the number of terrorist attacks. Although the data do not paint a clear picture, the linear fit line appears to indicate a positive relationship, just as the outbidding approach would expect. Of particular interest for our analysis are the cases where there

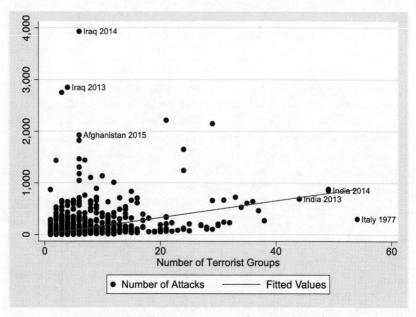

FIGURE 3.1 Terrorist groups and terrorist attacks.

---

[4] In robustness checks, we restricted our sample to those involving two or more groups – the cases where we can confirm potential competition – and our findings are consistent with those reported here.

are few groups and high numbers of attacks, such as Iraq in 2013 and 2014. In practice, these tend to be situations where a single group or a small number of groups has "cornered the market" with violence, conditions that we examine in detail in Chapter 6.

In our first set of models listed below, we examine the relationship between the number of active groups in a country and the number of attacks in that country, based on these measures derived from the GTD data. As Findley and Young (2012) and others have pointed out, however, identifying cross-national evidence of outbidding using the GTD's information on *both* the number of groups and the number of attacks is potentially problematic. This is because groups appear in the data pre-cisely *because they have committed terrorist attacks.* In other words, increasing numbers of groups would result in more attacks by default, biasing the results in favor of the outbidding hypothesis. We include models with the count of GTD groups strictly for comparison with later models, but, as an alternative, we also use a count of the number of active groups identified by the Uppsala Conflict Data Program (UCDP), version 1-2013 (Allansson, Melander and Themnér, 2017; Harbom, Melander, and Wallensteen, 2008). The UCDP includes information on actors involved in armed conflict that resulted in at least twenty-five battle-related deaths in a given year, where at least one of the actors is a government (Themnér, 2013). The project therefore collects informa-tion on groups frequently thought of as traditional rebel and insurgent organizations.

As with the GTD count, we simply count the number of active groups in each country during a given year to create our independent varia-ble. Other studies, including Findley and Young (2012) and Conrad and Greene (2015), have used similar measures as an alternative to counting groups in the GTD data. This second measure of competition allows us to examine if the number of rebel groups is statistically related to the number of individual attacks that a state experiences. The number of active groups ranges from one to ten. Roughly 38 percent of the observa-tions involve two or more active rebel groups. All of this suggests that the UCDP-based measure is capturing a different set of actors than the GTD, underlining the benefit of using it as an alternative test of the outbidding hypothesis. Figure 3.2 shows the relationship between this alternative measure and the number of terrorist attacks that a state experiences. The data points have been jittered to clarify the distribution. Once again, the linear fit line appears to indicate a positive relationship, albeit less obvious than before.

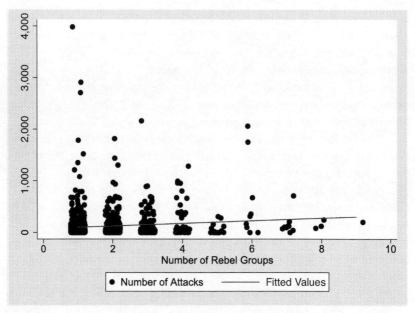

FIGURE 3.2 Rebel groups and terrorist attacks.

In our second set of analyses, we examine the evidence for Proposition 2.2. It states that per-group violence strictly decreases in the number of groups. Our empirical expectation is as follows:

Hypothesis 3.2 *States with more active militant groups experience fewer terrorist attacks per group than states with fewer groups.*

To test this hypothesis, we still require data on the number of groups (the independent variable) and, again, we use the counts derived from the GTD and UCDP data. But we also require a measure of per-group violence rather than the aggregate violence occurring in each country. There are two ways to capture this with the existing data. First, we could directly attribute attacks to specific groups and count the number of incidents each group is responsible for in a given year. Second, we could calculate the per-group violence rate for each country-year, dividing the number of attacks in a given year by the number of active groups.

The first solution has both theoretical and measurement problems. On the theoretical side, Proposition 2.2 is less robust to the individual level. For example, with asymmetric group capacity, adding another group may

TABLE 3.1 *Group-level attacks.*

	Min	Max	Median
Average attacks per terrorist group	1	917	5
Average attacks per rebel group	0.125	3,933	17
Number of terrorist groups	1	54	2
Number of rebel groups	1	10	1

cause a high-capacity group to increase its violence output. Measuring at the state level mitigates this problem, as we expect the per-group average to go down.

On the measurement side, for many of the attacks listed in the GTD, the name of the group or perpetrators responsible for the attack is also listed. However, there are a number of issues with using this group-level information that have been outlined by previous studies. In many cases, the proper name of a group is not reported, so generic information about the identity of the perpetrators is listed instead. This includes broad categorizations like "Islamists" or "students." It also has more specific descriptions like "Hutus" that do not refer to a formal organization. Even including such informal group names, nearly three-fifths of attacks listed in the GTD were neither claimed nor attributed (LaFree, Dugan, and Miller, 2014). Researchers have subsequently pointed out the inherent biases that may result from using these group-level attributions and claims of responsibility to examine certain research questions (Kearns, Conlon, and Young, 2014). Again, using the per-group average avoids these concerns. As such, we present our analysis below using the per-group average as the dependent variable.[5]

We begin the analysis with some summary observations (Table 3.1). The highest rate of violence experienced by a country using GTD groups is 917 attacks per group – experienced by Iraq in 2015. The median rate of attacks is five per group. The highest rate of violence experienced by a country using UCDP groups is Iraq in 2014, which is only listed as having one rebel group. The median rate of attacks per UCDP group is seventeen attacks.

Although we are primarily concerned with the bivariate relationship between group numbers and violence, in later tables we include a series

---

[5] Nevertheless, we examined Hypothesis 3.2 using the group-level attributions of violence as a robustness check. Regardless of the approach that we use, the main conclusions we draw from our empirical analysis do not change.

of variables to control for many state-level characteristics that could reasonably be expected to influence both the number of active groups and the amount of violence. This includes a measure of *Ethnic fractionalization* and a measure of *Religious fractionalization*, as countries with more ethnic groups or more religious groups may be at a higher risk of conflict by default (Alesina et al., 2003). Both variables range from 0 to 1 and capture the probability that any two individuals chosen at random from the population would be from different ethnic or religious groups. Higher values therefore indicate greater ethnic or religious fractionalization. We also include an ordinal measure of *Physical integrity rights*, ranging from 0 to 8 with higher values representing higher levels of respect (i.e., fewer violations) (Cingranelli and Richards, 2010). Previous research has found that government abuse of these rights can lead to higher levels of militant and terrorist violence (Walsh and Piazza, 2010).[6] It is possible that our hypothesized relationships are only relevant in the most serious cases of conflict, so we include a measure that indicates whether the country experienced a *Civil conflict* in a given year. This binary indicator is created from the UCDP dataset and equals 1 if an "intrastate conflict" or "internationalized intrastate conflict" occurred. We also include the natural log of the country's real GDP per capita and population, as both the economy and the population size can potentially influence the likelihood of violence, as well as the effectiveness of government countermeasures (Eyerman and Hart Jr., 1996). Data on GDP per capita and population size are drawn from Gleditsch et al. (2002) and the International Monetary Fund (International Monetary Fund, 2015) respectively. We also include a measure of the level of democracy in the country, drawn from the Polity project (Marshall and Jaggers, 2006). The measure ranges from -10 to 10 and uses a variety of information, including the competitiveness of the state's political institutions, to classify a state as more or less democratic. Lower values represent more autocratic governments and higher values represent more democratic ones.

Finally, to account for basic inertia in state-level violence, we include a moving average of the amount of attacks that a state has experienced since 1970 or the first year of its independence. Violence in one year

---

[6] Although an analysis that incorporates the concept of *state capacity* in addition to state behavior is warranted, that is the central focus of Chapter 4. Here, we build the basic model of competitive violence (comparable with previous empirical models) and then extend this model in Chapter 4 by incorporating state capacity as a key explanatory variable.

may not only lead to more violence in subsequent years, but particularly high levels of violence may also signal particularly chaotic environments ripe for the entry of new groups. Including the full range of control variables significantly reduces the sample size (up to 43 percent in the case of the rebel group models). This is primarily due to limitations in temporal scope for some of the variables. Nevertheless, we confirmed that our conclusions are not sensitive to the addition or deletion of individual controls.

Unless noted, we rely on a negative binomial approach, which is suited for cases where the dependent variable is a count. Our dependent variables are either a count of attacks at the country level or a count of per-group attacks. The negative binomial is preferred to the standard Poisson model because terrorism and violent attack data tends to be highly overdispersed. In all models we calculate robust standard errors clustered on the country.

ANALYSIS: COUNTRY LEVEL

The following tables and figures summarize our empirical exploration of the propositions derived in Chapter 2. The first set of analyses examine whether there is evidence that increasing numbers of militant groups lead to an increase in aggregate violence at the country level. In Table 3.2, we examine the bivariate relationships between our counts of militant groups and the count of violent attacks that a state experiences. The first column lists the results when we use the GTD count of terrorist organizations. As expected, the relationship is highly significant and positive. In other words, more active groups are associated with more violence overall.

Figure 3.3 shows the substantive effects of increasing numbers of active groups on the amount of violence a state experiences. The line shows the relationship across a range of values for the independent variable and emphasizes the positive relationship between the two variables. With one or two active groups, the predicted number of attacks is relatively low (twenty-two and twenty-nine predicted attacks, respectively). But by the time a state has seven active groups, the number of predicted attacks is well over 100. As we discussed in the previous section, however, this positive relationship may be due to inherent bias when using GTD groups to construct the independent variable. As an alternative, in the second column in Table 3.2, we test the relationship using a count of rebel groups from the UCDP project. Although the coefficient for the

TABLE 3.2 *DV: Total number of attacks.*

	Model 1 β (S.E.)	Model 2 β (S.E.)
Number of terrorist groups	0.261*** (0.062)	
Number of rebel groups		0.184 (0.120)
Constant	2860*** (0.252)	4.451*** (0.315)
N	2101	976

Robust standard errors in parentheses
* $p < 0.10$, ** $p < 0.05$, *** $p < 0.01$

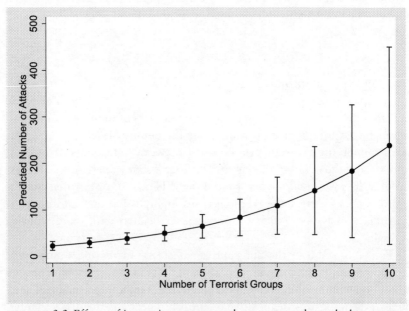

FIGURE 3.3 Effects of increasing group numbers on annual attacks by country.

variable *Number of rebel groups* indicates a positive relationship, it is just barely outside of conventional levels of statistical significance. We should emphasize here that the *Number of rebel groups* is really intended as a robustness check and we believe it does not capture our theoretical concept as well as the *Number of terrorist groups*. The threshold for being counted as a rebel group (twenty-five battle-related deaths) is a

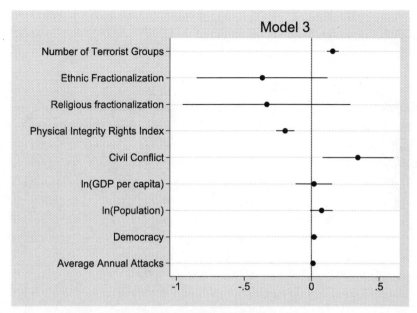

FIGURE 3.4 DV: Total number of attacks.
Source: Coefficients with 90 percent confidence intervals

pretty high bar and, therefore, a count of rebel groups is likely to be an *undercount* of active militant groups in many contexts. Nevertheless, the evidence provided in Table 3.2 and Figure 3.3 offers mixed findings, much like the previous findings in the literature on political violence.

In Figure 3.4, we move beyond the simple bivariate relationships to examine if there is any evidence for the hypothesized relationship when we control for a variety of other factors. The figure shows the coefficient estimates for all covariates, along with their 90 percent confidence intervals. We focus now on the model that includes the count of terrorist groups specifically. Even after including the other variables, *Number of terrorist groups* continues to have a highly significant ($p < 0.01$) and positive effect. The presence of a civil conflict and the average number of annual attacks in the state also positively influence the amount of violence, as expected. Higher levels of respect for *Physical integrity rights*, however, appear to have a pacifying effect on the aggregate violence.

Although not shown here, the relationship between the *Number of rebel groups* and the number of attacks is statistically insignificant, and yet the coefficient is consistently positive. Interestingly, only when *Physical integrity rights* is added to the model does the relationship become insignificant. This supports our contention that the behavior of the

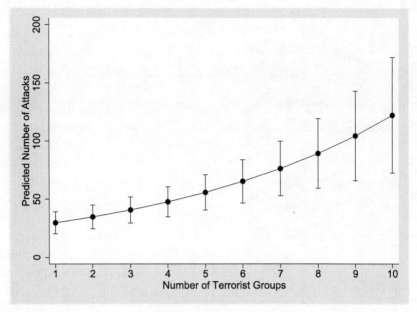

FIGURE 3.5 Multivariate results.

government must be taken into account, a matter that we return to in the next chapter.

Figure 3.5 summarizes the substantive effects of our key independent variable. We once again see a clear positive relationship between the number of GTD groups and the amount of violence. An increase from one active group to five active groups increases the predicted amount of attacks by 87 percent, and this difference is statistically significant. In this first set of tables and figures, therefore, we have growing evidence in favor of the outbidding hypothesis: more groups leads to more violence, and this appears to be the case even when using alternate operationalizations of the number of groups.

We also analyze how sensitive these findings are to changes in the model specifications. We complete a series of robustness checks, beginning with the inclusion of observations with zero terrorist attacks. Although we are theoretically interested in *differences* in levels of violence, rather than the occurrence or onset of violence, we nevertheless expand the analysis to include country-years where no violence occurred. The relationship between the independent variable and dependent variable is still highly significant, even after accounting for the disproportionate amount of zeros in the data with the aid of zero-inflated negative binomial models. The zero-inflated analysis also helps address reporting bias issues that have been identified in previous work on terrorism (Drakos and Gofas, 2006). In another series of models, we restrict the analysis to observations where at least two groups were active. Arguably, only cases with this baseline of competition are useful for our tests. When restricting the sample in this way, the results are still comparable with those reported here. We also test the robustness of the results by lagging all independent variables by a single year, and, again, the results are similar to the main set of models in this chapter. Finally, we estimate models with country fixed effects and those results are also comparable. Combined, the evidence supports the basic outbidding hypothesis: more groups leads to more aggregate violence.

ANALYSIS: GROUP LEVEL

In the preceding analysis, we considered violence at the aggregate, country-level. Now we turn to the per-group average violence committed. In Figure 3.6, we present the coefficient estimates from multivariate

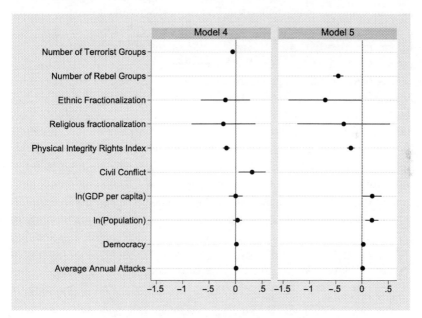

FIGURE 3.6 DV: Average group attacks.
Source: Coefficients with 90 percent confidence intervals

models using the same set of independent variables, but this time the dependent variable is the average amount of violence committed by each group in a given country-year. In Model 4, the independent variable is the number of terrorist groups active in the same country. The influence of this variable is negative and statistically significant ($p < 0.01$). We find the same effect and level of significance when using the number of rebel groups in Model 5. Figure 3.6 therefore provides strong preliminary evidence in favor of Proposition 2.2: group-level violence strictly decreases in the number of groups. In other words, when there is an increase in either the number of terrorist groups (defined by GTD) or the number of rebel groups (defined by UCDP), groups engage in fewer violent attacks on average. In both models, *Physical integrity rights* significantly reduce group-level violence. The measure of *Civil conflict* is not included in Model 6 because rebel groups are, by definition, engaged in civil conflict.

Figure 3.7 outlines the substantive effects of our key independent variables. Although the marginal effect of increasing group numbers in Model 5 appears to be just that – marginal – the evidence from Model 6 suggests a strong substantive effect: an increase from one to five active groups in a country, for instance, leads to an 84 percent reduction in average group attacks. This effect is statistically significant.

Before we discuss some of our additional robustness checks, it is important to emphasize the significance of the results presented in this most recent set of analyses. We have offered evidence of a relationship that is *counterintuitive* given the expectations of the contemporary outbidding literature. Although increasing competition appears to lead to more violence overall, we see evidence of violence *declining* as a per-group rate. It is important to point out that these latter empirical results are strongly biased *against* our hypothesis. According to the outbidding approach, increasing numbers of active groups signals an intensification of conflict and competition, which should result in groups engaging in greater quantities of violent attacks. And once again, using only the GTD data (as we did in Model 4) should bias the results in favor of a *positive* relationship. More active groups – considered active precisely because they use violence – should mean more violence by default.[7] But the results indicate a significant relationship in the opposite direction, a relationship likely to be underestimated. We conclude, then, that even if a particular

---

[7] Another way to think about this is that we do not allow groups to reduce their violence to zero.

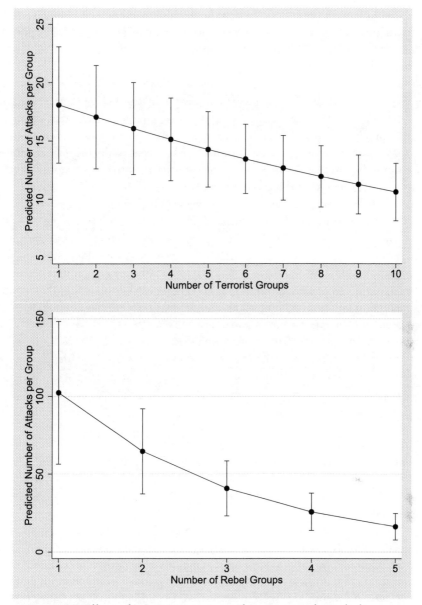

FIGURE 3.7 Effects of increasing group numbers on annual attacks by group.

group increases its use of violence in the face of growing competition, this effect is not consistent across groups and, on average, the opposite effect is more likely.

As with the country-level analysis, we also conduct robustness tests to further gauge the sensitivity of these results. The most important robustness check is the attack attribution approach mentioned previously. Again, these results are comparable with those reported here – increasing numbers of active groups significantly reduce the number of attacks attributed to a particular group in the GTD data. In this approach, we also controlled for group-level characteristics with information from the Big Allied and Dangerous dataset (Asal and Rethemeyer, 2008). Doing so results in a loss of up to 78 percent of the original observations, but allows us to account for (1) the membership size of each group, (2) the age of the group, and (3) whether the group espoused an Islamist ideology. In separate models, we also include a group-level indicator of the amount of attacks that each group committed in the most recent year that it appeared in the data. Using these group-level controls, the model with a count of UCDP rebel groups remains consistently significant and negative. The model with a count of terrorist groups is also negative, though sometimes outside of conventional levels of significance. Finally, we conducted our central analysis presented in this chapter with lagged independent variables and country fixed effects and we also used a restricted sample of observations with at least two active groups. In these robustness checks, the vast majority of the results are nearly identical to those presented here. In summary, there appears to be robust evidence that group-level violence declines, on average, as competition increases.

INSURGENCY IN NORTHEAST INDIA

Thus far, we have derived expectations that increasing competition may drive an aggregate increase in violence, while also resulting in a per-group decline in violence. In the previous section we presented large-n empirical evidence of both effects.

In Chapter 2, we argued that the decline in a single group's violence is largely attributable to a decline in the marginal utility derived from each individual attack. This decline in utility is driven, in turn, by an increasingly saturated marketplace for violence. Groups operating in such environments are likely to find that an individual attack does not offer the same return on investment as it may have when there were fewer active groups competing for the attention of the media, the government, and the public.

Such a decline in the utility of violence can occur for a variety of reasons. First, with more aggregate violence, the demonstrative value of a single attack is diminished. In an environment where violence is commonplace, individual attacks simply do not offer the same purchase as they do when violence is a more novel occurrence. We have also seen specific terrorist tactics decline in popularity when they are used too frequently. Suicide attacks, for instance, rose in prominence during the Lebanese Civil War. The group that pioneered the tactic's modern usage, Hezbollah, saw a great deal of media coverage and attention in return. But as the tactic spread throughout the conflict and into other conflicts, its value declined (Lewis, 2012). Even a particularly novel form of violence, then, can eventually become mundane given enough overuse. This is undoubtedly the case for less innovative, "everyday" terrorist attacks as well. While terrorist groups may gain some immediate benefits from launching different *types* of attacks, "more of the same" offers little value in particularly competitive environments (Conrad and Greene, 2015).

To explore the causal mechanisms at work in this process, we examine in detail a single case: the Garo National Liberation Army (GNLA), an insurgent organization that has operated in Northeast India since 2009. The GNLA offers a compelling test case for a number of reasons. First, the time period that we examine – in particular, the years 2012 and 2013 – involved a significant change in our independent variable: the competitiveness of the political landscape in the state of Meghalaya and an increase in active groups more broadly in the Northeast region of India. Although the GNLA maintained somewhat of a position of prominence in 2012, the number of groups operating in the states of Meghalaya and Assam "mushroomed" toward the end of that year (Routray, 2015). The Naga Rengma Hills Protection Force (NRHPF) formed in late 2012 to represent the Rengma Nagas, one of the region's many ethnic groups. Shortly thereafter, the Dima Jagi Nyso Army (DJNA) formed. But in 2013, the number of active groups exploded to include the United People's Liberation Front (January), the United People's Liberation Army (February), the Karbi National Liberation Army (September), the United Karbi People's Front (October), and the United Dimasa Kachari Liberation Front (November), among others (Routray, 2015). This rapid expansion of groups continued well into 2014. In total, the GTD database lists an increase of nine Indian terrorist groups from 2012 to 2013 (indicating either entirely new groups or groups that resumed attacks after maintaining a low profile during the previous year). Further, the GNLA explicitly acknowledged that many of these groups, while often representing different ethnic groups, were viewed as direct competitors for resources and public support ("GNLA labels victims informers," 2012). The South Asia Terrorism Portal similarly indicates a rising amount of group activity and aggregate levels of violence during these years, with annual fatalities more than doubling between 2011 and 2013 in the state of Meghalaya alone ("Meghalaya Assessment-2014," 2014). This period of time, then, provides a critical change in our independent variable – the number of groups active in the region – as well as substantial evidence of a correlation between group numbers and aggregate violence.

The second benefit of examining the GNLA during these years is that, unlike some other groups, there is substantial evidence that the group's capabilities and opportunities to use violence did not decline. On the contrary, as the overall violence in the region expanded and the GNLA reduced its level of violence, its other activities expanded. By late 2012, authorities had discovered that the group had spread its operations into the neighboring states of Assam and Nagaland (Lyngdoh, 2012). The increasing overall activity of the organization during 2012 and 2013 undermines the alternative hypothesis that any decline in group violence can be attributed to a decline in capabilities or opportunities.

Likewise, increased counterinsurgency operations offer little explanatory value. Despite heightened vigilance by authorities as the level of violence rose during 2013, a state government report issued in November of that year concluded that the state's security forces were suffering from a severe manpower shortage ("Meghalaya: The hills run red," 2013). In particular, the central government in New Delhi frequently removed forces from the region and redeployed them to other parts of the country ("Meghalaya: The hills run red," 2013). The unreliability and understaffing of the security forces during this time provided ample opportunity for the GNLA to escalate its use of violence, particularly as a way to capture the public's attention in an increasingly chaotic and crowded environment.

And yet, the GNLA did not increase its use of violence despite its increasing capacity and opportunity to do so. This suggests that the GNLA's *willingness* to use violence may have been the deciding factor. The group, in fact, dramatically reduced its violence at the same time that the number of groups in the region, as well as overall levels of violence, were rapidly increasing. We argue that the GNLA therefore intentionally and strategically scaled back its use of violence as a direct response to the escalation of competition at this critical time. The case of the GNLA therefore offers a glimpse into the competing processes that we have already outlined: despite growing levels of violence, individual groups may, on average, reduce their violent attacks.

GNLA's Background

The Garo National Liberation Army emerged in 2009 in a region already suffering from decades of insurgent and terrorist conflicts. The Northeast region of India is comprised of seven states, known as the "sister states": Assam, Manipur, Meghalaya, Nagaland, Arunachal Pradesh, Tripura, and Mizoram. A plethora of ethnic groups consider the area to be home and, as such, many of the insurgent campaigns over the years have focused on securing "homelands" or autonomy for these groups. One example is the long-running terrorist campaign of the United Liberation Front of Assam, which has waged war against the Indian government in an effort to secure independence for the Assamese people. Many of the people in the region, in fact, do not identify as Indians at all, but rather with their local identities (Mukherjee, 2014). Complicating and exacerbating the situation is the fact that the region borders both China and Burma, and several of the ethnic groups traverse these international borders. Violence in the area became especially pronounced during the 1990s as several insurgent organizations fought not only against government forces but also against one another. Violence between Naga and Kuki groups, in particular, emphasized that claims to statehood and autonomy are often seen as a zero-sum game by ethnic groups in the region. That zero-sum game between Naga and Kuki groups resulted in the deaths of more than 1,000 civilians between 1992 and 1997 ("Dynamics of ethnic conflicts in Manipur," 2012). Many of the groups in the region therefore view other groups as competition even when they do not technically "compete" against one another for the support of a single audience.

The GNLA was formed and led by former Deputy Superintendent of Police Pakchara Sangma, also known as "Champion" Sangma. The stated original purpose of the organization was to pursue a separate state for the Garo people, an ethnic group residing primarily in three western districts in the state of Meghalaya. The GNLA's Commander-in-Chief Sohan Shira said in a video released by the organization: "Garoland is our birth right, we are born with this right and we will die with this right. Garoland can be carved out of [the] existing state of Meghalaya ... we don't demand more or less but from within the existing boundary ... We will struggle till we achieve Garoland" ("GNLA justifies demand for Garoland, firm about dialogue," 2014). Although launching a violent campaign from its outset, its attacks were actually rather sparse for the first few years of the group's existence. In 2010, its first full year of operation, for instance, the GNLA was only involved in a few terrorist incidents. The most high profile of these incidents included a bomb blast at a shopping center in Tura in the West Garo Hills District. Although the bomb injured eight people, no one was killed. A single perpetrator was arrested. Later in the year, the GNLA were responsible for the murder of two migrant coal miners. Despite its sporadic attacks in the early years, the GNLA is credited with ushering in a new era of violence in Meghalaya and the broader region ("Incidents and statements Garo National Liberation Army (GNLA): 2010–2012," 2012). Meghalaya was allegedly "returning to peace" before the GNLA's ascension began a steady increase in the level of violence ("Incidents and statements Garo National Liberation Army (GNLA): 2010–2012," 2012).

Although not a central concern of our analysis, the GNLA may actually have emerged in part due to the competitive environment in the region. The Garo Hills had long been used by a variety of insurgent, terrorist, and criminal organizations as a transit route across the border with Bangladesh ("Meghalaya: Renewed terror," 2013). Meghalaya's Chief Minister Mukul Sangma alleged that some of these external groups may have, in turn, "trained and nurtured" terrorist organizations like the GNLA that are indigenous to the area ("Meghalaya: Renewed terror," 2013).

No matter the reasons for its creation, when the GNLA began operations in 2009 the state and the region were already crowded marketplaces for insurgency and terrorism. Among the most high profile of local organizations was the Hynniewtrep National Liberation Council (HNLC), representing the majority Khasi tribe. Also in existence at the time was another Garo organization, the Ahick National Vounteer Council (ANVC), which had signed a cease-fire with the government in 2004. Although not actively engaged in armed combat, the group continued to operate a variety of criminal activities in the region ("Meghalaya Assessment-2009," 2009). Within a few years, the ANVC would come to be viewed as the GNLA's primary competitor. A variety of other groups, most of whom represented Khasi or Garo tribes, operated largely under the radar. Although the situation in Meghalaya was relatively peaceful, it was undoubtedly primed for competition along organizational and ethnic fault lines.

As the GNLA tentatively entered this scenario in 2009, it began ramping up its use of violence over time – particularly against government targets. By mid-2011, the group was making regular attacks on state police forces, killing three police officers in June of that year, two in

July and five in October, as well as eleven civilians over the entire year ("Meghalaya: The hills run red," 2013).

By early 2012, the Garo National Liberation Army was the most active insurgent organization in the state of Meghalaya ("SBI manager kidnapped in Meghalaya," 2012). While the group had clashed with forces since its inception three years earlier, its profile rose dramatically during 2012. The group does not appear at all in the Uppsala Conflict Data Program's armed conflict dataset for the years 2009–2011. But in 2012, the GNLA finally crossed UCDP's threshold of being associated with twenty-five battle deaths and it was included for the first time (Themnér and Wallensteen, 2013). In January and February, the organization embarked on a "killing spree," murdering nearly ten people in separate incidents, including a fifteen-year old and a sixty-year old. The murders were allegedly committed to send a message to other villagers about the price of not cooperating with the group. During the early part of 2012, bodies were recovered "every other day" in the Garo Hills and West Khasi Hills ("GNLA labels victims informers," 2012). Throughout the first half of the year, the GNLA also intensified its attacks on security personnel and kidnapped government officials and civilians ("Declaring GNLA as terrorist outfit is for namesake, formality: Conrad," 2012; "Garo Hills on high alert following GNLA ambush," 2012). Amid this surge in violence, the Indian government officially declared the GNLA a terrorist organization under the Unlawful Activities (Prevention) Act. When asked about the decision to declare it a terrorist group, Leader of the Opposition Conrad Sangma seemed to acknowledge that the GNLA was not operating in a vacuum: the "government is determined to eliminate GNLA but if GNLA is eliminated today, another outfit will come" ("Declaring GNLA as terrorist outfit is for namesake, formality: Conrad," 2012).

Rise in Competition

The GNLA's violent campaign in 2012 coincided with increased public competition between the group and its primary rival for support of the Garo people: the Achik National Volunteers Council (ANVC). Some actually consider the GNLA to be an offshoot of the ANVC because the GNLA's Commander-in-Chief, Sohan Shira, was a former operative of the ANVC ("GNLA to take its demands directly to Centre, UN," 2012). Although in early 2012 the ANVC was technically under a ceasefire, it continued much of its activities in pursuit of an autonomous arrangement for the Garo people ("Centre unlikely to accede to Garoland, says G K Pillai," 2012). As such, it viewed itself as the natural rival to the GNLA and attempted to undermine the GNLA's rise to prominence by publicly criticizing the spate of attacks committed by the group in January and Febraury ("GNLA labels victims informers," 2012).

The ANVC would go on to claim that it was the main organization representing the Garo people, while the GNLA was declining in popularity. In April, one of ANVC's deputy commanders stated that "ANVC is gaining ground [on the GNLA]; accept it as this is a fact" ("ANVC(B) ask GNLA to surrender 'before time runs out'," 2012). The commander seemed to suggest that the GNLA's violent campaign was actually harming its relations in the Garo Hills, alleging that the "GNLA has no ideology nor do they go by any principle" ("ANVC(B) ask GNLA to surrender 'before time runs out'," 2012). He added that "how many [come] for your funeral will prove how much support you have." The GNLA, on the other hand, accused the ANVC of engaging in illegal tax collection from the local people and it accused the organization of working with state police to implement its extortion schemes ("ANVC(B)'s irrational taxes taking toll on bus fares: Sohan," 2012). Sirhan Sohan claimed in June that the ANVC was working with the state police to "finish those groups fighting for Garoland so that [it] can be supreme tax collector of Garo Hills and Garo Hills will be under [its] rule" ("ANVC(B)'s irrational taxes taking toll on bus fares: Sohan," 2012).

Meanwhile, the GNLA seemed to demonstrate a sensitivity to some of the ANVC's charges that it was a violent criminal organization rather than a political one dedicated to the cause of the Garo people. In June, when security forces arrested militants purportedly belonging to the GNLA, Sohan sought to distance the organization from the individuals, claiming they were in fact ANVC operatives ("ANVC(B)'s irrational taxes taking toll on bus fares: Sohan," 2012). As the aggregate violence in the region surged, the GNLA found competition from outside its own tribe as well. Although emphasizing their "brotherhoodness" with other tribes in the region, the GNLA explicitly stated for the first time that the simultaneous pursuit of homelands for other groups, especially the Khasi tribe, was undermining the GNLA's own cause of establishing Garoland ("GNLA to take its demands directly to Centre, UN," 2012). Amidst the rising competitive environment and the ANVC's public denunciation of the group, the GNLA formed a tentative alliance with the United Liberation Front of Assam (ULFA). The move was an effort to expand its control into neighboring Assam ("Joint combing operation for GNLA,

ULFA rebels," 2012). According to local police, the GNLA was attempting to recruit new supporters in the borderlands between the two states in an effort to strengthen their position in the Garo Hills ("Joint combing operation for GNLA, ULFA rebels," 2012).

The GNLA therefore did not wither under growing competition in 2012, but actually seemed to strengthen as an organization. The group declared all-out war on the police and threatened to kill all police informers in the Garo Hills ("GNLA declares war on Meghalaya police," 2012) as it ramped up its efforts. And by late in the year, authorities had discovered evidence that the group was spreading its operations into the neighboring states of Assam and Nagaland (Lyngdoh, 2012). Security forces were reportedly surprised at the extent to which the organization had penetrated into these areas (Lyngdoh, 2012). Further, the group's expansion and acceleration of its activities continued despite the arrest of its founder, Champion Sangma, midway through the year. The GNLA appeared to lose little ground following the arrest, as the group's Commander-in-Chief Sohan Shira took over as the driving force. If anything, Sangma's arrest only renewed the group's desire to demonstrate its capabilities. In October, the group attacked a local politician using a roadside improvised explosive device (IED) ("Saleng seeks security cover," 2013) and was involved in a number of clashes with security forces. Despite the wave of violence in Meghalaya and surrounding regions, and an unprecedented number of militant groups actively targeting the state, the GNLA closed out 2012 as the most high-profile organization in a rapidly escalating conflict.

Decline in Violence

By 2013, the perception and the reality of the GNLA's use of violence began to diverge. Although Champion Sangma had been imprisoned for months, an editorial in the *Meghalaya Times* in May 2013 concluded that the group was "uncontrollable," noting that local police forces had failed to make any substantial arrests of the organization's rank and file ("GNLA dares Legislator with death sentence: is Meghalaya really safe," 2013). The editorial also noted that Sohan Shira continued to operate at large as the de facto leader of the organization. The GNLA's behavior turned particularly bold when they publicly issued a "death sentence" against Meghalaya legislator Limison Sangma for his opposition to the group ("GNLA dares Legislator with death sentence: is Meghalaya really safe," 2013).

But while the group was portrayed by the media, politicians, and security forces as the most important threat to peace in the region, the group engaged in relatively little violence. From January through June of that year, the group only seemed to be involved in minor incidents, including one in which GNLA militants lobbed a hand grenade at a politician's residence ("Saleng seeks security cover," 2013). Their first major attack did not occur until June, when the group blew up a public bus in the North Garo Hills district. Notably, however, the militants who committed the attack forced all of the passengers off the bus before destroying it ("GNLA vents ire on bus, says 'this is against Govt'," 2013). Emphasizing the increasingly competitive and chaotic environment in which it was operating, police forces responding to the bus blast initially thought it was the work of a brand new organization, the United Achik Liberation Army (UALA). Although neither the UALA nor the GNLA officially claimed responsibility for the attack, passengers on the bus said the perpetrators identified themselves as members of the GNLA ("GNLA vents ire on bus, says 'this is against Govt'," 2013).

Contrary to the public perception of the group, then, the GNLA seemed to have restrained, rather than intensified, its overall use of violence as 2013 continued. The group also seemed to be acutely aware of the potential backlash that could occur if civilians were unnecessarily harmed in any attack. Even in late 2012, after Champion Sangma had been arrested, he publicly exhorted the group to refrain from violence during local elections ("GNLA to support Congress in Garo Hills: Champion," 2012). He stated, "I have made instructions to my cadres asking them not to create any problem during the [September] elections" in the Garo Hills region. The GNLA did indeed refrain from election-related violence, suggesting that the group was not "uncontrollable" after all. On the contrary, the group continued to refocus its efforts away from violent attacks over the next couple of years. Although it had been the most active group in Meghalaya in 2012, the group doesn't even appear in the UCDP dataset in 2013 as it was associated with only a handful of deaths during that year (Themnér and Wallensteen, 2014).

Yet the reduction in violence was a reflection of neither a decline in capabilities nor a successful counterinsurgency campaign. As mentioned previously, the group actually strengthened and expanded its operations into neighboring regions throughout 2013. The group also strengthened its relationship with the Assam-based United Liberation Front of Assam (ULFA), coordinating on subversive activities across state lines ("Security forces foil ULFA–GNLA terror plan," 2012). The alliance with ULFA appears to have dramatically increased the GNLA's weapons caches and expanded opportunities for training of its members ("Security forces foil ULFA–GNLA terror plan," 2012). Throughout 2013, authorities made a number of seizures of weapons and armaments, and the amount of materials found seemed to increase each time. During a single raid in early 2014, security forces discovered a cache one-third the size of all the arms seized from the group in the previous year. A separate raid on Sohan Shira's private residence "yielded an assortment of items including explosive devices, mobile phones, detonators, high-tech communication sets and wads of Indian and Bangladesh currencies," all signs of a thriving insurgency ("Meghalaya: The hills run red," 2013). Despite these seizures, the capabilities of the organization only seemed to grow. In one of the few high-profile attacks of 2013, the GNLA killed five security personnel in an ambush in the South Garo Hills ("Meghalaya: The hills run red," 2013). The attack was one of the most devastating since the GNLA's inception and prompted renewed scrutiny of the group.

Yet despite the growing attention placed on the group by security forces, increased vigilance is not a satisfying explanation for the group's dramatic decline in overall violence. A government report issued in November found that increased attention on the GNLA and other groups in Meghalaya was actually stretching the police forces thinner. The report noted an "acute shortage of manpower [due to] the dual task of maintaining law and order and engaging in counter insurgency operations" ("Meghalaya: The hills run red," 2013). Even though some argued that the number of security forces was adequate, it was often conceded that the security forces were not deployed in a logical or efficient manner. An October editorial suggested that "there is a deficit in deployment and establishment of Police Stations in some parts of the State [and] this is squarely the failure of the State Government and the State Police administration" ("Meghalaya: Renewed terror," 2013). Additionally, the direct antagonism between the GNLA and the police forces did not disappear in 2013. In some ways it intensified. In June, the group declared a "street war" against counterinsurgency forces, which was followed by a relatively high number of clashes ("Meghalaya: Renewed terror," 2013). Yet, despite a concerted campaign against state forces, the first death inflicted by the group did not occur until November, in the South Garo Hills ambush. Despite maintaining and expanding its military capabilities, the group seems to have largely refrained from inflicting casualties during 2013.

This clear change in behavior for the organization continued even as the competitive environment escalated. In November, the ANVC blatantly attacked a joint GNLA–ULFA camp, despite the fact that the ANVC was still under a ceasefire ("ANVC(B) boldly claims of attacking GNLA camp," 2013). The ANVC leadership said the reason for the attack was that they were concerned with the proliferation of new militant groups in Meghalaya. Shortly thereafter, the ANVC itself splintered and produced a brand new organization, the United Achik Liberation Army (UALA), further increasing the number of groups and the amount of violence in Meghalaya.

The GNLA had already seen the writing on the wall and had made the strategic decision to restrict its own use of violence in such a crowded and charged atmosphere. But if the group had seen a declining utility for violence in late 2012 and 2013, its perception of the utility of violence was changed irreparably following an incident in June 2014. Members of the GNLA murdered a thirty-five-year-old woman, Josbina Sangma, while her four children watched in the village of Chokpot in South Garo Hills. Although the murder itself was fairly routine for the organization (Sangma was accused of being a police informant), the brutal nature of the crime quickly became national news and resulted in a sweeping public backlash against the GNLA. For the first time, "the whole nation stood aghast" at the GNLA and the entire political situation in the Garo Hills, which had largely remained under the radar ("The chilling Chokpot killing," 2014). The Chokpot killing, in turn, led to the central government's decision to suspend nascent peace talks with the group ("Surrenders bring hope for peace," 2015).

Although the group accepted responsibility for the killing, the Chokpot incident seemed to further cement the group's changing view of violence against civilians. In November, when it was accused of perpetrating an IED blast that killed two police officers, the GNLA went to extensive lengths to claim they were not involved ("GNLA denies role in IED blast, Salgro Arengh's group claims responsibility," 2014). And as if to punctuate how the competitive environment had altered their utility for violence, the attack was subsequently claimed by a completely new and unknown organization, Salgro Arengh ("GNLA denies role in IED blast, Salgro Arengh's group claims responsibility," 2014). Although continuing a variety of activities over the next few years, the GNLA would never again achieve the level of violence seen during its height in 2012.

National Socialist Council of Nagaland

Rather than being a unique case, the Garo National Liberation Army may represent a broader trend of how growing political competition influenced other groups in the region during the same time period. One group, which developed close operational ties with the GNLA – the National Socialist Council of Nagaland (NSCN) – exhibited similar behavior to that of its ally in the face of competition ("GNLA declared 'terrorist organization', police dept jovial," 2012). The NSCN emerged in the late 1970s with the goal of establishing a separate state for the Naga people of Northeast India and North Burma. The proposed political entity would bring together the Naga across interstate and international borders, and would be known as Nagalim.

Over the years, the group was no stranger to political competition, including internal competition. The original NSCN fractured multiple times, producing new factions in 1990, 1998, 2005, and 2011. These schisms often resulted in more violence as the factions frequently turned on one another. By 2012, the dominant factions were the Isak-Muivah faction (NSCN-IM), and its primary rival, the Khaplang faction (NSCN-K). Other smaller factions continued to operate in the region as well.

Despite several of the groups being in some stage of ceasefire or peace negotiations with New Delhi, violence was still endemic. In January 2012, one of the groups – most likely NSCN-IM – attacked a polling station in Manipur during local elections, killing five people ("Five killed by rebel gunmen at polling station near Imphal," 2012). The NSCN-IM had agreed to a ceasefire with the central government in 2001, but as its alleged use of violence grew in 2012, New Delhi claimed that the group was demonstrating a "misinterpretation of [the] ground rules" of that agreement ("National Socialist Council of Nagaland – Isak-Muivah, Centre discuss ceasefire violations," 2012). The group was also increasingly active in training Maoist insurgents in Manipur and Assam, in cooperation with the People's Liberation Army (PLA) ("Maoist recruit Assamese youths," 2012).

But despite the expansion of its violent activities in 2012, by mid-year there was evidence that the NSCN-IM and many of the groups in the region were growing weary of the noisy, competitive environment in which they were forced to operate. One newspaper estimated there were as many as forty distinct insurgent groups operating in Manipur alone in 2012 ("Five killed by rebel gunmen at polling station near Imphal," 2012). And the NSCN constellation of factions itself had recently expanded, as the Khole-Kitovi faction (NSCN-KK) split from the NSCN-K. These two organizations, in turn, began attacking each other in earnest as 2012 progressed. At least four militants were killed in June when NSCN-KK operatives ambushed a village housing NSCN-K members in the middle of the night ("4 killed in National Socialist Council of Nagaland factional clash," 2012). Both groups, along with the NSCN-IM, were technically under ceasefire with the government in New Delhi, but continued to war with one another as well as with other groups in the region. Just days later, for instance, the NSCN-K was involved in a shootout with members of another Naga group, the Zeliangrong United Front (ZUF). Four militants were killed, along with two civilians, in the exchange of gun fire ("Brawl among Naga militants kills 6," 2012). The NSCN-K was also accused of bringing outside organizations into the mix. Allegedly, the United Liberation Front of Assam had expanded its operations into Manipur thanks to the protection and support of the NSCN-K ("Indian government panel says northeast group harbouring rebels," 2012).

With new schisms, rivalries, and alliances emerging seemingly everyday in mid-2012, the utility of violent activity seems to have declined for the NSCN-IM in particular. In July in Manipur, a contractor was abducted and blame was placed on the NSCN-IM almost immediately. But although such abductions were fairly routine for the organization, the group publicly denied the allegations, saying that "pointing [an] accusing finger . . . without any concrete evidence can never be accepted" ("NSCN-IM deny allegation of contractor's abduction," 2012). As the group's involvement in violent activities declined over the next year, the chaotic environment in Manipur was a contributing factor. In fact, nine additional groups became active between 2012 and 2013, significantly increasing the NSCN-IM's level of competition (START, 2016). The simultaneous explosion of violence in the Meghalaya region also generated new, indirect competition as it grabbed many of the region's and the nation's headlines during that year.

But there was also evidence that the group was growing weary of the competition from local ethnic groups and the political organizations that represented them. While involved in seemingly endless peace talks with New Delhi for years, in 2012 representatives of the Meiteis ethnic group accused the government of appeasing the Nagas at their expense ("Dynamics of ethnic conflicts in Manipur," 2012). The United Committee of Manipur (UCM) – a Meitei umbrella organization – declared that the peace talks should not threaten the territorial integrity of Manipur and stated that "a peaceful parting of the Nagas in Manipur and the Meiteis as good neighbours, was the only way to avert a catastrophic situation" (Ahanthem, 2014, 8). In many ways, then, the peace process involving the NSCN-IM was potentially exacerbating intergroup conflict between the Nagas and the Meiteis. Meanwhile, the Kuki National Front (KNF) and the Kuki National Organization (KNO) threatened to resume their violent struggle against the NSCN-IM and others since the land claims made by the Meitei and Naga people directly competed with the Kukis' own territorial aspirations ("Incidents and statements involving NSCN-IM: 1992–2012," 2012; "Kuki-Naga ethno-centrism in Manipur," 2013). Despite interethnic conflict seemingly ending in the 1990s, many suggested that the situation was particularly "tense" in 2012, threatening to erupt into full-scale conflict at any moment (Kipgen, 2013).

While the futility of launching violent attacks in such an atmosphere must have been apparent by 2012, like the GNLA, the NSCN-IM suffered significant public backlash from a single incident later that year. In December, one of the NSCN-IM's members allegedly molested a well-known actress. The crime prompted Manipur authorities to send a special delegation to New Delhi to discuss the activities of the NSCN-IM specifically ("Manipur: All-party delegation to meet Centre on militancy," 2012). The group later condemned the molestation. It then spent much of 2013 actively lowering its profile, engaging in 75 percent fewer attacks than in 2012 (START, 2016). While the group finally signed a peace agreement with New Delhi in 2015, it continued to engage in violent acts. Yet its use of violence would never reach the levels seen earlier in the decade, when there were half as many active groups.

Ultimately, then, we see a similar trend among key groups in Meghalaya and Manipur. As the political competition and overall violence increased dramatically in 2012 and 2013, violence committed by the GNLA and the NSCN-IM declined precipitously. Notably, neither group died out and they continue to engage in a variety of criminal activities today.

CONCLUSION

This chapter has provided a variety of evidence in support of our main thesis: while increasing numbers of militant groups may lead to aggregate increases in violence by default, per-group violence should decline on average. The reported statistical effects are robust across categories of militant groups and conflict types, as well as alternative model specifications.

In the second section, we presented evidence that as the number of terrorist organizations increase in a country, that country will experience greater amounts of terrorist attacks. However, there is no significant relationship between the number of traditional rebel groups and the aggregate amount of violence. This mixed finding mirrors the inconsistency of previous findings on the outbidding effect and suggests a closer look is necessary.

In the third section, we examined the outbidding process at the group level and the results demonstrate that increasing group numbers are significantly associated with decreasing numbers of attacks by individual groups. This effect is evident whether analyzing terrorist organizations or rebel organizations. We also noted that the empirical analysis is inherently biased against our hypothesis and, therefore, the results reported are likely conservative estimates of the actual relationship.

We also examined the microfoundations of our theoretical expectations by considering the multi-faceted insurgencies in Northeast India. As our analysis shows, groups such as the Garo National Liberation Army and the National Socialist Council of Nagaland seem to have intentionally scaled back their use of violence in the face of growing political competition. At the peak of their own campaigns against the state, both groups chose to restrain their use of violence for strategic purposes. Chaotic political environments in Meghalaya and Assam in 2012 and 2013 – with new militant groups seemingly emerging overnight – apparently convinced the GNLA and NSCN that the utility of violent attacks was in rapid decline. Interestingly, in both cases, a single attack or set of attacks resulted in significant public backlash, hastening the change in strategy. And while those years witnessed some of the greatest volumes of violence in contemporary India, the experiences of the GNLA and NSCN support our conclusion that group-level violence may actually decline concurrent with a broader wave of violence.

Although our analysis thus far is an interesting first pass at the outbidding problem, there are many aspects of competitive political violence we have not yet addressed. Indeed, we have focused entirely on incentives among competing groups. Yet governments can intervene in a variety of ways, ranging from policing efforts, to intercepting contributions to groups, to directing military operations to hamper a group's effectiveness.

Existing groups must consider how their actions incentivize other groups to form, and governments must also consider how their counterterrorism policies affect those decisions. The next three chapters push forward on these topics.

4

Outbidding, Capacity, and Government Enforcement

In recent years, scholars have increasingly turned their attention to how competition among political organizations influences their behavior. Outbidding has been a popular approach to the empirical puzzle and the last two chapters formalized and provided evidence for the mechanism. Yet most recent studies on intergroup competition – ours thus far included – implicitly assume that such competition occurs in a vacuum. A key actor has largely been ignored: the state. Not only are states the ostensible targets of group violence, but they can actively influence group recruitment processes (e.g., Goodwin, 2001; Kalyvas and Kocher, 2007; Lichbach, 1995; Mason and Krane, 1989). If groups use violence as a recruitment tactic in competitive environments, then state efforts to intercept or discourage volunteers should undermine the outbidding process. On the other hand, ineffective enforcement on the part of the state may create additional opportunities for groups to use violence to outbid one another.

Conflict in Algeria helps illustrate this principle. A key factor driving violence in the Algerian Civil War was the competitive dynamic between the Islamic Salvation Army (AIS), the Armed Islamic Group (GIA), and other groups. The GIA infamously engaged in brutal terrorist attacks as the groups competed against one another for control of the conflict. The government signed a collective truce in 1997 but could not stem the flow of recruits to the groups. Still seeing a pool of available resources, the groups continued to output violence to capture those goods. The state's role as a strategic actor therefore influenced the competitive dynamic between the groups themselves. As a result, by the time the truce was signed, "the government succeeded in turning a conflict between Islamist guerrillas and the security forces into a pitiless struggle between the GIA and the AIS"(Martinez, 2000, 19).

Similarly, competition between the various Irish republican groups involved in the "Troubles" created incentives for these groups to use violence as a means of distinguishing themselves. The IRA's assassination of Lord Mountbatten, for instance, may have been a response to increased violence committed by the competing Irish National Liberation Army (McCauley and Segal, 1987). But Northern Ireland differed from Algeria in a critical way. The central British government had much greater reach whereas the Algerian government's enforcement was feeble. In particular, British use of informants placed a dam in front of the recruitment stream. Violence levels correspondingly tapered off (Sarma, 2005).

Algeria and Northern Ireland are but two cases. Yet their differences suggest an underlying mechanism that may have much broader implications. Government policing reduces the number of citizens that can join a group. Moreover, citizens ought to internalize that enforcement and some may not want to try joining at all, further thinning out the pool of available resources. With less to compete over, groups might then wish to lower the effort they exert in violent competition.

To explore this richer strategic interaction, we develop a model of outbidding that explicitly incorporates a state's effort to stymie recruitment. Organizations wish to recruit from a pool of citizens. But whether citizens try to join an organization depends on expectations about the state's effort to police the recruitment process. In turn, the state's enforcement effort depends on expectations of how many wish to join. This creates a complicated strategic environment that a model can help adjudicate.

We find that, in equilibrium, fewer individuals ultimately join an organization as the cost of policing decreases. This is because, as predicted, greater enforcement both deters some individuals from volunteering and catches others who try. Consequently, competing organizations have a smaller pool of resources to outbid each other for, resulting in less competition. As traditional outbidding theory postulates, adding another group still increases expected violence. However, *the additional amount of violence is smaller when the state can police more efficiently.*

This comparative static generates a natural testable hypothesis, which we then investigate empirically. Our theory states that the effect of an additional group is conditional on the state's ease of enforcement. We therefore build upon the previous chapter's statistical model of competitive violence, using data on terrorist attacks and multiple indicators of governmental capacity. Consistent with our hypothesis, additional groups predict greater violence, but state capacity mitigates the effect. When state capacity is low, we find the addition of a single terrorist group can lead to an increase in the expected number of terrorist attacks. By contrast, when state capacity is high, the difference in violence attributed to the addition of groups is often negligible.

Conveniently, our test allays concerns about previous empirical findings in the outbidding literature. At present, this literature shows some positive links between the number of organizations and total violence (e.g., Conrad and Greene, 2015; Nemeth, 2014; Phillips, 2015). But this empirical relationship is also consistent with an alternative causal mechanism: high levels of grievances cause more individuals to want to join political violence organizations (e.g., Araj, 2008; Brym and Araj, 2006; Rasler, 1996; Walsh and Piazza, 2010). This would naturally lead to both additional group formation and additional violence, independent of competitive incentives. Thus, the concern is that competition does not explain the link between groups and violence, but rather, it is a spurious correlation caused by a third factor (Chenoweth, 2013, 368).

When multiple mechanisms lead to the same empirical implication, one solution is to investigate a hypothesis implied by one mechanism but not the other (Fowler and Montagnes, 2015). The previous chapter took one step in that direction, investigating violence at the group level. We continue with that theme but in a different direction by using this chapter's conditional effect as a discriminating hypothesis. Under the outbidding mechanism, violence increases more quickly in the number of groups as enforcement becomes more difficult. Under the alternative mechanism, organizations are not competing with one another. In turn, enforcement should not have an interactive effect because it only deters membership; it does not discourage violence at differential rates depending on the number of active groups. We find support for the conditional effect, increasing our confidence that competition is indeed a major driver of political violence.

To outline the remainder of this chapter, the next section further motivates how state policing and enforcement shapes the marketplace for violence. We use the lessons from that section in developing an extension of Chapter 2's model. The section following derives an empirically testable hypothesis from a key comparative static of the model and discusses how to best test that hypothesis. We then show evidence that strong enforcement capability mitigates competition. Finally, the conclusion discusses how policing is only one counterterrorism strategy and that we will need to go further to understand all of outbidding's second-order effects.

ENFORCEMENT AND RECRUITMENT

In short, the trouble with many treatments of outbidding is that they largely assume such competitive dynamics occur in a vacuum. Specifically, little attention is paid to how state responses to terrorism may influence groups' capabilities and incentives to use violence in competitive environments. At the same time, a separate body of literature has focused on how the effectiveness of state enforcement directly impacts the ability of non-state groups to recruit new members and supporters (e.g., Goodwin, 2001; Kalyvas and Kocher, 2007; Lichbach, 1995). Governments that engage in indiscriminate violence, for example, are more likely to "push" the average citizen into supporting a non-state actor (Mason and Krane, 1989). Increasing numbers of potential recruits and supporters, in turn, should intensify intergroup competition as they vie for these new "resources."

More important for this chapter's extension, the literature has also shown that the effectiveness of state enforcement, including the ability to use violence in a discriminate fashion, is partially a function of state capacity (e.g., Fearon and Laitin, 2003; Hendrix and Young, 2014). Higher capacity states incur lower marginal costs of enforcement, allowing them to more efficiently curb terrorism (Hendrix and Young, 2014; Blankenship, 2016). And Fjelde and Nilsson (2012) find that intergroup violence is likely to flourish when state authority is weak. Depending on the nature of state enforcement, then, we should expect intergroup competition to lead to increased violence under certain circumstances but not others.

A couple of anecdotes illustrate our point further. During the Algerian Civil War, competitive violence among various militant factions was central to the conflict. In fact, some scholars have argued that the primary target of the two most prominent groups – the AIS and the GIA – was not the state but each other (Hafez, 2000). Their stated *raison d'être* was the overthrow of the Algerian government, of course. But they violently disagreed over what should replace it. While the GIA pushed for full Sharia law to be established after the government's defeat, the AIS sought to simply restore the electoral process that had predated the war. It was this disagreement and the related threat to each other's survival that led both groups to focus intensely on outbidding the other. Although the conflict had already been raging for several years by the mid-1990s, the GIA famously declared war on the AIS in January 1996, marking a new phase in the war. As the conflict escalated, the groups increasingly targeted civilians and non-combatants. Such targets made up 13 percent of all attacks in 1992, but by 1997 they accounted for 79 percent of attacks (Hafez, 2000).

The state attempted to finally end the violence in 1997 by signing a truce with the AIS. There were few to no enforcement mechanisms, however, and the truce essentially relied on the AIS policing itself. As a result, the agreement was not implemented effectively. Specifically, various militant factions allied with the AIS proved difficult to rein in, and they continued to recruit aggressively and even escalated their battles against one another and against the GIA. The overall level of violence increased well into 1998 as a result, with hundreds of civilians being massacred within months of the truce. One incident alone allegedly involved the killing of ninety-eight civilians in a single night (Whitney, 1997). Violence continued even further into 1999, when the government finally signed a comprehensive agreement that granted amnesty to militants who renounced violence. While this gesture did not put an end to recruitment – public backlash against the GIA's brutal tactics played a large part – the state had begun the process of lowering the costs of defection from the various groups. These lower costs, in turn, further reduced the value of competitive violence and contributed to the eventual termination of the conflict (World Peace Foundation, 2015).

Similar to Algeria, many analysts have suggested that surges of violence during the "Troubles" in Northern Ireland can often be attributed to competitive pressure in a crowded environment. This competitive pressure was especially evident by the late 1970s when the IRA had devolved into a number of competing organizations. In an effort to remain relevant and demonstrate their capabilities, several of the organizations engaged in escalating displays of violence in an effort to "one up" the others. Competitive violence, in fact, was in large part to blame for the failed 1973 Sunningdale Agreement (Sawyer, 2008). According to some analysts, the overall level of violence in the country did not experience a marked decline until one of the militant groups achieved a virtual monopoly over the others. During the mid- to late 1970s, when the groups battled one another for supremacy, the IRA killed Lord Mountbatten, allegedly in an effort to outbid the INLA's recent surge of violence. Although there were likely multiple motivations for the assassination, it cannot be denied that the incident generated "tremendous publicity" for the group, so that observers could not "but be impressed by IRA skills" (Pockrass, 1987, 349). Although the assassination is often cited as a particularly intense period of the conflict, overall violence began to subside in the ensuing years as competition among the groups became less pronounced.

But something else was at work during this period besides the changing competitive dynamic among militant groups. Whereas the Algerian government was late to the game in effectively countering recruitment by militant groups, the British government intervened relatively early in the Troubles. The Royal Ulster Constabulary (RUC), Northern Ireland's police, took a page from Michael Collins' playbook by embedding informants into nearly every militant group. These witness-informants, known as "supergrasses," were especially helpful in undermining recruitment.

The story of William Black helps illustrate this point. The RUC arrested Black in November 1981. Black became a supergrass and, over a short period of time, began feeding information to the agency about local Republican terrorists and their supporters. The RUC built a number of cases around Black's information and, in less than a year, a mass trial against his targets began. Noting that Black had facilitated so many cases against those standing trial, the judge overseeing the trial referred to Black as a "dangerous and ruthless terrorist" (Hillyard and Percy-Smith, 1984, 343). Despite the judge's implied concerns about the character of the individual providing the bulk of the testimony, the trial nevertheless proceeded. In total, the court accused thirty-eight people of nearly 200 distinct charges. Most of the charges were related to the commission of forty-five specific instances of violence. The prosecution relied, at least in part, on Black's testimony. Of those tried, thirty-five were convicted and four received life sentences in prison.

The first-order effect of the arrests caused great damage to the IRA. But they also had a critical second-order effect. The RUC's use of supergrasses, and William Black in particular, created "a climate of fear and distrust amongst those who engage in political violence" that extended to those even considering taking a role in the organization (Hillyard and Percy-Smith, 1984, 351). Thus, Northern Ireland's capable enforcement mechanisms had a reverberating deterrent effect. The government would later couple the use of supergrasses with preliminary versions of disarmament, demobilization, and reintegration programs, as well as amnesty offers. The combined effect was a significant increase in costs for joining these groups and a significant decrease in costs for defecting from them.

The same techniques have been effective in addressing political violence in a number of cases, including contemporaneous successes against the Red Brigades in Italy (Hillyard and Percy-Smith, 1984).

We offer these anecdotes simply as a way to illustrate that there is much more to the story of competitive violence than the literature or the earlier model has considered. In both the Algeria and Northern Ireland cases, competitive violence was undoubtedly a central feature of each conflict. Militant groups often focused more on distinguishing themselves from other groups than on defeating the government. However, intergroup competition in both cases also depended heavily on the effectiveness of government policy. Specifically, when government policy reduced incentives to join groups (or made it easier to leave them), each group's utility for demonstrative displays of violence was significantly reduced. Indeed, after the use of informants in Northern Ireland became widespread, much of the IRA's violence shifted to internal targets. A large number of attacks were subsequently intended to intimidate and punish alleged "touts." Successful counter-recruitment policies therefore had a dramatic effect on group operations and their use of violence, in addition to the direct effects on the recruitment/retention process.

Yet many models of outbidding and intergroup competition completely ignore the role of the state and its policies. Even two chapters ago, we presented a model where the only actors were n militant groups and explicitly ignored the state as an actor. Although we constructed the model in such a way for the purposes of abstraction, given what we have discussed in the current chapter, the omission of the state is certainly notable. In addition to that, our earlier model, as well as many existing approaches to competitive group behavior, also omits the civilian population. If the civilian population is the ostensible audience for competitive violence, then it follows that the full strategic dynamic between the population, the state, and the militant groups must be modeled to provide a comprehensive picture.

We therefore incorporate all these actors into a single model of competitive violence. In particular, the state's relative costs in countering militant group recruitment processes must be incorporated. Such costs could theoretically change the incentives for groups to engage in competitive violence, while simultaneously influencing the civilian population's utility for supporting or contributing to the groups. For the first time in our analysis, then, we extend the basic outbidding model to incorporate richer strategic dynamics.

Another common theme in existing studies is that measurement of competition is problematic. In particular, the most obvious way to measure terrorist competition – by counting the number of active groups – creates an important challenge for empirical analysis of outbidding. The theory expects that more terrorist organizations should be associated with more terrorism because of competitive pressures. However, as we have stressed, evidence of this link is also consistent with an alternative explanation: a number of factors may increase grievances among the population, leading more people to seek out opportunities to engage in terrorism, which might increase the number of active organizations by default. Indeed, an extensive literature finds that heavy-handed government activities can directly increase grievances among the population, resulting in a broader willingness to participate in terrorist violence (e.g., Burgoon, 2006; Piazza, 2009, 2011; Savun and Phillips, 2009; Walsh and Piazza, 2010). If this broader willingness leads to the formation of additional groups who engage in violence, we cannot conclude that competitive incentives are driving the increase. Instead, the increase in violence might be an artifact of more people being willing to engage in violence.

One way to distinguish between these competing mechanisms is to develop a hypothesis that follows from outbidding theory, but not from the alternative explanation. In the next section, we present a formal model that generates such a prediction by examining the circumstances under which increased competition is likely to cause the largest increases in violence. We then reconsider the empirical evidence with insights regarding the joint effects of competition and state enforcement on the amount of violence that a state experiences.

THE MODEL

To capture the aforementioned incentives, we now extend Chapter 2's model on two fronts. First, we include the target state's decision to exert effort and mobilize resources to prevent recruitment into the organizations. And second, we also explicitly model individual citizens' choice whether to join at all now that they face some risk of the state catching them in the process. These decisions still take place within the broader context among the groups.

To begin the formalization, the model consists of three sets of actors: $n \in \{2, 3, \ldots\}$ militant groups, a state, and a unit mass of citizens sympathetic to the ideological cause of those groups. As before, each militant group wants to acquire resources from the citizens and can use violence as a way to attract the resources to that group and away from other groups. The state wishes to minimize violence and recruitment. Citizens are willing to assist the groups but also worry about state interference.

Formally, the game begins with each of the n groups simultaneously choosing a level of violence. Letting i represent a generic group, we still denote each group's choice as $v_i \geq 0$. Afterward, the citizens observe the violence choices and select whether to attempt to join a group or not. The state then selects an effort level $e \geq 0$ at marginal cost $\alpha > 0$; higher values of α reflect greater agency loss or general difficulty in using governmental bureaucracy to enforce the law. As the state exerts more effort, it intercepts more of the contributions.

Payoffs are as follows. Let π be the mass of contributions that individuals attempt to give to the groups. To model the offsetting effect of effort, suppose that only $\frac{1}{1+e}$ portion of the contributions reach the groups.[1] Note that this functional form has many desirable qualities: (1) producing zero effort implies that all contributions are successful, (2) increasing effort decreases the portion of successful contributions, and (3) producing an arbitrarily large amount of effort implies that virtually none of the contributions are successful. It also captures the idea that enforcement has decreasing marginal returns. That is, the state can more cheaply capture the first percent of contributions, but each percent thereafter becomes increasingly more expensive to catch.[2] Overall, the state's utility equals:

$$-\sum_{i=1}^{n} v_i - \frac{\pi}{1+e} - \alpha e$$

That is, the state suffers the total amount of violence the groups produce, also has disutility for whatever share of resources reach those groups, and pays for its effort of enforcement. Note that dividing π by $1 + e$ captures the direct effects of enforcement. For example, it captures the benefits Northern Ireland enjoyed by using William Black's information to arrest and jail IRA operatives.

Now to the citizens. Just like before, they begin the interaction as undecided over how to allocate support, if they will lend any support at

---

[1] For risk-neutral actors, this is equivalent to all of an individual's contribution reaching the group with probability $\frac{1}{1+e}$.

[2] In fact, diminishing marginal returns is the key assumption and we could relax the model to a general functional form as long as we maintain it.

all. Unlike before, they also have an entry decision. Let $w > 0$ be the general payoff for remaining a civilian and not contributing to an organization; higher satisfaction with the status quo implies greater values of w, while higher grievances with the state correspond to lower values of w. Let j represent a generic citizen from the mass. Each citizen has a unique payoff for a successful contribution to an organization denoted $x_j \geq 0$. However, a citizen's worst outcome is if the state intercepts his contribution; we standardize such a citizen's payoff to 0 here without loss of generality.[3] This preference ordering leads to an interesting trade-off: citizens with sufficiently high affinities for contributing (i.e., citizens with values x_j sufficiently high) strictly prefer contributing *if they know they will be successful* but would rather not if enforcement is virtually guaranteed.

Let $f(x)$ represent the probability density function (PDF) of these values x_j, where $f(x)$ is strictly positive on the interval $[0, 1]$, with 1 representing the most sympathetic individual without loss of generality. To focus on the interesting cases, let the general payoff for remaining a civilian be less than the underlying sympathy of the most sympathetic individual. That is, $w < 1$. If this were not the case, no one would want to join under any conditions, rendering enforcement inconsequential and leading to an uninteresting theoretical case. Also, let $F(x)$ be the cumulative distribution function of $f(x)$, with $F(0) = 0$ and $F(1) = 1$. Note that the strictly positive PDF implies that $F(x)$ is strictly increasing. We also require that $F(x)$ be continuous to rule out any discontinuous "jumps" in ideological inclinations.

Finally, we modify each group's payoff in accordance with the state's enforcement capability. Citizens still divide their contributions according to a ratio contest success function. However, enforcement means that not all of these contributions reach the group. Let π be the quantity of support offered. Note that, unlike Chapter 2, the citizens endogenously determine π. But only $\frac{1}{1+e}$ portion of it falls into the hands of the groups. After factoring in the divisions and the cost of production, group i's overall utility equals:

$$u_i(v_i) = \left(\frac{\pi}{1+e}\right)\left(\frac{v_i}{v_1 + \ldots + v_n}\right) - mv_i$$

Note that i's payoff depends on both the quantity of contributions and the state's enforcement level, with more contributions increasing

---

[3] One might think that a citizen should receive a negative payoff here, but we can peg this at 0 because utility functions are identical across positive affine transformations.

the size of the pie (holding enforcement fixed) and greater enforcement decreasing the size of the pie. In comparison with Chapter 2's baseline model, this extension essentially swaps the exogenously given market size with one that endogenously forms through both citizen and state action.

Optimal State Enforcement

With the timing and payoffs defined, we turn to the game's solution. Because it is a sequential game of complete information, the appropriate solution concept is subgame perfect equilibrium. We therefore proceed with backward induction, beginning with the state's game-ending enforcement decision.

As the payoffs section foreshadowed, the state's chief tradeoff is between exerting greater effort at higher costs to stop more of the contributions and exerting less effort at lower costs to stop fewer of the contributions. Because enforcement has diminishing marginal returns – it is easier to find and stop the first contribution than the last – the state permits some number of contributions to exchange hands. The appendix formally analyzes the tradeoff, which results in the following equilibrium strategy:

Lemma 4.1 *In all subgame perfect equilibria, the state's level of enforcement effort is the maximum of $\sqrt{\frac{\pi}{\alpha}} - 1$ and 0. This amount weakly increases in the total quantity of attempted contributions (π) and weakly decreases in the state's marginal cost of effort (α).*

The comparative statics on the state's equilibrium effort generate most of the intuition. When the marginal cost of enforcement is high, the state finds reducing contributions to be relatively unattractive compared with absorbing negative effects of those contributions. The state therefore reduces its enforcement. Likewise, when only a few citizens are contributing, paying for an expensive dragnet to stop them is not worthwhile. Eventually, if the citizens contributing are so few and enforcement is too costly, the state chooses no enforcement at all. This is why the state chooses the maximum of $\sqrt{\frac{\pi}{\alpha}} - 1$ and 0; 0 represents the case where enforcement is just not worthwhile. It also explains why the relationships are weak; if the state's optimal effort level is 0, then small changes to the game's parameters do not alter its decision.

Lemma 4.1 demonstrates an important element of the outbidding puzzle that the baseline model does not capture. Large values of α yield no enforcement whatsoever. The baseline model therefore implicitly captures those cases through incidental omission of an enforcement decision. But our motivating cases indicate that such anarchic situations are not universal, so we ought to investigate how the enforcement decision could spill over into the other actors' decisions. In fact, when α is small, the state can enforce at a cost-effective rate. Thus, the total pool of resources available to the groups would seem to decline. This does not play into the groups' violence calculus in the baseline model at all.

Of course, the state's enforcement decision is only one determinant of the net pool of resources. As such, our next step is to understand how the citizens operate under such a scenario.

Optimal Citizen Contributions

The state's enforcement decision generates an interesting tradeoff for the citizens. Recall the payoffs for and probabilities of successful contribution, failed contribution, and no contribution. Now hold fixed a level of effort e. Then citizen j with entry value x_j strictly prefers to join if:

$$\left(\frac{1}{1+e}\right)(x_j) + \left(1 - \frac{1}{1+e}\right)(0) > w$$

$$x_j > w(1 + e)$$

Thus, citizens' decisions have three intuitive properties. They are more likely to join when enforcement is small than when it is large because the government will not catch them as often. They are less likely to join when their wealth is large because it represents too great an opportunity cost to sacrifice. Lastly, they are more likely to join when their value for contributions is large.

Figure 4.1 diagrams the decision-making process. Hold fixed a level of enforcement. All citizens that value successful membership below w never join – even without enforcement, these citizens care too little about the ideological cause to give to an organization. Citizens above w are conditionally willing to join. However, enforcement creates reluctance. Consider an individual with a value just above w. They are willing to join if they know enforcement will not catch their effort. But even a small amount of enforcement makes the gamble not worth pursuing, as their utility for a successful contribution is only slightly greater than not

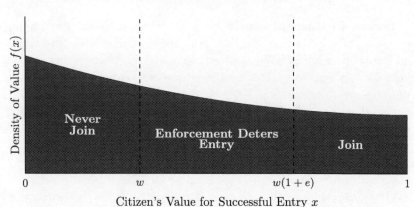

FIGURE 4.1 Distribution of citizen values and their entry decisions.

joining at all. This logic continues through all citizens with values up to $w(1+e)$. The corresponding middle group defines the second-order benefits of enforcement, like the chilling effect that William Black's testimony had on IRA recruitment. Only those above $w(1+e)$ join. Note that as enforcement increases, e becomes larger, and the deterred middle group expands as well.

The above intuition treats enforcement as exogenous. But enforcement is an endogenous choice by the state. Indeed, enforcement looks particularly attractive because it acts as a double whammy to the groups' cause – it reduces the number of individuals who join (by shifting the second cutpoint to the right) *and* it catches more of the individuals who do.[4] In fact, if the distribution function has a significant bulge in Figure 4.1's middle region, the deterrent effect may reduce the quantity of resources reaching the groups by a larger margin than the actual enforcement itself.

This takes us to the next strategic dilemma. How do the citizens decide whether to join, knowing that this decision in turn affects the state's enforcement choice? We now address that. The key is describing a particular pivotal citizen. For a certain level of enforcement, this pivotal citizen is indifferent between contributing and not contributing. Moreover, if the only citizens that contribute are those with greater values, then the government would want to produce that certain level of enforcement. These self-reinforcing behaviors allow an equilibrium to form.

---

[4] Actually, it is a triple whammy: later, we show that higher anticipated enforcement convinces the organizations to commit less violence.

In fact, we can define that pivotal citizen using the following equation:

$$\frac{x}{\sqrt{1 - F(x)}} = \frac{w}{\sqrt{\alpha}} \tag{4.1}$$

Let x^* be the unique solution to Line 4.1.[5] Then the following lemma provides a summary for α sufficiently low:[6]

Lemma 4.2 *In all subgame perfect equilibria, all citizens with values $x_j < x^*$ do not join, and all citizens with values $x_j > x^*$ join.[7] The proportion of individuals joining increases in the marginal cost of enforcement α.*

Intuitively, there is a pivotal citizen with a value for successful entry of x^*. All citizens with values greater than them join, and all citizens with values smaller do not. The proportion of individuals joining is therefore $1 - F(x^*)$. Given this, the state produces an enforcement level that makes the individual x^* exactly indifferent between joining and not joining. This makes not joining optimal for individuals with values less than x^* and joining optimal for individuals with values greater than x^*. The equation $\frac{x}{\sqrt{1-F(x)}} = \frac{w}{\sqrt{\alpha}}$ defines the point that creates this indifference.

Two comparative statics help further make sense of Lemma 4.2's claims. To begin, note that the left-hand side of Line 4.1 strictly increases in x. Thus, if the right-hand side increases, x^* must increase to maintain the necessary equality. In turn, suppose the citizens' value for not joining w increases. Then so too does x^*. That is, fewer individuals want to join because they are more satisfied with their life outlook. Meanwhile, imagine that the marginal cost of enforcement α increases. Then x^* *decreases*. This is because the citizens anticipate lower enforcement and so the marginal citizen is more inclined to enter. Increasing the cost of enforcement in this manner plays into our key comparative static later.

Optimal Political Violence under Enforcement

All that remains is each group's violence decision. The groups are forward looking and can anticipate total contributions and enforcement.

---

[5] We prove the uniqueness of the solution in the appendix.

[6] Specifically, if $\alpha < 1 - F(w)$. If α is greater than that cutpoint, the game hits a corner solution in which the state chooses no enforcement even if all individuals for which $x_j > w$ (a necessary condition for entry by Lemma 4.2) join. We focus on the case where $\alpha < 1 - F(w)$ for lack of substantive cases where states completely forgo enforcement. Changing enforcement does not change violence locally, but moving it enough eventually shifts the parameters into the interior solution we just described.

[7] What the citizen with $x_j = x^*$ chooses to do is immaterial because this has zero measure.

In particular, Lemma 4.2 tells them to expect $1 - F(x^*)$ to join. Meanwhile, within the interior solution, Lemma 4.1 instructs them to expect $\sqrt{\frac{1-F(x^*)}{\alpha}} - 1$ in enforcement effort. As such, only $\frac{1}{1+\left(\sqrt{\frac{1-F(x^*)}{\alpha}}-1\right)}$ portion of the $1 - F(x^*)$ citizens reach the groups.

This line of reasoning allows us to make some direct connections to the baseline model. Before, we assumed that the parties competed over the exogenous π quantity of resources. With the endogenous entry and enforcement decisions that quantity becomes:

$$(1 - F(x^*)) \left(\frac{1}{1 + \left(\sqrt{\frac{1-F(x^*)}{\alpha}} - 1 \right)} \right) = \sqrt{\alpha(1 - F(x^*))}$$

Substituting that value for π into Chapter 2's original results, we can make the following claims about the individual groups' decisions and the overall violence produced.

Lemma 4.3 *In equilibrium, each group produces* $v^* \equiv \frac{(n-1)\sqrt{\alpha(1-F(x^*))}}{mn^2}$ *of violence. The overall violence produced therefore equals* $\frac{(n-1)\sqrt{\alpha(1-F(x^*))}}{mn}$.

Although the proof for this is a simple substitution into Chapter 2's framework, it is worth reiterating the groups' thinking here. Part of each group's calculation is to consider the sum of the resources *successfully* contributed. They do not base their decisions on expecting to divide $1 - F(x^*)$ of resources because they know they will never have access to all of that. This explains the scaling to $\sqrt{\alpha[1 - F(x^*)]}$.[8] The rest of the logic follows from Chapter 2's results.

How Does Enforcement Capacity Affect Violence?

Although Lemma 4.3 gives each group's violence strategy and overall violence production, we still have not explored how competition impacts that rate. Moreover, we also do not know how enforcement affects competition, which in turn affects violence. The following proposition addresses both of those questions:

---

[8] A necessary condition for the parameters to fall in the interior solution is that $\alpha < \pi \leq 1$, so the enforcement transformation cannot cause the groups to produce more violence than they would otherwise.

Proposition 4.1 *The sum of equilibrium violence* $\frac{(n-1)\sqrt{\alpha(1-F(x^*))}}{mn}$ *strictly increases in the number of groups* n. *Moreover, the rate at which overall equilibrium violence increases in* n *increases in the marginal cost of state enforcement* α.

There are two implications to unpack from Proposition 4.1. We begin with the comparative static on violence as a function of the number of groups. This is the same finding as Chapter 2. Adding groups creates greater competition, which in turn leads groups to produce more collective violence even as each one individually scales back; a new group's production simply outstrips the sum reductions by the rest of the groups. Adding enforcement to the mix does not change the fact that competition still plays a role in each group's decision.

However, Proposition 4.1's second claim is new, both to this project and the outbidding literature in general. It makes a prediction about how fast equilibrium levels of violence will rise with the introduction of another group. Specifically, higher marginal costs of state enforcement lead to less enforcement, more individuals joining, and more of those recruits reaching the groups. These factors all lead to a greater increase in equilibrium violence with the introduction of another group.

Figure 4.2 illustrates this relationship. Increasing the marginal cost leads to more violence regardless of the number of groups, but note that the gulf widens as that marginal cost increases. Intuitively, this occurs because each group's violence decision is pegged to the overall pool of expected resources. Adding another group does not change the size of this pool, so the additional group causes a larger increase when the pool is bigger than when the pool is smaller.

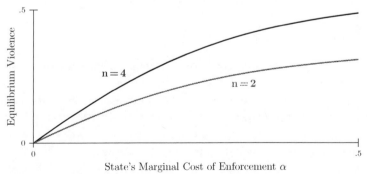

FIGURE 4.2 Equilibrium violence as a function of enforcement capacity.

We can see this by examining the difference between equilibrium violence for four groups versus two. When the marginal cost of enforcement approaches 0, the state exerts effort to block almost all citizens from joining. Lots of competition or little competition, the groups do not see much point in producing violence to accumulate resources that never come to fruition. Overall violence is very low, with only a slight bump when more groups exist. Compare that with a situation where the marginal cost of enforcement is large. Now more citizens will successfully join a group. Investment becomes worthwhile and so the effect of competition becomes more evident.

Going deeper into the proposition, as foreshadowed, higher marginal costs of enforcement have a double effect on how competition affects violence rates. The equilibrium violence quantity $\frac{(n-1)\sqrt{\alpha(1-F(x^*))}}{mn}$ makes clear the direct effect. After all, we measure the cost of enforcement through α. As α decreases, enforcement effort increases, and the government intercepts a greater share of contributions. But α also has a hidden effect with x^*. Lower marginal enforcement costs deter more citizens from trying to join, which increases x^* and therefore decreases the equilibrium violence quantity through another causal pathway.

As we transition to statistical analysis below, it is important to emphasize that Proposition 4.1's comparative static tracks the marginal cost of enforcement, not level of enforcement chosen in equilibrium. This provides us with empirical leverage we would otherwise lack. It is difficult to acquire reliable realized enforcement quantities for states prone to terrorist violence. In contrast, researchers can readily construct proxies for state enforcement *capacities*, and Proposition 4.1 directly connects them to changes in violence behaviors. Thus, by modeling enforcement as an endogenous choice, we have derived a primitive that generates greater empirical leverage. We exploit that leverage below.

HYPOTHESIS AND RESEARCH DESIGN

The comparative statics derived from our model suggest that the number of active terrorist organizations and the marginal cost of state enforcement have a multiplicative effect on the amount of violence that a state experiences. Importantly, this implication allows us to make a distinction between the alternative explanation that state enforcement increases grievances among the civilian population, which leads to a greater number of active organizations and a greater amount of violence by default. Under such a mechanism, enforcement should not have an interactive effect because it only deters membership; it does not discourage violence at differential rates depending on the number of active groups. Our model, however, predicts a *joint* influence of the cost of state enforcement and the number of active groups on the amount of violence. In other words, this expectation allows us to identify evidence for a causal process driven by intergroup competition rather than a broader pattern of grievances leading to violence. Our central expectation, then, is as follows:

Hypothesis 4.1 *States with more active terrorist organizations experience more terrorist attacks than states with fewer organizations, and this effect is augmented by increasing marginal costs of state enforcement.*

To examine the empirical evidence for our hypothesis, we first require data on the number of terrorist attacks that states experience, since our comparative statics and hypothesis include expectations about the level of *aggregate* violence at the state level. We construct a count of domestic attacks, drawn from the GTD (START, 2016).[9] We focus on the aggregate amount of violence rather than the per-group average because the implications of the model in this chapter are focused on country-level violence. The number of attacks that states experience in a single year ranges from a minimum of 0 to a maximum of 524. The vast majority of country-years (our unit of analysis) involve zero attacks. When our dependent variables are combined with the covariates described below, we have more than 1,000 country-year observations spanning the time period between 1990 and 2007.[10]

Independent Variables

The key explanatory concepts that we develop in this chapter are (1) competition among terrorist groups and (2) marginal enforcement costs incurred by states. For the first concept, we use the measure introduced in the previous chapter that counts the number of active terrorist groups operating in a country in a given year. We previously found a clear link

---

[9] Domestic attacks are those where the suspected perpetrator nationality is the same as the location of the attack. In robustness checks, we also test our expectations on the full range of attacks, including international attacks. The results are comparable to those reported here.

[10] In the most expansive model included in this book, the sample includes observations for 124 different countries during the time period.

between the number of terrorist groups and the amount of violence and, as such, we focus on that measure instead of the count of rebel groups. We also noted in Chapter 3 that the number of rebel groups is not an ideal measure of our concept of interest. Among the models presented in this chapter, between 40 percent and 44 percent of observations involve at least one active terrorist group, with the maximum number of groups being twenty-four.[11] We also construct an alternative version of this variable, described in the section on robustness at the end of the empirical analysis.

For the second concept, state enforcement costs, we use several different measures. Importantly, neither our comparative statics nor our hypothesis are about the *quantity* of enforcement. Instead, we are interested in capturing the *costs* of such enforcement. We have therefore chosen a series of measures capturing state capacity and efficiency more broadly. First, we include a measure of *Bureaucratic quality* drawn from the International Country Risk Guide (ICRG). The variable is measured on a scale from "0" to "4," with higher values indicating bureaucracies that have greater "strength and expertise to govern without drastic changes in policy or interruptions in government services" and those that are largely "autonomous from political pressure" (Howell, 2011). A wide range of literature has concluded that the quality of a government's bureaucratic institutions significantly impacts its ability to implement economic, environmental, and human rights policies (e.g., Cheon, Urpelainen, and Lackner, 2013; Perkins and Neumayer, 2007). Similarly, governments with low bureaucratic quality face significant challenges in implementing security policies. These states have "limited administrative reach" (Blankenship, 2016, 6), hindering their ability to monitor the civilian population (Scott, 1998) and apply selective enforcement. For a variety of reasons, then, the marginal cost of state enforcement against terrorist groups is higher with a poorly functioning bureaucracy. Scholars have found evidence that higher-quality bureaucratic institutions are indeed associated with lower risks of terrorism and other forms of political violence (e.g., Blankenship, 2016; Goodwin, 2001; Hendrix, 2010; Hendrix and Young, 2014).

There is a potential concern about endogeneity when using the measure in our analysis. The experts charged with coding the variable

---

[11] There were twenty-four active groups in India in 1995.

might observe violence in a country and discount bureaucratic quality accordingly. This would pose a problem for our research design. To examine this issue in greater depth, we regressed the bureaucratic quality measure on the average annual attacks that a country experienced in our data. Higher average attacks were actually associated with *higher* levels of bureaucratic quality, which may be consistent with research that finds more developed countries are targeted more often with terrorist attacks (e.g., Kurrild-Klitgaard, Justesen, and Klemmensen, 2006). Nonetheless, the fact that higher bureaucratic quality is associated with more attacks makes our findings in this chapter even more startling.

As an alternative, we also use a more objective measure of a government's *Relative political reach*, which is the ratio of public participation in the formal (taxed) economy to expected participation (Kugler and Tammen, 2012). Greater participation in the formal economy indicates a higher capacity and efficiency in monitoring and "reaching" the civilian population. This greater efficiency, in turn, lowers the marginal costs of enforcement. The variable ranges from .02 to 1.8, with higher values indicating greater government reach.

While *Bureaucratic quality* and *Relative political reach* are conceptually comparable, we include an alternative measure that serves as a proxy for state enforcement costs. The variable, *Regime durability*, is a count of the number of years since the last major institutional change in a state's political structure, measured as a three-point change on the democracy–autocracy scale compiled by the Polity project (Marshall et al., 2002). A state's value on the scale for a given year is determined by several factors, including the competitiveness and exclusivity of the state's political institutions. The scale ranges from "-10" (highly autocratic) to "10" (highly democratic), so a three-point change indicates fairly significant institutional changes. The maximum value of the variable in our data is 202 years.

The durability of a regime proxies for costs of enforcement because, as Olson (1982) notes, there are "start-up costs in creating any organization" that subside over time. In older regimes, power is more likely to be consolidated (Diamond, 1994; Linz and Stepan, 1996), interest groups and bureaucracies are more likely to be entrenched (Olson, 1982), and marginal costs of enforcement are likely to decline. By contrast, regimes that have recently experienced major political transitions must focus on consolidating power, often incurring significant costs of enforcement. Because of these inefficiencies and associated grievances,

TABLE 4.1 *Correlation matrix of key variables.*

	Bureaucratic quality	Relative political reach	Regime durability	Average attacks
Bureaucratic quality	1.00	–	–	–
Relative political reach	0.02	1.00	–	–
Regime durability	0.54	−0.01	1.00	–
Average attacks	0.03	0.04	0.07	1.00

a wide range of literature has found younger regimes are at greater risk of experiencing political violence than older regimes (e.g., Eyerman, 1998; Hegre et al., 2001; Piazza, 2013; Svolik, 2009; Tarrow, 1994). By focusing on *Regime durability*, we therefore examine if a government's broader consolidation of power influences the amount of terrorism that a state experiences.

Although we use each of these measures as an alternate means of capturing our main concept, Table 4.1 shows that there is little overlap across the three indicators. The correlation between most of the variables is near-zero in most cases, with the highest correlation (0.54) between *Bureaucratic quality* and *Regime durability*. There is also little correlation between the average number of attacks a state experiences and any of the three measures. In other words, the bar appears to be high to find results that support our hypothesis.

In our analysis, we are not only concerned with the independent effects of state enforcement costs and terrorist competition, but the conditional effects as well. We therefore construct a series of interaction variables using the various measures of state enforcement costs and the number of active terrorist organizations.

Control Variables

Following the analysis in the previous chapter, we include the same series of control measures capturing the level of violence and the broader political environment. In addition, we include a measure to isolate marginal state enforcement costs from total government capacity and resources. We include each government's total tax revenue, measured as a percentage of the country's Gross Domestic Product (GDP) (World Bank, 2015). This is a critical control because a government's revenue directly influences its bureaucratic capacity and may also influence the likelihood that a state experiences political violence (Kirk, 1983). Controlling for total revenue helps avoid a spurious finding.

Because our dependent variable is a count of attacks, we once again use a negative binomial approach. In all cases, robust standard errors clustered on the country are estimated. And in all of our models, the independent variables are lagged by a year to account for the proper temporal order.

EMPIRICAL ANALYSIS

Our central expectation is that states with higher numbers of terrorist organizations and greater marginal costs for state enforcement will experience the most terrorist attacks. In such environments, where the state incurs high marginal costs and multiple terrorist groups exist, groups will rely more heavily on violence in an effort to secure resources from the civilian population. Table 4.2 displays the results of the central tests of our argument. For each model, the dependent variable is a count of the number of terrorist attacks in a given country-year. The models differ in the measure used to capture the enforcement costs of the state. Model 1 features the ICRG measure of *Bureaucratic quality*, while Model 2 includes the measure of *Relative political reach*. Model 3 uses an alternative operationalization with the Polity measure of *Regime durability*.

In all three models, the measure capturing enforcement costs is insignificantly associated with the dependent variable. But because each of the measures is interacted with the *Number of groups*, the interpretation is not straightforward. The results for each constituent term capturing enforcement costs indicate that the influence of the variable on the number of attacks is insignificant *when there are zero terrorist groups*. This is not a surprising finding given that little to no terrorism occurs when there are no active terrorist groups.

On the other hand, the coefficient for the constituent term *Number of groups* is positive and highly significant across all three model specifications. The interpretation of these results is the reverse of our previous interpretation: states with greater numbers of terrorist organizations experience more terrorist attacks *when the marginal cost of state enforcement is highest*.[12] In other words, additional terrorist competition has a strong relationship with the amount of violence that

---

[12] In Model 3, the specific interpretation is that states with greater numbers of terrorist organizations experience more terrorist attacks *during and immediately after regime transitions*.

TABLE 4.2 *Competition, enforcement, and terrorist attacks.*

	DV: Number of terrorist attacks		
	Model 1	Model 2	Model 3
Bureaucratic quality	−0.13	−	−
	(0.29)	−	−
Relative political reach	−	−0.54	−
	−	(0.66)	−
Regime durability	−	−	0.01
	−	−	(0.01)
Number of groups	0.45**	0.50**	0.52***
	(0.20)	(0.20)	(0.14)
IV*Number of groups	−0.03	−0.20	−0.01**
	(0.06)	(0.18)	(0.01)
Tax revenue	0.02	−0.01	0.01
	(0.02)	(0.02)	(0.02)
Ethnic fractionalization	0.04	−0.15	−0.17
	(0.79)	(0.70)	(0.72)
Religious fractionalization	−0.38	−0.32	−0.51
	(0.71)	(0.72)	(0.65)
Physical integrity rights	−0.12*	−0.16**	−0.17***
	(0.07)	(0.07)	(0.07)
Civil conflict	0.77***	0.93***	0.89***
	(0.23)	(0.22)	(0.20)
ln(GDP per capita)	−0.11	−0.25	−0.26
	(0.19)	(0.14)	(0.17)
ln(population)	0.46***	0.46***	0.3***
	(0.11)	(0.15)	(0.12)
Average attacks	0.04***	0.03***	0.03***
	(0.01)	(0.01)	(0.01)
Democracy	−0.03	−0.02	−0.01
	(0.03)	(0.03)	(0.03)
Constant	−0.73	1.49	0.74
	(1.69)	(1.42)	(1.53)
Observations	996	984	1,139

* $p < 0.10$; ** $p < 0.05$; *** $p < 0.01$ (two-tailed)
(Robust standard errors, clustered on country in parentheses)

states experience when governments incur particularly high costs of enforcement. This piece of information serves as preliminary evidence in support of our hypothesis.

To fully explore the relationship between terrorist competition, state enforcement costs, and terrorist violence, however, we must examine the interaction terms from each model. The coefficients for each multiplicative term (*IV* ∗ *Number of groups*) are only statistically significant in one of the three models. But as Brambor, Clark, and Golder (2006) point out, we cannot draw conclusions about the interactive effects by examining the coefficients alone. We must examine the substantive effects of the interaction for a range of both independent variables.

In Figure 4.3, we plot the marginal effects of the number of terrorist organizations on the amount of terrorism that a state experiences, across a range of values for each measure of state enforcement. Each graph therefore corresponds to one of the three models, differing in the measure of state enforcement costs that is used. Each line in the graph represents the marginal effects given a specific number of terrorist groups (0, 1, 2, 3, and 4).[13] Across all three plots, greater numbers of terrorist organizations are associated with higher predicted counts of terrorist attacks. For the first and third graphs (those using *Bureaucratic quality* and *Regime durability*), the slopes at the bottom of the graphs are relatively flat. This indicates that when there are 0, 1, 2, or 3 groups, the amount of violence does not vary much as the cost of state enforcement decreases. The slopes at the top (*Number of groups* = 4) of these graphs, however, are clearly negative, indicating that as competition becomes particularly intense, we begin to see lower enforcement costs having a pacifying effect on the amount of violence a state is likely to experience.

The pattern is most evident in the graph that includes *Relative political reach*, where negative slopes are apparent across several of the plots representing specific numbers of terrorist organizations. Importantly, across all three graphs, we see a great deal of convergence as the relative costs of enforcement decrease (as we move from left to right on the graphs). In other words, when a state has relatively low costs of enforcement,

---

[13] The range of values for the key independent variables were chosen because there is relatively high confidence in these estimates. When estimating results for states with more than four organizations, the confidence intervals are often too wide to safely draw conclusions. Nevertheless, the patterns identified here are visually evident at higher numbers of terrorist organizations and greater values of *Regime durability*.

adding one or two or three terrorist organizations doesn't influence the amount of violence that a state experiences to a great degree. But when states face particularly high costs of enforcement (or have recently experienced major institutional transitions in Model 3), additional terrorist organizations can have dramatic consequences for the amount of violence that a state experiences. As an example, using the results from Model 2, a state with one active terrorist organization with the lowest value for *Relative political reach* has a .31 probability of experiencing at least one terrorist attack.[14] If that same state instead has four active organizations, the probability rises to .53, and the difference is statistically significant. A similar pattern appears in Model 3, where a state with one active terrorist organization that experienced a regime change in the previous year has a .18 probability of suffering at least one attack. The same state with four active organizations has a .40 probability of experiencing one or more attacks. For regimes that experienced a regime change thirty-five years ago, the probabilities are .20 and .34, respectively.

The additional control variables included in Models 1 through 4 offer largely intuitive results. Across all four models, an increase in *Physical integrity rights* significantly reduces the amount of terrorism that a state experiences, consistent with the findings of Walsh and Piazza (2010), among others. Likewise, regardless of the model specification, intrastate conflict significantly increases the amount of terrorism that a state experiences in a given year. It is important to note that we find support for our hypothesis even after controlling for intrastate conflict. In other words, the interactive effect of state enforcement costs and terrorist competition operates independently of whether there is a full-blown civil conflict. Additionally, the effect is independent of the overall capacity of the government, represented by total tax revenue as a percent of the country's GDP. The evidence from Table 4.2 and Figure 4.3, then, indicates that enforcement costs and competition among terrorist organizations have a strong joint effect on the amount of terrorism that a state experiences.

Finally, in a series of models not included here, we examine whether the findings from the previous chapter hold if we remove the interaction terms from the models. That is, we want to see if our hypotheses from Chapter 3 regarding country-level and group-level violence

---

[14] All probabilities are calculated while holding the other covariates in each model constant at their median values.

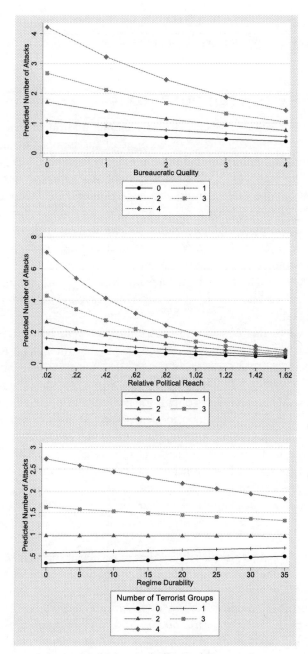

FIGURE 4.3 Marginal effects of competition.

hold when we control for *Bureaucratic quality*, *Relative political reach* and *Regime durability*. Indeed, we still find that aggregate violence increases as group numbers increase, while per-group rates of violence decline.

ADDITIONAL EVIDENCE

In a series of robustness checks, we examine additional evidence for our hypotheses. First, instead of a count of the number of active terrorist groups, we substitute a measure of the year-to-year change in that number. Although our model generates implications based on the static number of groups, Conrad and Greene (2015) argue that accounting for changes in the number of groups can be a useful proxy for the competitiveness of a political environment. The models including *Regime durability* and *Relative political reach* and the change in the number of groups are comparable to those reported in this book.

Second, we include a lagged dependent variable in our models to account for simple inertia in recent violence and we find that our conclusions do not change.

Third, we further consider the possibility that state repression is driving violence more generally. Although there is no theoretical reason to believe that state repression influences the *interaction* of government enforcement costs and intergroup dynamics (the central premise of our hypothesis), we nonetheless control for government protection of physical integrity rights in the main models presented in this chapter. In the robustness checks, we substitute a measure of the level of "political terror" committed by the government (Wood and Gibney, 2010). In either case, our hypothesized relationship holds, regardless of the direct effect of state repression on violence.

Fourth, we include country and year fixed effects in the models. In all models except one, the trends are comparable with those reported in this book.

Fifth, we consider the possibility that our causal process is only applicable once there is some baseline of violence. As such, we analyze each model on the subset of observations with at least one terrorist attack (in other words, we drop observations with no violence). The models including *Bureaucratic quality* and *Regime durability* are comparable with those reported in the book when restricting the sample in this way.

Sixth, we address the abundance of zero observations by modeling them as a split population. We use a zero inflated approach, modeling the inflation stage as recommended by Drakos and Gofas (2006). In all cases, the results are robust to this modeling strategy.

Seventh, we include an additional control capturing the overall capacity of the country. We include in the models the number of military personnel in the country (Singer, Bremer, and Stuckey, 1972) and we find no important differences from our main models.

Finally, we treat our key independent variables as indicators of a latent variable capturing the marginal costs of enforcement in each state. Our approach thus far has implicitly assumed the existence of such a variable, but we have treated our three indicators as individual proxies instead of measuring the marginal costs directly. In robustness checks, we use a structural equation model (SEM) approach to predict a latent measure based on our observable measures of bureaucratic capacity. We create two separate measures by alternatively combining *Relative political reach* or *Bureaucratic quality* with *Regime durability*. We then substitute the linear prediction of the latent variables into our original models and the effects are once again consistent with those reported in this chapter. In the vast majority of our results, then, the particular model specifications or measurement choices do not change our primary conclusion: states experience greater levels of violence when there are more terrorist groups and higher marginal costs of enforcement augment this effect.

CONCLUSION

How does state enforcement alter incentives for competition? This chapter extended the baseline model to analyze the strategic dilemmas of competing political violence organizations, citizens sympathetic to their cause, and a state trying to reduce new membership. Higher levels of enforcement simultaneously deter citizens with moderate interest from attempting to join and catch a portion of the more extreme individuals who try. Anticipating these effects, competing groups produce less outbidding violence when the state's marginal cost of enforcement effort is lower. Thus, although outbidding still occurs, enforcement mitigates the effect on violence.

Our formal model's results give us new leverage to empirically test outbidding theory. Many mechanisms could explain why more groups correlate with more violence, but our theory is unique in that we expect that outbidding violence is conditional on anticipated levels of enforcement. Measuring the ease of enforcement through bureaucratic quality, political reach, and regime durability, we find the conditional effect in the data. The addition of new terrorist groups can dramatically increase the expected amount of terrorism a state experiences when the costs of state enforcement are high. But this effect is often negligible when state enforcement costs are low. These results increase our confidence that competition is a broad driver of political violence, especially since alternative explanations do not predict this conditional effect.

Following our baseline model, the implication for counterterrorism strategy is straightforward. Conventional wisdom in academic and policy circles recommends an "enemy of my enemy" approach whereby states support moderate groups (or moderate factions within groups) in an effort to counter the most extreme groups. Our analysis, however, provides additional support for the outbidding thesis that increased competition can lead to more violence. Additionally, our model has identified specific conditions under which such competition is most likely to result in more violence. By focusing on mechanisms that lower state costs of enforcement – through improved intelligence sharing, for instance – states may be able to reduce incentives for groups to engage in competitive violence. And according to our results, such a strategy would have the most pronounced effect in environments where many organizations operate simultaneously. The costs of state enforcement, then, provide the crucial context that makes violence more or less useful to organizations.

The results also generate a key implication for policymakers, which we have echoed throughout this chapter. Increasing enforcement capabilities has direct costs to the state and reluctant or budget-strapped policymakers might think twice about taking enforcement efforts very far. Nevertheless, the model indicates that such individuals may wish to rethink their investment efforts. Greater enforcement capabilities mean that the government will want to spend more on those activities when they become necessary. The primary effect of that spending is to stop contributions from reaching militant groups. But the benefits accrue beyond that. Anticipating that enforcement could intercept their attempt to reach one of those groups, marginal contributors choose to keep to themselves. But both the direct and deterrent effects of enforcement feed into the groups' outbidding decisions. Recognizing that the pool of resources will diminish, the groups commit less violence overall. As such, shrewd policymakers ought to consider all three of these benefits as they think of ways they can decrease the costs of implementing enforcement.

This chapter has largely conceived of domestic government institutions as the vehicle through which enforcement operates. But there are other institutions that may facilitate similar enforcement results. To the extent that some international organizations directly augment or supplement state enforcement efforts, these organizations become an integral part of counterterrorism policy. The United Nations Security Council, for instance, mandated in UNSC 1373 that member states change their domestic laws to strengthen counterterrorism enforcement. Because the resolution was binding under Chapter VII of the United Nations Charter, many states increased their counterterrorism enforcement capabilities simply as a means of compliance.

Likewise, international organizational efforts in places like Afghanistan have provided the only true source of enforcement until the national government could transition into the role of enforcer. NATO's International Security Assistance Force (ISAF) was tasked with the management of the fight against the Taliban, as well as the development and training of the Afghan National Security Forces. The contributions of ISAF therefore facilitated two purposes: direct deterrence of political violence and contributions to the enforcement capacity of the new Afghan government.

Of course, our work is not done. Formalizing enforcement opens up new questions that were not originally apparent. Enforcement is an inherently reactive strategy. States must wait for citizens to want to join militant groups before intercepting them. Yet states also have many *proactive* policy levers. Given the subtle consequences of enforcement, one may naturally wonder whether reducing grievances, setting up defenses, and offensively attacking existing groups have unforeseen consequences. Our next two chapters delve into those topics.

APPENDIX

We now prove the three key lemmas before turning to the chapter's main proposition.

Proof of Lemma 4.1

Recall that the state's objective function is:

$$-\sum_{i=1}^{n} v_i - \frac{\pi}{1+e} - \alpha e$$

The first-order condition of this with respect to e is:

$$\frac{\pi}{(1+e)^2} = \alpha$$

$$e^* = \sqrt{\frac{\pi}{a}} - 1$$

The second-order condition of this is $-\frac{2\pi}{(1+e)^3}$, which is negative. This implies that the value for e^* is a maximum.

However, it is possible that e^* is less than 0, which is an impossible effort to produce. In that case, the first- and second-order conditions give that the state's utility is strictly decreasing in e. Consequently, the state maximizes its payoff with $e = 0$. Therefore, the state chooses $e = max\left\{\sqrt{\frac{\pi}{a}} - 1, 0\right\}$.

Proof of Lemma 4.2

As the main text indicated, a citizen j strictly prefers contributing if:

$$\left(\frac{1}{1+e}\right)(x_j) + \left(1 - \frac{e}{1+e}\right) > w$$

$$x_j > w(1+e)$$

By analogous argument, they strictly prefer not contributing if $x_j < w(1+e)$ and are indifferent when $x_j = w(1+e)$.

Note that a citizen's preference can depend on e, and e in turn depends on the number of citizens who volunteer, as π reflects that quantity. We can solve this feedback loop by proving that a critical citizen x^* exists such that all citizens with $x_j > x^*$ contribute and all citizens with $x_j < x^*$ do not.[15] Consider a proof by contradiction. If this were not the case, then there must exist a citizen with value x' and a different citizen with value x'' such that $x'' > x'$ and the citizen with x'' does not contribute but the citizen with x' does. But $x' > w(1+e)$ implies $x'' > w(1+e)$, so both citizens must contribute, a contradiction. Therefore, a citizen x^* exists such that all citizens with $x_j > x^*$ contribute and all citizens with $x_j < x^*$ do not.

Although the above proof by contradiction may seem unimportant, it means that we can rewrite π from the proof for Lemma 4.1 as $1 - F(x^*)$,

---

[15] What the citizen with $x_j = x^*$ does is immaterial because that citizen has no probability mass.

where $x^* = w(1 + e^*)$ for the interior solution. Thus, we need to find the individual such that if all individuals with values x_j greater than them join and the state produces optimal effort, that individual is indifferent between contributing and not contributing. Or:

$$x^* = w\left[1 + \left(\sqrt{\frac{1 - F(x^*)}{\alpha}} - 1\right)\right]$$

$$\frac{x^*}{\sqrt{1 - F(x^*)}} = \frac{w}{\sqrt{\alpha}}$$

The right side of the equality is a value strictly between 0 and infinity. The left side of the inequality strictly increases in x, equals 0 for $x = 0$ and approaches infinity as x approaches 1. The intermediate value theorem therefore guarantees a unique solution. Call x^* that implicit solution.

Figure 4.4 demonstrates how changing inputs alters the solution. The line plots $\frac{x}{\sqrt{1-F(x)}}$, which starts at 0 and breaks toward infinity as x approaches 1. When α is small, as α_1 illustrates, x^* must be large to compensate. This results in fewer contributions because only individuals with values greater than x^* contribute. Increasing α, as α_2 illustrates, decreases the overall value of $\frac{w}{\sqrt{\alpha}}$. The value $\frac{x^*}{\sqrt{1-F(x^*)}}$ must maintain equality, however. And because $\frac{x}{\sqrt{1-F(x)}}$ increases in x, the only way to do this is to decrease x^*. More individuals contribute under these circumstances.

That said, there is the possibility of a corner solution. As Figure 4.1 illustrated, individuals with values below w do not contribute under any circumstances. As such, if the solution requires x^* to fall below w (because α is sufficiently large), instead all citizens with values greater

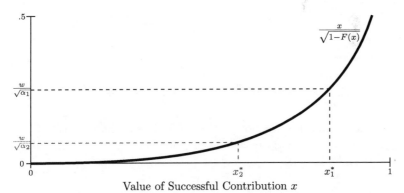

Value of Successful Contribution x

FIGURE 4.4 Illustration of the equilibrium implicit function.

than w contribute and all citizens with values less than w do not.[16] The state knows that $1 - F(w)$ individuals are contributing, but opts not to exert effort because its marginal cost is too high.

Proof of Lemma 4.3

This proof matches the analogous proof in Chapter 2 but now includes an endogenous market size. By backward induction, the groups anticipate $1 - F(x^*)$ individuals to join, with the state only permitting $\sqrt{\frac{\alpha}{1-F(x^*)}}$ to make it to the market (in the non-corner solution). Thus, the groups compete over $\sqrt{\alpha[1 - F(x^*)]}$ resources. Consequently, each organization i's objective function is:

$$\sqrt{\alpha[1 - F(x^*)]}\left(\frac{v_i}{v_1 + \ldots + v_n}\right) - mv_i$$

That is, group i receives a share of the resources equal to its portion of all violence committed, minus its costs of producing that violence. The first-order condition of this objective function is:

$$\sqrt{\alpha[1 - F(x^*)]}\left(\frac{v_1 + \ldots + v_n - v_i}{(v_1 + \ldots + v_n)^2}\right) - m = 0$$

With n organizations, n symmetric first-order conditions must be fulfilled simultaneously. Substituting $v_i = v_{-i}$ into the first-order condition generates:

$$\sqrt{\alpha[1 - F(x^*)]}\frac{(n - 1)v_i}{(nv_i)^2} - m = 0$$

$$v_i^* = \frac{\sqrt{\alpha[1 - F(x^*)]}(n - 1)}{mn^2}$$

This is a maximum because the second-order condition is:

$$-\frac{2\sqrt{\alpha[1 - F(x^*)]}(v_1 + \ldots + v_n - v_i)(v_1 + \ldots + v_n)}{(v_1 + \ldots + v_n)^4}$$

All values within the fraction are positive, so the leading negative sign makes the overall quantity negative. Thus, each organization commits $v_i^* = \frac{\sqrt{\alpha[1-F(x^*)]}(n-1)}{mn^2}$ violence.

----

[16] Specifically, this requires $\frac{w}{\sqrt{1-F(w)}} > \frac{w}{\sqrt{\alpha}}$, or $\alpha > 1 - F(w)$.

Proof of Proposition 4.1

By Lemma 4.3, there are n groups producing $\frac{\sqrt{\alpha[1-F(x^*)]}(n-1)}{mn^2}$ violence, for a total of $\frac{(n-1)\sqrt{\alpha(1-F(x^*))}}{mn}$ violence. Taking the derivative of this with respect to n yields:

$$\frac{\sqrt{\alpha[1-F(x^*)]}}{mn^2}$$

This is always positive for the parameter values. Thus, violence is increasing in n.

Further, this value is itself increasing in α. Proving this requires a little bit of work. Specifically, we want to show that:

$$\frac{\partial}{\partial\alpha}\left(\frac{\sqrt{\alpha[1-F(x^*)]}}{mn^2}\right) > 0$$

By the chain rule, this is:

$$\left(\frac{1}{2mn^2\sqrt{1-F(x^*)}}\right)\left(\frac{\partial}{\partial\alpha}(\alpha(1-F(x^*)))\right)$$

And by the product rule, we have:

$$\left(\frac{1}{2mn^2\sqrt{1-F(x^*)}}\right)(1-F(x^*))\alpha\left(\frac{\partial}{\partial\alpha}(1-F(x^*))\right) \qquad (4.2)$$

The difficult part comes from the fact that x^* is the implicit solution to:

$$\frac{x}{\sqrt{1-F(x)}} - \frac{w}{\sqrt{\alpha}} = 0 \qquad (4.3)$$

Thus, x^* is a function of α. With that in mind, another round of the chain rule to Line 4.2 yields:

$$\left(\frac{1}{2mn^2\sqrt{1-F(x^*)}}\right)(1-F(x^*))\alpha\left(-f(x^*)\frac{\partial x^*}{\partial\alpha}\right) \qquad (4.4)$$

In turn, the crux of the problem is finding $\frac{\partial x^*}{\partial\alpha}$. The implicit function theorem gives this as the negative of the derivative of Line 4.2 with respect to α divided by the derivative of Line 4.2 with respect to x. That is:

$$\frac{\partial x^*}{\partial\alpha} = -\frac{\frac{\partial}{\partial\alpha}\left(\frac{x}{\sqrt{1-F(x)}} - \frac{w}{\sqrt{\alpha}}\right)}{\frac{\partial}{\partial x}\left(\frac{x}{\sqrt{1-F(x)}} - \frac{w}{\sqrt{\alpha}}\right)}$$

$$\frac{\partial x^*}{\partial\alpha} = -\frac{w}{2\alpha^{\frac{3}{2}}\sqrt{1-F(x)}}$$

Substituting this into Line 4.4 yields:

$$\left(\frac{1}{2mn^2\sqrt{1-F(x^*)}}\right)(1-F(x^*))\alpha\left(\frac{f(x^*)w}{2\alpha^{\frac{3}{2}}\sqrt{1-F(x)}}\right)$$

Each of these terms is positive. Thus, the rate at which violence is increasing in n is faster when α is larger.

5

Outbidding as Deterrence: Endogenous Demands in the Shadow of Group Competition

The Syrian Civil War began rather inauspiciously in February 2011. An eleven-year-old boy, Naief Abazid, was arrested by local authorities in Daraa after scrawling anti-government graffiti on a school wall. Grievances against the government had been growing thanks to a recent economic crisis that had gripped the country. In fact, many alleged that the Syrian government's policies had exacerbated the growing poverty and inequality. The crisis, in this view, was simply the latest manifestation of "extreme repression" that Syria had suffered following Bashar al-Assad's rise to power in 2005 ("My Arab Spring: Syria's revolution betrayed," 2016). That repression was on full display as the arrest of Abazid exploded into a serious political crisis. Security forces opened fire on crowds who gathered to protest the boy's detention, killing two people. Protests then began to spread to the major cities of Syria, including Damascus and Homs. The growing protests triggered a vicious cycle, in which Assad's forces became increasingly violent. By May, more than 500 civilians were allegedly killed, with 2,500 people detained ("Syria protests: Rights group warns of 'Deraa Massacre'," 2011).

As the crisis erupted into a full-blown civil war, the number of militant groups opposing the Assad regime mushroomed. By one estimate, as many as 1,000 distinct armed opposition groups fought against the regime and against one another ("Guide to the Syrian rebels," 2013). Through the war's most violent period in 2014, and even as late as 2016, Assad continued to strike a defiant tone. In September 2016, shortly before ceasefire talks were set to begin, he vowed that he would reclaim "every inch of Syria" (Ensor, 2016). But as the myriad of armed groups continued to fight, and with no end apparently in sight for the conflict, Assad's tone notably began to change. In 2017, he declared that the

Syrian government was ready to negotiate "on everything" and admitted that a number of "mistakes [were made] on the part of the government" ("Bashar al-Assad: Everything on table in Astana Talks," 2017). And throughout 2017, as the Russian-designed "de-escalation zones" were put into effect around the country, Assad referred to them as a chance for "reconciliation" ("Assad says de-escalation zones chance for rebels to 'reconcile'," 2017).

Despite being in a stronger position relative to previous years, Assad was essentially opening up the possibility for reform. While it remains to be seen whether Syria will return to (or increase) its prewar repression, the civil war undoubtedly demonstrated to Assad the danger of such heavy-handed overreach. The sheer quantity and diversity of opposition that sprang up during the war reduced the utility of broadly repressive policies.

This chapter incorporates the source of an audience's grievances. We extend the core model so that the interaction begins with the target choosing a policy. All else equal, the target wants to capture more of that policy – be it territory, economic extraction, or regional political influence. However, as the target captures more of the policy, more individuals wish to volunteer to join a militant group. Groups observe the audience's level of antipathy to the target and then exert effort – in the form of violence – to accumulate more of the resources.

The revised model produces a number of results, some intuitive and others counterintuitive. To begin, as the target captures more of the policy, violence increases. This is due to the competition effect. The amount of violence groups produce increases in proportion to the resources available to capture; naturally, groups are willing to spend more when they can acquire more. In addition, the standard outbidding effect arises. That is, holding fixed the target's policy demands, adding groups causes more violence.

However, these two intuitive results combine to create a counterintuitive implication: increasing the number of groups may lead to a *decrease* in violence actually produced. How is that possible? Suppose that only a couple of groups compete with one another. Then for any policy captured, the target expects violence to be relatively small, as competition will be minimal. As a result, the target will have maximal demands. The high demands lead the audience to provide high contributions. The groups in turn produce high levels of violence, though the abundance of contributions primarily drives that decision, not outbidding competition.

Now suppose many groups compete with one another. This time, for any policy captured, the target expects violence to be relatively large because the outbidding effect will be out in full force. As such, outbidding leads to deterrence – scared of the competition and the violence it produces, the target may minimize its policy demands. Consequently, equilibrium levels of produced violence are small. Violence would be large here if the target kept its policy demands constant between the two cases. Yet the target fears outbidding violence so much that it chooses to exit the arena instead.

Overall, whether more groups implies more violence depends on a seemingly unimportant detail. Indeed, *the shape of the distribution of audience preferences determines how the number of groups influences violence*. If citizens become radicalized at a sufficient and increasingly rapid rate as the state demands a greater share of the policy, the straightforward outbidding effect holds – more groups imply more violence. However, if citizens are especially sensitive to initial encroachments, the deterrence effect dominates – more groups can counterintuitively imply *less* violence.

Why is the shape of the distribution of citizen preferences pivotal? In brief, when citizens are sensitive to initial encroachments, a target state's demand becomes an all-or-nothing affair. That is, if it is worth suffering the great pain to demand the first bit of the policy in dispute, then it is worth demanding *all* of the policy. Thus, the pool of support the groups draw from is either large or non-existent. The outbidding logic means that group competition drives high levels of violence in the former case, and the violence grows worse as the number of groups increases. In turn, if the number of groups crosses a critical threshold, the target state switches from demanding everything to demanding nothing. The corresponding loss of potential support reduces violence.

This chapter's results force us to temper the generality of the previous two chapters' empirical findings. As we noted in this book's introduction, a model's conclusions are a function of its assumptions. Our baseline models of outbidding showed that more groups cause greater violence. Here, however, we show that such a relationship only holds when certain scope conditions are fulfilled. If governments can mitigate the anger of disaffected citizens and citizens are especially sensitive to initial encroachments, the deterrence effect dominates. The broad statistical trends we discovered earlier are consistent with most cases failing to meet those scope conditions.

Nevertheless, we must be careful not to confuse a statistical average with a general truth. Cases within the complete domain could run in the opposite direction. Figure 5.1 lends credence to that possibility. It shows the frequency of country-years in which there were four or more

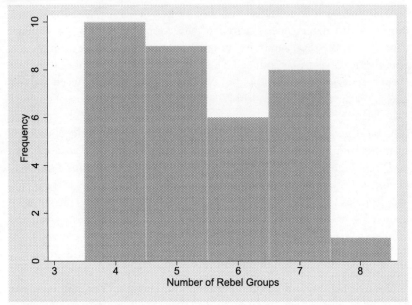

FIGURE 5.1 Country years with four or more rebel groups and no attacks.

rebel groups, and yet the GTD documents no terrorist attacks. Given the overproduction of violence by the Taliban in the twenty-first century, it is ironic that several of the country-years captured in Figure 5.1 occurred in Afghanistan during the 1980s. In total, there are twenty-five observations in the data where the number of rebel groups is unusually high and where no attacks are registered by the GTD.

As a result, any policy implications based on our earlier results require a caveat. Under certain alternative scope conditions, adding a group may not have the anticipated effect and can lead to situations that would appear in Figure 5.1. And while separating out those cases would be ideal, the scope conditions of this chapter's argument would make implementing a measurement for a large-n study prohibitively difficult. In short, a policymaker considering whether to manipulate the incentives of competitive violence within a particular market ought to consider the constraints of that specific situation. Qualitative outbidding researchers must also think carefully about how citizen preferences work on a case-by-case basis. Finally, for quantitative researchers, we urge caution in interpreting the results of regressions on outbidding.

Despite the difficulty of measuring citizen preferences, the model produces other results with straightforward applications. Indeed, the second implication informs the study of the effectiveness of terrorism. By some accounts, terrorism does not allow individuals to obtain the policy goals they seek (Abrahms, 2006). Rather, attacking civilians precludes opponents from making the desired concessions. Although the literature shows a number of counterexamples (e.g., Kydd and Walter 2002; Pape 2003), terror campaigns routinely fail to alter substantive outcomes. This creates a deeper puzzle as to why terrorist organizations commit those attacks in the first place.

Our model indicates that these results are consistent with outbidding creating a selection effect. Even if terrorism cannot alter policy outcomes, groups may still invest in violence if disgruntled individuals would provide financial and moral support to the perpetrators. More groups place more competitive pressure on each organization, causing overall violence output to increase. Target governments may recognize these effects ahead of time. Those that do and anticipate that the price of terrorism will be extreme choose not to disrupt the policy in the first place. Those that do and anticipate that the price of terrorism will be small may nevertheless capture the disputed policy objectives. They then write off the terrorist attacks as the cost of doing business. Terrorism works here, but its persuasive effect occurs off the equilibrium path.

Our next implication examines who benefits from outbidding violence. In this endogenous grievances model, those who wish to deter the state are the only real winners. As we outlined in Chapter 2, the existence of another group further reduces the rents the other groups can capture through the context. Because that additional group increases overall violence production, the state also loses, either because it reduces the policy it captures or suffers more damage to maintain the same policy outcome. But the state's loss is a gain for anyone with contrary policy preferences.

The final implication asks whether international organizations would benefit from eliminating a competing group. Suppose that such organizations only wish to reduce the quantity of violence produced. By Chapter 2's logic – and the standard conceptions of outbidding theory – having one less competing group would seem to only improve the outcome. However, this chapter shows that the reduced competition has a second-order effect of inducing the state to take more aggressive policy positions. The net effect can be a higher overall production of violence.

THE MICROFOUNDATIONS OF GRIEVANCES

Governments that overreach tend to generate higher levels of grievances among their populations, raising the likelihood of conflict. Early rational choice models suggested such conflict was a default outcome of governments becoming larger and more powerful. Rummel (1985), for instance, argues that concentration of power in any form tends to produce conflict because it leads to zero-sum games. By contrast, when power is more decentralized – or in Rummel's conception, people are more "free" – human interactions are represented by positive-sum games. As a result, political conflict is less likely.

A wide range of subsequent studies find empirical evidence for the link between government overreach and political violence. These studies use a variety of measurements to capture government abuses of civil and human rights. Countries that actively discriminate against ethnic minorities, for instance, tend to experience more domestic terrorism and also export more terrorism to other countries (Asal, Conrad, and White, 2014; Piazza, 2011). Meanwhile, Walsh and Piazza (2010) find that states that regularly abuse the physical integrity rights of their citizens suffer more incidents of terrorism. In their estimation, such abuses of power alienate domestic political movements, international observers, and significant portions of the general public. Many of these actors then choose to redress their grievances through the use of political violence. Notably, governments involved in high levels of activity *abroad* may also generate such grievances among *foreign* populations, and are more likely to be targeted by transnational terrorists as a result (Savun and Phillips, 2009). In contrast to such abuses, Burgoon (2006) provides evidence that states providing more benefits to their citizens – in the form of social services – experience lower levels of political violence. This relationship is so pervasive that the US National Strategy for Combating Terrorism argues that democratic governance can reduce grievances by giving citizens the opportunity to address social and economic issues through their power to vote.

Whether citizens wish to contribute to terrorist organizations under repressive policies depends on many issues, but the literature points to four that are particularly salient. First, citizens' wages (Bueno de Mesquita, 2005b; Bueno de Mesquita and Dickson, 2007) and general enjoyment of life form the basis of the judgment; both decline as a target state becomes more expansionary, whether directly through the modified policy or indirectly through economic distortions it may cause. Second, an individual's latent extremist tendencies matter; even minor policy demands may set off those predisposed to radical action. Third, repressive policies can motivate individuals to contribute to seek revenge for loved ones killed during hostilities (Bloom, 2005; Elster, 2005, 241–242; Ricolfi, 2005, 111); revenge should trigger more individuals to join as the external actor entangles itself deeper into civilians' affairs. Finally, in the framework of terrorism-as-public-goods, a citizen's desire to contribute depends on their altruistic preferences and willingness to engage in self-sacrifice (Azam, 2005; Elster, 2005; Pape, 2005, 187–198; Wintrobe, 2006). Although such individuals constitute a minority of any given population, a certain subset exhibits these traits (Berman and Laitin, 2008; Iannaccone and Berman, 2006).

Governments are aware that these actions influence terrorism and use policy levers to adjust prospective violence accordingly. China's efforts to manage ethnic conflict in the autonomous northwestern region of Xinjiang illustrate this. For centuries, Xinjiang's multi-ethnic population has posed significant challenges for the central administration. Many of the region's groups, including Kazakhs, Hui, and Kirghiz, have been "resistant to Han cultural assimilation" (Gladney, 1990). Over the last few decades, China has worked hard to bring the region fully into China's state, identifying it as part of the western "poverty belt" that includes Tibet. The government believes that economic underdevelopment has fueled grievances by the various groups in the region. Resolving the economic problems would therefore bring stability to the region.

To that end, China pushed various reforms to improve Xinjiang's economy, including its portion of the "Great Western Development Drive." Some of these policies have paid off. During the 1990s, Xinjiang experienced rapid economic development. Between 1991 and 1994 alone, regional GDP doubled. So too did investments in the region (Moneyhon, 2002). The increased economic productivity appears to have reduced dissent from some ethnic groups in the area, consistent with the overarching goal.[1]

More generally, governments can establish "spheres of influence" that the central authority respects in an effort to quell the motivators of violence (Staniland, 2012, 250–251). For instance, Pakistan has passed de facto control over portions of cities to the Muttahida Qaumi Movement (Lieven, 2011, 317). The Taliban received even larger segments until pressure from the United States made the effort too costly (Hoyt, 2015; Rashid, 2008, 385). Although the Pakistani military could have applied pressure to these opponents, the government preferred not to suffer the

---

[1] The economic drive may have contributed to the consolidation of the political marketplace by Uyghur groups. In particular, the East Turkestan Islamic Movement took control over the market and proceeded to increase total violence within that community. The next chapter provides an explanation for that behavior.

costs of terrorist and insurgent violence. Other examples include the relative peace between Afghanistan and the Mujahideen during the Soviet intervention (Staniland, 2012, 251) and the Soviet/Russian approach to Tatarstan's push for regional autonomy (Kondrashov, 2000, 142).

But whether modifications to any given policy result in a major change in violence rates depends on the distribution of citizen preferences. This distribution is pivotal to all of the formal results below, so it is worth describing what this means in greater detail. To begin, take a single individual. Consider their baseline happiness, extremist tendencies, vulnerability to revenge, and altruistic nature. If the opposing state vacates the policy entirely, that person will likely be satisfied and not want to contribute. On the other hand, an extremely aggressive policy demand will have that citizen rush to assist the organizations. Thus, at some point, that citizen is indifferent between contributing and not contributing.

Now consider an entire society's collection of those indifference points. Because happiness, extremism, vulnerability, and altruism are not uniform across a population, the indifference points vary as well. But how those points cluster determines which policy the government pursues and, in turn, whether more groups yield more violence.

Two possibilities further motivate a key distinction the model makes below. Consider the origins of discontent in Lebanon prior to the 1983 Beirut barracks bombings. Colin Powell, who was an assistant to Defense Secretary Caspar Weinberger at the time, wrote in retrospect that US operations against Shiite targets led the audience to "assume ... the American 'referee' had taken sides" (Powell and Persico, 1996, 291). In effect, by taking one step into the fray, Washington had mobilized a significant segment of the population against it. Social solidarity across a population for those affected by minimal incursions would create a similar effect (Wintrobe, 2006, 108–143).

Now consider a region where the average citizen lives a comfortable, happy life. These individuals still dislike a foreign state meddling in their internal affairs. Nevertheless, minor encroachments will not cause the vast majority of citizens to sacrifice their livelihoods. Only a few particularly radical individuals may begin to support an organization. But such a tepid response is not absolute. If the state begins completely uprooting the average person's livelihood, grievances eventually accumulate. Soon, large segments of the population begin aiding the resistance organizations.

These two cases show a clear distinction. Think of the underlying functions that take extremist proclivities and government meddling as their inputs and map them to actual contributions to a group. In the Lebanon case, proclivities were high for a large enough portion of the population that the initial encroachment catalyzed a flood of support to the market. Greater demands would have further stoked the fire, but that increase would not have resulted in as large of a jump as the first bit. In the hypothetical second case, the initial demand would only cause a modest bump to support levels. However, the real surge would not begin until the demands become burdensome. Both cases see support increase in the demand. But the rates at which they increase are unique.

From a formal perspective, the difference between the two is a subtle change in the functions' second derivatives. Yet the next section demonstrates that those second derivatives determine whether overall violence increases or decreases in group counts.

MODELING ENDOGENOUS GRIEVANCES

Following the above discussions, we now add two actors to Chapter 2's baseline model: a target state and a unit mass of citizens considering whether to contribute to an organization. These are the same actors as in the previous chapter, but we now explore a different strategic problem. The game consists of three phases:

1. the state makes a demand;
2. the groups observe the demand and each simultaneously chooses a level of violence;
3. the citizens observe the demand and levels of violence, and each decides whether to support a group.

More thoroughly, the state begins by demanding $x \in [0, 1]$. This represents the portion of the good it consumes. The previous section motivates its many interpretations. Greater discrimination against ethnic minorities, greater abuse of physical integrity rights, higher rates of economic extraction, more expansive foreign policy platforms, fewer social services provided to an outgroup, and greater efforts to forcefully assimilate all correlate with greater values of x.

The second phase features the familiar contest between the organizations. Each of $n \geq 2$ organizations chooses a level of violence $v_i \geq 0$.[2]

---

[2] We keep the number of groups exogenous to match the previous models' frameworks, which allows for a more direct comparison between the new and old results. It also fits with cases where militant groups remain dormant until a policy disagreement gives

Unlike Chapter 2, however, the state endogenously determines the size of the market that the groups compete over. Specifically, each citizen from the unit mass chooses whether to join a group or not. Following previous discussions, we assume that the citizen contributions are proportional to the quantity of violence that each group chose previously.

Payoffs are as follows. A citizen j receives $w_j(x)$ for remaining a civilian and (without loss of generality) 0 for joining a group. In accordance with the micromotives for terrorist recruitment, we assume each citizen's w_j is continuous and strictly decreasing in x. In words, the more the state demands, the less attractive civilian life looks relative to joining an organization. A variety of studies argue that as states engage in more repressive and coercive policies, the relative utility of engaging in political violence increases while the relative utility of peaceful submission decreases (Gurr, 1970; Lichbach, 1987; Muller and Weede, 1990) Repression has also been linked to extreme displays of political violence, such as terrorists' pursuit and use of weapons of mass destruction (Campbell and Murdie, 2018). Encroachment into the civilian population's domain may directly deny economic opportunities, exacerbate relative deprivation, lead to abuses of human rights, or trigger a variety of other outcomes linked to radicalization.

We also assume that $w_j(0) < 0$ and $w_j(1) > 0$ for all citizens. That is, the mass of citizens we are interested in prefer remaining citizens if the state demands nothing and will all volunteer if the state demands everything. Thus, these citizens are minimally sensitive to the state's decision and they may or may not join an organization depending on the demand.[3]

By virtue of these assumptions, each citizen j has a critical value of x for which $w_j(x) = 0$. Put differently, for each citizen, a particular state

them a message to convey. The Second Intifada illustrates this, with stark changes in violence outputs resulting from anticipated changes to Israeli policies. Aside from that, the general mechanism operates in situations where groups endogenously form and then choose violence outputs. Here, the state's choice determines both the number of groups that form and the violence they choose. Regardless, the central mechanism still applies. When groups face lower costs of entry, outbidding pressures are greater. Internalizing the threat of violence, the state reduces its policy demands.

[3] In practice, there may be citizens who prefer to remain civilians regardless of the demand. Such individuals have no impact on the results below. There may also be citizens who prefer to join an organization regardless of the demand. Including such individuals in notationally cumbersome and causes minor disturbances to the results below. We therefore exclude them from the formal analysis and instead note how their inclusion changes a few conclusions.

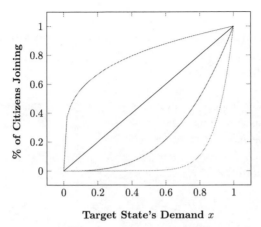

FIGURE 5.2 Cumulative probability distribution examples.

demand exists that leaves that citizen indifferent between remaining a civilian and joining a group. Although these indifference points might not appear important for determining the relationship between the number of organizations and the prevalence of violence, they prove to be critical. Let $f(x)$ represent the probability density function of these indifference points and $F(x)$ represent the cumulative distribution function (CDF). To permit greater analysis, suppose the explicit function is $f(x) = \lambda x^{\lambda-1}$, where $\lambda > 0$ is a parameter that determines its exact shape.

Known as a power distribution, this PDF form captures a wide range of distributions. Figure 5.2 illustrates four such possibilities. When $\lambda = 1$, the CDF of the probability distribution is uniform; each additional unit of demand radicalizes the same portion of individuals. This models a heterogeneous group, as there is no clustering of their preferences. When $\lambda < 1$, the function is concave; each additional unit the state demands radicalizes decreasingly more citizens. This corresponds to situations like the aforementioned Lebanon case, where initial incursions created a large outpouring of support. Note that as λ approaches 0, the group becomes increasingly homogeneous. Lastly, when $\lambda > 1$, the function is convex; each additional unit the state demands radicalizes increasingly more citizens. Going to the other extreme, as λ approaches infinity, the group again becomes increasingly homogeneous.

In sum, preferences are not uniform across populations. Some populations may be more sensitive to state demands. Correspondingly, they radicalize at a faster rate than others. *Ex ante*, the parameter λ may appear irrelevant to how violence changes as the number of groups increases. To the contrary, though, the presumed monotonic relationship between violence and the number of groups is sensitive to the alignment of preferences.

The organizations have identical preferences to before. Recall previously that each group i's objective function was $\pi \frac{v_i}{v_1+\ldots+v_n} - m v_i$, where $\pi > 0$ was the sum pool of resources and $m > 0$ was the marginal cost of violence production. This utility function remains the same, except now the citizens' decisions determine π.

Finally, given the above distribution of citizen preferences once more, we write the state's utility as:

$$x - \alpha \sum_{i=1}^{n} v_i - \beta z$$

The first component is simply the quantity of the policy the state takes. The second is the sum violence the organizations produced. Finally, the third component is the state's disutility for citizens joining the organization in general, which may result in additional costs that we do not explicitly model here. The placeholder z represents the portion of the citizens joining.

Because we have three theoretically distinct sources of value, we use scalars to allow the state to place its preferred weight on each of them. We standardize the value of the policy to 1. The state weighs the sum of violence by $\alpha > 0$. Finally, $\beta > 0$ captures the importance the state places on citizens joining. Higher values of α and β mean that the state cares more about those factors and less about the others.[4]

Beyond that, to maintain generality, we do not place any further functional form on the scalars. However, we offer some brief motivation. A state that has high resolve for the policy issue at hand would have low values for both α and β. If violence would personally target policymakers with control over the state's decision, α would trend higher. Finally, because the quantity of citizens joining represents a future problem for the state, β captures time preferences; the more patient a state is, the higher β would be.

---

[4] Setting the scalar for policy equal to 1 is without loss of generality because games are identical across positive affine utility transformations. Thus, we could have a scalar $\gamma > 0$ to capture the state's weight on the policy. But then we could divide all of the state's utilities by γ. This changes the scalars of the other factors to $\frac{\alpha}{\gamma}$ and $\frac{\beta}{\gamma}$. Both of these are strictly positive values, and thus we can simply have the α and β parameters from the model implicitly capture the γ weighting.

Citizen Decisions and Competition among Groups

We ultimately want to know how the number of competing groups affects total levels of violence. This was simple in the baseline model because we merely needed to solve for the competition phase for a general number of groups n and then investigate equilibrium violence as a function of n. Drawing similar conclusions is more complicated here because the state can anticipate violence and endogenously alter its demands. We therefore must solve the general competition phase for all possible demands from the state. Once we have that information, we can feed it into the state's utility function and optimize its demand.

Despite the addition of the state and the mass of citizens, the competition phase of the game remains almost identical to before. At the end of the game, each citizen compares their payoff for remaining a civilian versus joining a group given the state's demand. Any civilian j such that $w_j(x) > 0$ joins, whereas any civilian j such that $w_j(x) < 0$ does not.[5] Given the distribution of citizen preferences, we can write the quantity of citizens joining as $F(x)$.

Moving up a step, the organizations can anticipate that $F(x)$ portion of citizens will join a group, and each knows that its share of those $F(x)$ resources are proportional to the quantity of violence it commits. This optimization problem is identical to the original group contest, except the quantity of resources π is now endogenously formed as $F(x)$. Reformulating our results from Chapter 2 gives us this first result:

Lemma 5.1 *Suppose the state demands x. Each group produces $\frac{F(x)(n-1)}{mn^2}$ in violence. Overall violence therefore equals $\frac{F(x)(1-\frac{1}{n})}{m}$.*

To be clear, outbidding remains in full effect here. Holding fixed the state's policy demand, increasing the number of groups increases the total violence the groups commit. Despite that information, we cannot yet conclude that violence actually increases in the number of groups. The expectation of the additional violence caused by a group may cause the state to reduce its demands. Lemma 5.1 shows that this would have a countervailing effect – total violence increases in x, so shrinking the demand *reduces* violence.

---

[5] What a citizen does when indifferent is irrelevant because they have measure zero for the family of distribution functions analyzed.

Indeed, applying Lemma 5.1's violence levels to the state's objective function suggests that this countervailing effect may create a barrier to inference. To see this, Lemma 5.1 allows us to rewrite the state's utility as

$$x - \alpha F(x) \left(\frac{1 - \frac{1}{n}}{m} \right) - \beta F(x)$$

The first component still shows that the state benefits from demanding more of the policy. However, greater demands increase grievances, causing more citizens to join an organization and causing the organizations to commit more violence to compete for those resources. Thus, the latter two terms *decrease* in x. The state's dilemma is balancing the benefits of capturing more of the policy to the punishment of additional violence.

How Competition Can Reduce Violence

Surprisingly, how competition affects violence produced depends on the shape of aggregate citizen preferences. We begin with cases where $\lambda < 1$. Recall from Figure 5.2 that such values imply that the initial increases to the state's demand result in relatively large increases in citizen contributions; although further demands also further increase contributions, the rate of the increase in contributions declines. This leads to the first proposition:

Proposition 5.1 *Suppose that the rate of citizen contributions increases faster at lower demands than higher demands (i.e., $\lambda < 1$). If the state is sufficiently sensitive to violence (i.e., $\alpha > \frac{m(1-\beta)}{1-\frac{1}{n}}$), it demands none of the policy. If the state is sufficiently resistant to violence (i.e., $\alpha < \frac{m(1-\beta)}{1-\frac{1}{n}}$), it demands the entire policy.*

In short, when citizens are more sensitive to initial encroachments, the government's decision becomes an all-or-nothing affair. Substantively, the state views the problem as a decision between conceding all demands to the population or engaging in an extractive occupation.

There is a straightforward explanation for this. Consider the state's marginal value for taking the first bit of the policy. Given the distribution of citizen preferences, this results in a large spike in violence. Each additional bit of the policy taken causes a further increase in violence, but those jumps are smaller than the initial spike. Put differently, demanding each additional unit of the good results in less additional radicalization than the first portion. As such, if demanding that first amount proves worthwhile, demanding *all* of the good must be worthwhile.[6]

In turn, the state calculates its best course of action by substituting $x = 0$ and $x = 1$ into its utility function and checking which produces the larger value. The appendix shows that making this comparison generates the cutpoint on α seen in Proposition 5.1. Larger values of α imply that the state worries more about the violence it may suffer. Intuitively, then, the state finds the $x = 0$ option relatively more attractive as α grows larger.

Although this logic may be simple, altering the number of groups has an unexpected second-order effect:

Proposition 5.2 *Suppose that the rate of citizen contributions increases faster at lower demands than higher demands (i.e., $\lambda < 1$). The relationship between the number of groups and equilibrium violence is nonmonotonic. If the state's equilibrium demand is $x = 1$ and remains there with the addition of another group, then violence increases. However, increasing n can cause the state's equilibrium demand to shift from $x = 1$ to $x = 0$. Equilibrium violence drops to 0 and remains there for all subsequent increases in n.*

Figure 5.3 helps clarify Proposition 5.2's findings. If the state demands the entire policy, it does so because it cares little about the quantity of violence. Small changes to the level of violence does not impact the decision. Thus, if taking the whole policy looks much better than taking none of it, an additional group will not change the state's stance. The additional group may lead to more competition and more violence, but the state prefers absorbing that violence rather than relinquishing its demands. Thus, equilibrium violence initially increases in Figure 5.3. Competition has the effect that standard outbidding theory would predict.

However, this logic does not necessarily hold for yet larger group numbers. Violence accumulates as the number of groups continues to increase. Eventually, the total sum of violence may grow so large that the state prefers avoiding it entirely by capturing none of the policy. If so, violence drops precipitously. The increase in groups still increases

---

[6] Mathematically, this occurs because the state's utility function is convex. This also gives insight into how the results extend beyond the family of distributions we analyze here. The state never chooses a demand inside a concave region of the distribution. (The state's utility function includes a negative scaled version of the distribution, which makes the utility function *convex*.) Thus, the dropoff that occurs in Proposition 5.2 below extends to any distribution for which an increase in n causes the state to decrease its demand to the endpoint of the concave region or below.

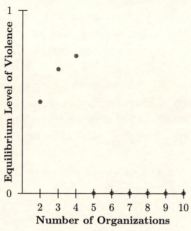

FIGURE 5.3 Equilibrium violence under Proposition 5.2.

competition. However, that increase in competition worries the state. Its only option to mitigate competition is to reduce the pool of resources the groups compete over. Because the best way to do this is to deplete the market entirely by demanding nothing, the net effect is a decrease in violence despite the increase in competition. Any further increases to the group count only reinforce the state's decision to withdraw.

The outbidding literature does not anticipate such a dropoff. What is missing? Current outbidding theory operates in a vacuum. More groups means more competition for scarce resources, which compels groups to exert greater effort to bring home those resources. But competitive incentives concern more than just the groups. Indeed, the target of the violence endogenously reduces grievances when it foresees outbidding pressures. In effect, competitive outbidding deters the state from expanding its policy demands, and the deterrent effect can sometimes trump the competition effect.

There are a few caveats worth highlighting about these results. First, relaxing an earlier assumption further complicates the relationship. Figure 5.3 shows that violence is flat once the number of groups exceeds the critical cutpoint. However, this is a consequence of the assumption that no citizen wishes to contribute if the government withdraws all demands. Suppose instead that some portion of citizens always want to contribute regardless of what the state's actions are. Increasing groups can still flip the state's decision from demanding the entire good to demanding none of it, just as Figure 5.3 illustrates. The corresponding loss of support means that outbidding violence declines as pictured. However, it is reasonable to think that a market could still exist even if $x = 0$. This would capture the idea that some individuals want to join militant groups for the sake of joining militant groups, without any real policy goals in mind. If so, then violence does not drop to 0 but rather maintains some positive value. Furthermore, after the dropoff, violence increases once again as the number of groups increases. This is due to the familiar competition effect.

Beyond that, there may not be a critical number of groups that results in a switch from a demand of $x = 1$ to $x = 0$. Instead, the state may prefer taking nothing or everything regardless of the number of groups. Recall from Proposition 5.1 that the state prefers taking none of the pie if $\alpha > \frac{m(1-\beta)}{1-\frac{1}{n}}$. One obvious way this can hold is if the state does not care at all about the policy goal and therefore weighs violence at a very high level. A more subtle way this can happen for all possible number of groups is if $\beta > 1$, which forces the right side of the inequality to be negative. Substantively, such β values mean that the state weighs all of the citizens turning against it as more important than securing the entire pie. Thus, the quantity of outbidding violence has no impact on the state's preference to choose $x = 0$.

The precise level of competition may still not matter in cases where the state does not mind turning the citizens against it. Note competitive violence minimizes when $n = 2$. Substituting that into the cutpoint yields $\alpha > 2m(1 - \beta)$. This can still hold if m is sufficiently small. Recall that m is the marginal cost of violence. If violence is cheap to produce, even two groups will produce massive quantities of it to capture marketshare. In turn, just those two groups are sufficient to convince the state to withdraw its policy claims to eliminate the market. Adding another group only reinforces the decision and thus the state maintains the demand $x = 0$ regardless of the number of groups.

Similarly, the state may throw caution to the wind and demand all of the good regardless of group competition. Proposition 5.1 states that this happens if $\alpha < \frac{m(1-\beta)}{1-\frac{1}{n}}$ for all n. Note that competitive violence has an upper limit and we can calculate the upper limit of its effect by taking the limit of the cutpoint as n approaches infinity. This yields $\alpha < m(1 - \beta)$. In contrast with the previous paragraph, if the marginal cost of violence is prohibitively expensive, even groups in environments with otherwise intense competitive pressures will not produce much of it. Consequently, provided that the state is not deathly scared of violence, it demands the entire pie regardless of the number of groups.

A similar consequence arises when α and β approach 0. This case represents a situation where the state does not care at all about suffering violence or spurring citizens to join a group and instead cares entirely about the policy demand at stake. Whether the number of groups is large or small is irrelevant because the state does not care about the specifics of competitive violence. It just takes the entire good no matter what.

When Competition Promotes Violence

The previous section only analyzed cases where citizen contributions increased faster at lower demands than higher demands. This made the state's policy demand an all-or-nothing affair. However, the state may prefer a moderate demand when citizen contributions increase slowly for initial demands and increase faster at higher demands. Substantively, these are cases where most citizens tolerate small policy grabs from the state but each additional demand upsets a larger portion of the citizens. Unlike before, taking the first bit of the pie does not imply that the state should take all of it. Instead, each additional amount carries with it greater punishment, which forces the state to find the proper balance. The following proposition explains how the state addresses its dilemma:

Proposition 5.3 *Suppose that the rate of citizen contributions increases slower at lower demands than higher demands (i.e., $\lambda > 1$). If the state is sufficiently resistant to violence (i.e., $\alpha < \dfrac{m\left(\frac{1}{\lambda} - \beta\right)}{1 - \frac{1}{n}}$), it demands the entire policy. If the state is sufficiently sensitive to violence (i.e., $\alpha > \dfrac{m\left(\frac{1}{\lambda} - \beta\right)}{1 - \frac{1}{n}}$), it demands $x^* = \dfrac{1}{\left(\lambda\left(\frac{\alpha\left(1 - \frac{1}{n}\right)}{m} + \beta\right)\right)^{\frac{1}{\lambda - 1}}}$.*

Intuitively, if the state does not mind suffering violence, it captures the entire policy. This rallies all of the citizens to contribute and competitive violence is correspondingly high, but the state believes the cost is an acceptable downside to maximizing its policy goals. The outcome is more interesting when the state is sensitive to violence. Here, the state feels the tradeoff and thus chooses a more moderate demand. The subsequent market is smaller than in the first case.

To understand the state's thinking, consider how the moderate demand changes as a function of the parameters. [7] Increasing the state's sensitivity to outbidding violence or general recruitment (by increasing α and β, respectively) causes the state to shrink its demands so as to avoid radicalizing as many civilians. Changes to the number of groups or marginal cost of violence also have intuitive effects, though the causal pathway is indirect. Additional groups and cheaper costs of violence (increasing n or decreasing m) exacerbate outbidding competition. Internalizing this, the government demands less under these conditions. Still, citizen contributions for the very first slice of the policy are small and do not feature the large jump seen in Proposition 5.1's case. As such, the state maintains a positive demand even as changes to those parameters make the government more reticent.

Of course, calculating equilibrium violence requires an additional step. Although adding a group causes the government to reduce its demands within the interior solution, outbidding simultaneously increases the amount of violence for a fixed market size. Given the cross-cutting effect, it is unclear whether the deterrence effect or competition effect dominates. Nevertheless, the following proposition gives clear conditions under which the traditional outbidding theory holds:

Proposition 5.4 *Suppose that the rate of citizen contributions increase is sufficiently slower for lower demands than higher demands (i.e., $\lambda > max\{\frac{1}{\frac{\alpha}{2m}+\beta}, 1 + \frac{\alpha}{\beta m}\}$). Then equilibrium violence strictly increases in the number of groups.*

Put differently, suppose that the initial portions of the demand radicalize very few citizens but capturing the latter portions of the policy leads to sharp increases in radicalization. Then violence assuredly increases as groups increase no matter the frame of reference.

Why does the competition effect dominate here? Refer back to Figure 5.2's illustration of different distribution functions. Proposition 5.4 covers cases where λ is sufficiently large, so consider the bottom-right-most distribution. Initial demands only radicalize a tiny fraction of the citizens. As such, the state is unlikely to have a small demand because it could take substantially more without driving more individuals to terrorism. However, contributions increase rapidly toward the end of the curve.

---

[7] All of the results discussed in this paragraph are from taking a simple derivative on x^* with respect to the proper parameter.

It is therefore unlikely that the state should capture the entire policy, as it could forgo just a small sliver and massively reduce the number of individuals it radicalizes.[8] In turn, the equilibrium demand falls toward the higher end but is not all-encompassing. Indeed, in such a case, the state will have a moderate demand regardless of the number of competing groups.

Now consider how an increase in the number of groups affects violence. The discussion of Proposition 5.3 already explained why the government's demand drops. However, for distributions with high λ values, the drop is barely noticeable. Recall again the bottom-right curve of Figure 5.2. Because total radicalization is mostly flat for lower demand values, the state must massively reduce its demands to have a tangible effect on recruitment. Such a reduction has a large policy cost for low marginal reward and so the state barely shrinks its demand. Correspondingly, total contributions barely change as well. The extra group still amplifies outbidding incentives among the other groups though. As such, the competition effect trumps the deterrence effect.

The appendix derives Proposition 5.4's cutpoints. The first requirement $\left(\lambda > \frac{1}{\frac{\alpha}{2m}+\beta}\right)$ guarantees that the state prefers to not take the whole policy even when only two groups compete. The second requirement $\left(\lambda > 1 + \frac{\alpha}{\beta m}\right)$ ensures that the competition effect dominates the deterrence effect conditional on being in that interior solution.

A careful reader will notice that Propositions 5.2 and 5.4 exclude values of λ just greater than 1 from the analysis. We omit such cases from the formal analysis because they largely have the same theoretical implications as the cases described above. Nevertheless, we now provide a brief summary:

- The state can prefer to capture the entire policy regardless of the number of groups. In this case, analogous discussion from Proposition

---

[8] One can observe this by checking Proposition 5.3's condition for the state to demand $x = 1$, which is $\alpha < \dfrac{m\left(\frac{1}{\lambda}-\beta\right)}{1-\frac{1}{n}}$. This assuredly fails when $\lambda > \frac{1}{\beta}$, which forces the numerator to be negative and thereby ensures that the always-positive α is greater than the right-hand side. This makes substantive sense. As λ approaches infinity, the distribution begins resembling a step function that is 0 for all inputs other than 1 and jumps to 1 at 1. This represents a near-infinite increase in violence costs for the smallest increase in demands. Thus, the state chooses a slightly smaller value.

5.2 applies – because the state's demand is not sensitive to the number of groups, equilibrium violence is strictly increasing in n.

- The state can prefer to capture the entire policy for a small number of groups but prefers a moderate demand for a large number of groups. Such an outcome exhibits the dropoff from Figure 5.3. Increasing n increases violence as long as the demand remains fixed at 1 but will decrease once the state takes a more conservative approach. Thus, the dropoff is not as steep as depicted in the figure.

- If the state's optimal demand is always in the interior, violence can strictly decrease in n if the second requirement of Proposition 5.4 $\left(\lambda > 1 + \frac{\alpha}{\beta m}\right)$ fails. This is because the state can make relatively small changes to its demand and yield a large reduction in contributions. It prefers to do that in situations with intense competition and thus the deterrent effect dominates the competition effect.

IMPLICATIONS OF OUTBIDDING-AS-DETERRENCE

With the model complete, we now turn to the lessons we can draw from it. Given the quantitative findings from the last two chapters, we begin with the limitations that this chapter's main result emphasizes. Afterward, we discuss some of the key comparative statics of the model, which provide substantive insight into the effectiveness of terrorism and who benefits from outbidding incentives.

Empirical Challenges for Outbidding Research

A commonly held implication of outbidding theory is that increasing competition leads to more violence. For example, Findley and Young (2012, 708) state that "the greater the number of opposition groups, the more likely any terrorist acts will occur during armed conflict." Stanton (2013, 1014) echoes this, saying that "outbidding arguments predict that terrorism is more likely in conflicts involving multiple rebel groups." Fortna (2015, 15) indicates that the "outbidding argument suggests that terrorism is more likely when there are several rebel groups active as part of the same struggle." It was also a central finding in earlier chapters' models.

Many empirical studies find a relationship between the number of groups and quantity of violence produced. Bloom's (2004) formulation of the theory applies it to Palestinian resistance to Israeli policies. Nemeth (2014) finds quantitative evidence to support the hypothesis. His connection hinges on whether the audience will respond favorably to violence, which was one of Bloom's key scope conditions. Our earlier results also corroborate the general outbidding logic.

Nevertheless, empirical estimates of the average relationship between additional groups and violence output tell us little about individual cases. Other data-generating processes may exist where adding an extra group results in a decline in violence. The presence of such groups increases the difficulty of finding a relationship in the data. But conditional on discovery, it simultaneously does two things. First, it underestimates the relationship for cases that follow the standard competition data-generating process. Second, it misestimates – and indeed suggests the opposite relationship – for those that follow the alternative explanation.

This chapter's mechanism provides such an alternative explanation. If the target of violence manipulates the size of the market, a selection effect can arise. Thus, an increase in the number of groups leads to a decrease in violence produced. Given that this mechanism creates noise in the data, it is perhaps unsurprising that some operationalizations of outbidding theory fail to find a relationship (Findley and Young, 2012; Fortna, 2015; Stanton, 2013). In fact, Findley and Young anticipate this exact explanation, stating that "it may also be the case that there are heterogeneous dynamics at work in which the number of groups increases terrorism in some countries ... but decreases it in others" (719). This chapter's model supports that assertion. In *some* cases, violence increases in the number of groups.[9]

From a research design perspective, in an ideal world, we could find a way to subset the cases where this chapter's scope conditions are met to obtain better estimates of the outbidding effect one would wish to measure. More specifically, per Proposition 5.4, the model shows that the straightforward relationship holds when citizens are sufficiently insensitive to initial encroachments but become increasingly resistant as the state presses forward. That is, the parameter λ must be sufficiently large. A more precise quantitative test of traditional outbidding theory therefore first requires operationalizing λ. From there, the data either could be subsetted to remove cases that do not meet the scope condition or

---

[9] True to that, Findley and Young find support for outbidding when focusing on Israel, in line with Bloom's qualitative assertion.

the regression models could include an interaction term to allow the relationship between groups and violence to depend on λ.[10]

Thus, outbidding theory needs to think about these demand curves for terrorism. One potential way to get at this is through the use of survey data. Because outbidding is inherently tied to public opinion, researchers have worked with survey data to link public support to violence (e.g., Kaplan, 2015). Yet a proper measure of λ requires deeper survey data than what is standard. The rate at which citizens increase their support for a cause is not a mere snapshot. Put differently, the level of support for a single, already-implemented policy is not the necessary piece of information. Rather, the rate of increasing support is the distribution of preferences among citizens, reflecting where they would go from supporting to not supporting militants.[11] As such, the theory indicates that surveys must be carefully constructed to obtain the right information.

To illustrate, suppose we wanted to quantify support for groups that target Israel. A survey that asks whether Palestinians currently support political violence today is not sufficient. It must also ask whether Palestinians would support these organizations if Israel retracted or expanded its policy demands. From here, we could estimate a value of λ by tracing the rate at which the increase in support increases. This is not standard practice – it relies on thinking through a counterfactual and working through a second derivative. Neither of these are obvious components of outbidding theory at the outset.

Although careful survey methods provide some hope, it is worth detailing the assumptions a researcher has to make to allow for the inferences to be valid. As λ grows larger, the state's demand weakly

---

[10] The model provides a best-case scenario by assuming that the distribution remains either convex or concave throughout the support. In practice, we cannot eliminate the possibility that real-world distributions do not shift in between. For example, initial encroachments could quickly jump support levels due to a subset of radical individuals who are eager to fight. Middling demands could still increase support but at a moderate rate, reflecting a comfortable middle-class majority's reluctance to commit to the cause. Yet the increases could accelerate toward maximal demands once again. Because concavity drives the main propositions' results, adding a group can either increase or decrease violence, depending on whether the current optimal demand falls in the convex or concave region. This also explains why adding squared, cubed, and higher-order exponential terms cannot adequately test a theory without strong *ex ante* guidance on how many convexity/concavity transitions a set of militant group competitions should have.

[11] A deeper issue here is that the vast majority of a population does not typically support militant groups. In turn, choosing the right sample to obtain a useful measure is a challenge.

increases for some parameter spaces. Intuitively, large values of λ mean that virtually no one contributes for all but the largest demands that the state can make. As such, the state makes an onerous policy demand. But when λ is small, the state suffers the deleterious consequences of violence much sooner. This incentivizes the state to moderate its demands.

Now consider whether the state can solicit that information directly by asking potential contributors to the organizations. These individuals wish to minimize the target state's demands but become willing to contribute if the state overextends its reach. Suppose that the target state is unsure of how those potential contributors would react to various levels of encroachment – that is, the state faces incomplete information over the audience's resolve.

Incentive compatibility issues indicate that a public opinion poll will struggle to elicit truthful revelation from a strategic audience. To understand why, suppose the state took such a poll at face value. If citizens indicated great latent animosity, the state would internalize the threat and reduce its demands. But if citizens signaled relatively weak preferences except for the most egregious demands, the state would take more. Expressed in this manner, the incentive to misrepresent becomes clear. As long as less-resolved citizens care at all about losing even a small share, they would want to lie and mimic a more-resolved citizen's message. In turn, capturing the citizens' true underlying preferences requires assuming that citizens are not considering the deeper strategic dimensions of the poll.

Although incentives to misrepresent are commonly understood in the crisis bargaining literature (Fearon, 1995), the literature on terrorism and coercion seems to overlook it. In an interview with a *New Yorker* reporter, a Hamas leader claimed that their "biggest problem is the hordes of young men who beat on our doors, clamoring to be sent. It is difficult to select only a few. Those whom we turn away return again and again, pestering us, pleading to be accepted" (Hassan, 2001). Researchers often take these comments at face value (Bueno de Mesquita, 2005b; Spaniel, 2018b) and the Hamas leader may have told the truth in that particular instance. However, he has a clear incentive to overrepresent the popularity of Hamas, both to gain yet more followers and increase its coercive capacity.

The Effectiveness of Terrorism

An open question in the political violence literature is whether terrorism succeeds in coercing opponents. For Abrahms (2006) the answer is a firm no. A quick analysis of the empirical evidence appears to support this argument. Abrahms investigates twenty-eight terrorist groups as designated by the US State Department and finds that they only obtained 7 percent of their combined forty-two policy goals. He concludes that "the poor success rate is inherent to the tactic of terrorism itself" (43–44).

This view is controversial. Responding to Abrahms, other scholars argue that the apparent lack of terrorism success is an artifact of restrictive data choices (Thomas, 2014) or is far from universal (Rose, Murphy, and Abrahms, 2007). Pape (2003) also gives a comprehensive list of suicide terrorism campaigns and finds success, though Abrahms argues that these cases are limited to a few groups and three target states.

However, this chapter's model indicates that there is a deeper problem in estimating the effectiveness of terrorism. In short, a selection problem means that observational data can lead to the wrong inference. Terrorism could be effective despite the data suggesting that terrorists flounder.

This chapter added an endogenous market to the theory of outbidding. With it comes the ability of the target state to reduce the output of violence. All it must do is demand less of the policy in dispute, shrink the market of support, and benefit from the lower effort that terrorist groups exert. In turn, if the violence produced in equilibrium is great, it is the result of the state strategically choosing to endure that violence. After all, if it did not want to suffer that much, it could have relinquished the policy entirely.

Put this way, terrorism is just the cost of doing business for the state in the model. In cases where we observe violence, the state finds the price worth capturing a greater share of the policy in dispute. In cases where we observe no violence, it is precisely because violence would be so intense that the state has no choice but to do everything in its power to avoid provoking terrorist organizations. Violence therefore appears to negatively correlate with policy concessions despite the exact opposite relationship being true.

In this light, coercive bargaining failure may actually *improve* an organization's welfare. That is, if we view coercion failure or the failure to achieve strategic goals as the government capturing more of the good, this can mobilize a larger share of the population. In turn, the organization will have a larger pool of resources and recruits to capture. So, while groups may rarely achieve their strategic priorities, their "success rate" in achieving process goals appears to be much higher.

Worse for the terrorist organizations, group competition is a double whammy for their overall utility. As in the main model, holding fixed the size of the market, each organization's payoff decreases as the number of groups increases. This is because the extra competition from an additional group drives more resources elsewhere, taking away resources from the others.

In an endogenous market, competition also has a second-order effect that further starves all organizations of resources. The model shows that the state's demand weakly decreases in the number of groups. This is because the fear of additional violence deters the state from capturing more of the policy. But this means that the groups face additional competition for *fewer* resources.

Limited Aims

So far, we have seen that an additional group hurts both the state and the competing organizations. The tradeoff is in changes to the policy:

Remark 5.1 *The state's demand weakly deceases in the number of groups.*

That is, more groups generate a greater deterrent effect. Because citizens have a preference for lower policy demands, they therefore benefit on this dimension.[12]

More generally, the citizens' policy outcome improves from any increase in the net production of violence. Increasing the number of groups is one way to do that. As alluded to in Chapter 2, this gives further theoretical justification for the particular contest success function we use. From a design perspective, the Tullock (1980) ratio function we use maximizes aggregate effort (Dasgupta and Nti, 1998) for a reasonable set of requirements for the contest. Consequently, if the citizen contributors wished to maximize violence output from the groups, adopting the distribution we model accomplishes that goal.[13]

---

[12] By the model's parameterization, citizen welfare weakly increases in the number of groups. We do not emphasize this result because citizens may also be the inadvertent victim of an attack. In turn, if they value their own welfare relatively high compared with the policy space, they may prefer a world with fewer groups. The cleanest direct interpretation of the model therefore applies to a breakaway group committing attacks within the central government's capital. In that case, the citizens who may support the groups are not to suffer directly from a group's attack.

[13] As noted in Chapter 2, the contest function that maximizes output in sufficiently asymmetric cases involves excluding the groups with the highest marginal costs (Franke et al., 2013).

In any case, digging deeper into Remark 5.1's logic reveals a deeper credibility issue that the citizens face. The earlier discussion of incentives to misrepresent hinted at this. Citizens would collectively benefit if they could threaten to join an organization regardless of whether their demands are met. If the target state were to believe those threats, it would further recede its demands; violence, after all, increases in the number of citizens contributing. All citizens would benefit from this. However, such threats are not inherently credible – the only citizens that contribute are those for whom the actual payoff for contributing exceeds the payoff for not.

It is worth emphasizing that the state's limited aims are not the result of some bargaining process.[14] In the standard crisis bargaining framework (Fearon, 1995), states with all of the proposal power ask for less than their ideal policy outcome because the opponent can implement a less favorable outcome via war. Here, the state faces no such rejection constraint; if the state wants to capture the entire policy good, it may. But the model shows that a state sometimes wishes to limit its share despite having free rein, recognizing that the cost of violence may exceed the marginal value of an additional portion of the policy good.

Some illustrations may help drive home this point. Many European countries chose not to participate in the Iraq War because even a successful invasion would increase the chances of terrorist attacks against the homeland. France and Germany were, in particular, vocal about this concern (Dettke, 2009, 157–158; Parmentier, 2008; Pauly, 2013, 12–13).[15] Observing this exact result from the Iraq War has increased reticence in engaging elsewhere in the Arab World. The Madrid train bombings on March 11, 2004 are a frequently cited example of a terrorist attack stemming directly from a government's policy on the Iraq War. Notably, the Spanish government changed its policy in apparent response to the attacks, quickly withdrawing its military forces from Iraq. But even seemingly unrelated attacks, such as the assassination of Dutch filmmaker Theo van Gogh, have been subsequently linked to motivations generated by the Iraq War (Nesser, 2006). In the United States experts have debated how much US foreign policy in Iraq inspired operations like the 2015 San

[14] Cunningham (2011), for example, argues that concessions can strengthen a target state's preferred faction when facing multiple competing groups. She then finds that states are more likely to grant self-determination when facing divided movements than united fronts. This chapter's model highlights an alternative mechanism: increased competition disincentivizes larger claims.

[15] This was also a point of objection for doves in the United States.

Bernardino attack. Concerns about the counterproductivity of US policy in the Middle East may help explain the country's relative restraint in the Middle East since the "termination" of wars in Iraq and Afghanistan.

Induced limited aims have a deeper effect on crisis bargaining, one that the literature does not fully appreciate. The vast majority of crisis bargaining models assume that states bargain over a unit interval with diametrically opposed interests. If bargaining fails and war begins, the winner takes the entire interval. This chapter's model indicates that this is not always the case. One could imagine that the interaction analyzed here is the subgame following the state emerging victorious, either from a civil or interstate war. Even free from the bounds of organized conflict between regular armies, the state sometimes chooses to limit its demands.

The handful of models that incorporate moderate preferences (Bils and Spaniel, 2017; Schultz and Goemans, 2019; Spaniel and Bils, 2018) demonstrate a couple of interesting findings. First, moderate preferences reduce a country's coercive bargaining power. Such countries find less overall value in fighting a war, making them willing to accept smaller offers during a negotiations phase. This again serves to the benefit of the citizens, who want to minimize the opposing state's share of the policy, whether through war or peace. Second, the possibility of moderate preferences generates an interesting signaling dynamic. States especially fearful of terrorism may wish to capture small amounts even through peaceful means while actively shunning more generous offers. They therefore do not have the standard incentive to misrepresent their private information. Citizens once again benefit here – the state does not lie to capture more, which would otherwise again reduce citizen welfare.

In any case, this chapter provides better microfoundations for the interval two states bargain over. Incorporating explicit preferences into crisis bargaining models may help yield new insights that remain hidden in the implicit form.

International Organizations and Group Elimination

Chapters 2 and 4 provided straightforward implications for how international organizations could reduce violence outputs. Eliminating a group reduces the basic competition incentive, which in turn reduces violence output. Meanwhile, raising the cost of violence directly convinces groups to do the same. In short, raising the barriers to terrorism yields the desired outcomes.

This chapter's model begins to show the limitations of those straightforward policy implications. Consider an international organization or institution whose sole goal is to reduce terrorism. Removing a group here can have a perverse second-order consequence that causes terrorism levels to rise. Within the model, outbidding acts as a deterrent. Scared of violence, the target state takes positive steps to quell citizen furor, which removes the groups' incentive to compete. As such, if the international organization removes a group, it could inadvertently kill the deterrent. The target state responds by increasing its demands, raising citizen furor, and suffering violence afterward. In turn, policymakers must be cautious in exploiting the implications from earlier chapters. Removing a group is an effective strategy when doing so will not cause the target state to alter its behavior. But it may fail when target states become more belligerent as a result.

The core problem here is misaligned incentives between such an organization and the target state. One might suspect that, if removing a group causes an increase in violence, the target state is worse off. This is false. The target wishes to strike the correct balance between acquiring more of the policy and suffering less violence. The organization may not care much about the former but cares about the latter. Much like how others warn that humanitarian institutions can inspire rebel groups to act more aggressively against their governments and thereby raise the risk of war (Kuperman, 2008; Spaniel, 2018a), group removal provides a mitigation effect. Knowing it will not have to absorb the full consequences of expansive aims, the state balances toward capturing more of the policy. Hence the tension.

Unfortunately, this result means that empirical findings on group reduction are subject to the Lucas (1976) critique. Strategic organizations only reduce group numbers when they expect violence to go down – for example, going from four to three groups or three to two groups in Figure 5.3. In cases where violence will increase or stay steady, the investment is not wise. Thus, we would expect to see a negative relationship between elimination and violence. From such a result, it may be tempting to conclude that organizations should engage in greater efforts to eliminate militant groups. However, a policymaker who naïvely follows this advice could jeopardize a relatively stable situation by eliminating the deterrent that keeps the target state honest.

CONCLUSION

This chapter extended the baseline competition game to permit the target state to change its aggravating policy in anticipation of outbidding violence. Doing so reduces the total contributions that the organizations compete over and thus mitigates the incentives to outbid one another. As a result, the target state faces a stark tradeoff. The more of the policy it takes, the more violence it expects to suffer in return. Thus, the state must decide how best to balance its desire to move the policy closer to its ideal point and avoid the costs associated with achieving that goal.

The severity of competition determines how the state makes its decision. Holding the state's policy choice fixed, adding a group increases violence levels per the standard outbidding logic. Thus, more groups make maintaining any particular policy demand look less attractive. In turn, those additional groups have an unclear net impact on violence. Although outbidding leads to an increase, it is possible that the deterrent effect dominates.

By formalizing that tradeoff in this chapter, we discovered an unexpected result. In the context of this framework, the relationship between group numbers and violence depends on the shape of citizen preferences for contributions. If most citizens refuse to provide assistance unless the state makes substantial policy demands, then the outbidding effect reigns supreme. This is because the state is inclined to take a moderate approach to the policy so as not to induce those citizens to contribute. Further moderating the policy has diminishing marginal returns on reducing those contributions. That is, to reduce contributions by any notable amount, the state must drastically cut its policy demand. Thus, although adding another group causes the state to moderate its policy slightly, it does not move the needle by much. The outbidding effect therefore dominates.

In contrast, if most citizens provide assistance for even small encroachments by the state, then the policy becomes an all-or-nothing affair. Adding a group here can be pivotal to the state's decision. Indeed, when the competition becomes so strong that the corresponding violence overwhelms the value of the entire policy, then the state switches from taking everything to taking nothing. Violence drops to 0 because the groups no longer have any prize to compete for. In sum, greater competition can counterintuitively yield less violence under these circumstances due to the intervening deterrent effect.

If there is indeed a threshold where more competition results in lower levels of violence, then, in some cases, proliferation of groups may not be a wholly negative outcome. This aligns with a fairly common policy position that recommends pitting rebel factions against one another. A classic treatise on counterinsurgency tactics, for instance, says that "the goal of the counterinsurgent's psychological warfare should be . . . to divide their ranks . . ." (Galula, 2006, 86). Yet the key implication – that the rivals will defeat each other – may not be the mechanism actually at work. Instead, as this chapter has shown, division and fragmentation of movements may indirectly produce restraint on the part of the government through a long-run deterrent effect.

Of course, as Chapter 3 showed, empirical violence increases in the aggregate as more groups compete. Nevertheless, our findings here indicate that we ought to interpret that statistical result with caution. What is true *on average* is not true in every case. Positive expectations may still hide negative counterexamples. Unfortunately, the cause of this chapter's exception to the rule is prohibitively difficult to capture in quantitative analysis. It is all the more remarkable that we can find Chapter 3's statistical result despite our inability to filter out those cases.

On a more positive note, the model also generated a couple of insights better-ready for empirical consumption. First, terrorism may be a powerful deterrent tool even if it appears otherwise. This is because, given the incentive structure we study, those willing to incur the price of terrorism as the cost of doing business are those that ignore the threat. Where terrorism would succeed, the potential target opts out of the conflict before it begins. Terrorism therefore exhibits a "hidden hand" of coercion similar to what the sanctions literature has discovered (Drezner, 2003) and speaks to the selection problems inherent in political violence more generally (Fearon, 2002).

We also demonstrated that citizens benefit from outbidding competition. Holding fixed a policy demand, more groups create more competitive pressures and therefore raise overall violence production. Internalizing the threat, the target state relaxes its grip over the policy. The groups lose out here because they compete over fewer rents due to the smaller market. But citizens emerge victorious by obtaining a more attractive policy outcome.

This logic has important sway in ongoing policy debates. As the United Kingdom debates how to exit the European Union, a sticking point is the border between the Republic of Ireland and Northern Ireland. With both the Republic of Ireland and the United Kingdom a part of the European Union, the border that divides the Irish island is essentially meaningless. But departure from the European Union could mean a hard border put into place, which could resurrect tensions not seen since the

Troubles. Many groups could sprout overnight to attempt to claim true successor status to the Irish Republican Army. British politicians have correspondingly been reluctant to implement any sort of hard border on the island. But this has caused second-order bargaining complications with the European Union, as the lack of a hard border would allow trade with the United Kingdom to go through an Irish back door.

In any case, the fact that this chapter's strategic environment showed how more groups could yield less realized violence raises a deeper question. Is this chapter's framework an isolated case, or might there be more counterexamples as well? We delve deeper into alternative outbidding concerns in the next chapter and demonstrate that the deterrence effect is not unique. Indeed, violence may be larger when a single group tries to convince would-be challengers not to enter the political violence marketplace.

APPENDIX

This appendix gives proof for the four propositions within the chapter.

Proof of Proposition 5.1

Recall that the state's objective function is:

$$x - \alpha F(x) \left(\frac{1 - \frac{1}{n}}{m} \right) - \beta F(x)$$

The first-order condition is:

$$1 - \alpha f(x) \left(\frac{1 - \frac{1}{n}}{m} \right) - \beta f(x) = 0$$

Substituting $f(x) = \lambda x^{\lambda - 1}$ and solving for x yields:

$$x^* \equiv \left(\frac{1}{\lambda \left(\frac{\alpha \left(1 - \frac{1}{n} \right)}{m} + \beta \right)} \right)^{\frac{1}{\lambda - 1}}$$

The second-order condition for a maximizer is:

$$-\frac{\lambda x^{\lambda - 2}(\lambda - 1)(\alpha(n - 1) + \beta m n)}{m n} < 0$$

Recalling that $\lambda > 0$, $x > 0$ for any interior solution, and $n \geq 2$, this simplifies to:

$$\lambda > 1$$

Therefore, if $\lambda < 1$, the function is convex on the interval and so the solution to the optimization problem must be a corner. Substituting $x = 0$ into the utility function outputs 0; substituting $x = 1$ into the utility function outputs $1 - \frac{\alpha\left(1 - \frac{1}{n}\right)}{m} - \beta$. In turn, $x = 0$ is the optimal demand if:

$$0 > 1 - \frac{\alpha\left(1 - \frac{1}{n}\right)}{m} - \beta$$

$$\alpha > \frac{m(1 - \beta)}{1 - \frac{1}{n}}$$

By analogous argument, demanding $x = 1$ is optimal if $\alpha < \frac{m(1-\beta)}{1-\frac{1}{n}}$. This completes the proof of Proposition 5.1.

Proof of Proposition 5.2

The change in violence is straightforward within a given case. If $x = 0$ for two consecutive values of n, equilibrium violence equals 0 in both cases. If $x = 1$ for two consecutive values of n, then we must substitute $F(1) = 1$ into Lemma 5.1's equilibrium violence calculation. This is $\frac{1 - \frac{1}{n}}{m}$. Taking the derivative of it with respect to n yields $\frac{1}{mn^2}$, which is strictly positive. Therefore, violence strictly increases in n if the demand remains static at $x = 1$.

However, the cutpoint complicates the relationship because it is also a function of n. Recall that the demand equals 0 if $\alpha > \frac{m(\frac{1}{\lambda}-\beta)}{1-\frac{1}{n}}$. If $\frac{1}{\lambda} - \beta < 0$, this must hold. Otherwise, the right-hand side is strictly decreasing; one can observe this by noting that the derivative of the right-hand side with respect to n is $-\frac{m(\frac{1}{\lambda}-\beta)}{(n-1)^2}$, which is negative when $\frac{1}{\lambda} - \beta > 0$. What this means is that a value of n may exist for which $\alpha > \frac{m(\frac{1}{\lambda}-\beta)}{1-\frac{1}{n}}$ for all n values greater than it but $\alpha < \frac{m(\frac{1}{\lambda}-\beta)}{1-\frac{1}{n}}$ for all n values less than it. Thus, crossing the threshold shifts the demand from $x = 1$ to $x = 0$. This causes a drop in violence – violence goes from being some positive amount to 0.

See the main text for proof of parameters for which no such shift in the demand can occur.

Proof of Proposition 5.3

If $\lambda > 1$, the second-order condition for a maximizer holds. That maximizer is x^*. However, the state cannot demand more than 1. The maximizer falls below this upper bound if:

$$\left(\frac{1}{\lambda\left(\frac{\alpha\left(1-\frac{1}{n}\right)}{m}+\beta\right)}\right)^{\frac{1}{\lambda-1}} < 1$$

$$\alpha > \frac{m\left(\frac{1}{\lambda}-\beta\right)}{1-\frac{1}{n}}$$

Thus, if $\alpha > \frac{m\left(\frac{1}{\lambda}-\beta\right)}{1-\frac{1}{n}}$, the state demands $x = x^*$. By analogous argument, if $\alpha < \frac{m\left(\frac{1}{\lambda}-\beta\right)}{1-\frac{1}{n}}$, the state demands $x = 1$.[16]

Proof of Proposition 5.4

Reworking Proposition 5.3's cutpoint on α in terms of λ yields $\lambda > \frac{1}{\frac{\alpha\left(1-\frac{1}{n}\right)}{m}+\beta}$; if this holds, the state prefers making the interior demand x^*. Because the right-hand side decreases in n, this condition is hardest to fulfill when n is minimized – i.e., $n = 2$. Therefore, if the condition holds for $n = 2$, it holds for all n. Substituting $n = 2$ yields $\frac{1}{\frac{\alpha}{2m}+\beta}$. This is sufficient for the state to always make the interior demand.

Conditional on making the interior demand, we must investigate how violence changes as a function of n. Recall that equilibrium violence equals $F(x)\left(\frac{1-\frac{1}{n}}{m}\right)$. Substituting for $F(x)$ and then x^* yields:

---

[16] Due to the concavity of $F(x)$ and the state's linear evaluation of the policy, x^* is strictly positive and we therefore do not have to worry about it falling below the lower bound.

$$\left(\cfrac{1}{\lambda \left(\cfrac{\alpha\left(1 - \frac{1}{n}\right)}{m} \right) + \beta} \right)^{\frac{\lambda}{\lambda - 1}} \left(\cfrac{1 - \frac{1}{n}}{m} \right)$$

Taking the derivative of this with respect to n shows that equilibrium violence increases in n if:

$$-\cfrac{\left(\frac{mn}{\lambda(\alpha(n-1))+\beta mn} \right)^{\frac{1}{\lambda-1}} (\alpha(n-1) - \beta mn(\lambda - 1))}{\lambda n(\lambda - 1)(\alpha(n-1) + \beta mn)^2} > 0$$

$$\lambda > 1 + \cfrac{\alpha\left(1 - \frac{1}{n}\right)}{\beta m}$$

The right-hand side is increasing in n. As such, the condition becomes harder to fulfill as n increases. Taking the limit as n approaches infinity, the condition must hold for all n if $\lambda > 1 + \frac{\alpha}{\beta m}$.

Together, these are the conditions appearing in Proposition 5.4. If they both hold, then the state always selects the interior demand x^* and violence always increases in n given that demand.

A General Result

We now give some brief details on how the result extends past the distributional forms considered in this chapter.

Proposition 5.5 *Suppose:*

1. *The game begins with the state selecting a policy $x \in [0, 1]$.*
2. *The volunteer curve is strictly increasing and strictly concave in x (i.e., $f(x) > 0$ and $f'(x) < 0$), with $F(0) = 0$ and $F(1) = 1$.*
3. *In the following subgame, equilibrium violence is (i) equal to 0 if $x = 0$, (ii) strictly increasing and weakly concave in x, and (iii) strictly increasing in n.*

Then the state chooses $x = 1$ for sufficiently small n and chooses $x = 0$ for sufficiently large n. Equilibrium violence is nonmonotonic.

Proof:　Let $v(F(x), n)$ be the function that maps the number of volunteers and competing groups to a quantity of equilibrium violence in a general competition subgame. Then the state begins the game by optimizing $x - \alpha v(F(x), n) + \beta F(x)$. Let $g(F(x), n) = \alpha v(F(x), n) + \beta F(x)$. Assumptions (2) and (3ii) ensure that $g(F(x), n)$ strictly increases in x (because both components strictly increase in x) and strictly concave (because one component is strictly concave and the other is weakly concave, and the sum of a strictly concave and a weakly concave function is strictly concave).

In turn, $x - [g(F(x), n)]$ is strictly convex. This is because:

- x is weakly convex
- $[g(F(x), n)]$ is strictly concave, and the negative of a strictly concave function is strictly convex
- The sum of a weakly convex and a strictly convex function is strictly convex.

Consequently, the x that maximizes $x - [g(F(x), n)]$ must be one of the constraints – i.e., $x = 0$ or $x = 1$. Thus, finding the optimal x is merely a comparison between the utility of these two choices. So the state chooses $x = 1$ if:

$$1 - \alpha v(F(1), n) - \beta F(1) > 0 - \alpha v(F(0), n) - \beta F(0)$$

Assumption (2) permits substituting $F(0) = 0$ and $F(1) = 1$, while Assumption (3i) permits substituting $v(F(0), n) = 0$:

$$1 - \alpha v(1, n) - \beta > 0$$
$$\alpha < \frac{1 - \beta}{v(1, n)}$$

Analogously, it chooses $x = 0$ if the inequality is flipped. This demonstrates the claim about equilibrium strategies.

Now we prove the nonomotonicity of violence in n. Assumption (3iii) states that $v(F(1), n)$ strictly increases in n. Thus, increasing n has the effect of increasing the denominator, which in turn decreases the overall value of the cutpoint. As such, the state is willing to choose $x = 1$ for some α values when n is sufficiently small but instead chooses $x = 0$ for those same α values when n is sufficiently large.

Increasing n therefore has the same effect as described in the main model. As long as n is below the critical threshold that makes the state prefer selecting $x = 0$, the state selects $x = 1$ and violence increases in n per Assumption (3iii). But once n exceeds the threshold, violence drops to 0 per Assumption (3i).[17]

[17] In fact, Assumption (3i) can be relaxed to merely requiring that $v(F(1), n) - v(F(0), n)$ strictly increases in n. One can derive this by not assuming that $v(F(0), n) = 0$ and then solving for the cutpoint as done in the proof.

6

Cornering the Market: Counterterrorism in the Shadow of Group Formation

Thus far, we have explored many facets of competition in the marketplace for political violence. Chapter 2 developed the foundations of outbidding. Chapter 4 explored how government efforts to intercept contributions and recruits attenuate competition. And the previous chapter investigated how competition among multiple groups may cause governments to soften their otherwise objectionable policies. Regardless, the central theme has been that active competition drives violence.

Yet the empirical record shows important counterexamples.[1] Sometimes single, monolithic groups initiate widespread violence without any apparent competition driving the decision.[2] Take Sri Lanka as an example. A number of militant Tamil youth movements had formed in the 1970s and the early 1980s, and those groups often actively competed with one another. Their tactics escalated from political assassinations in the late 1970s to a multi-party guerrilla war in the next decade.

Soon thereafter, a Sri Lankan government crackdown demolished those organizations. Only the Liberation Tigers of Tamil Eelam (LTTE) remained in a position to consolidate power (Abeyratne, 2004). But the lack of active competition for the LTTE did not result in a reduction in violence. Instead, the LTTE became even more violent and waged a campaign of suicide terrorism throughout the 1990s. Between July 1987 and February 2000, the group executed 168 suicide attacks in India and Sri

---

[1] More generally, global terrorist group numbers declined dramatically over the past few decades, yet violence increased at a comparable rate (Pedahzur, Eubank, and Weinberg, 2002).

[2] This is in contrast to the previous chapter, where fewer groups could produce more violence in equilibrium due to the state's endogenous demand. Regardless of the ultimate output, active competition determined the groups' effort.

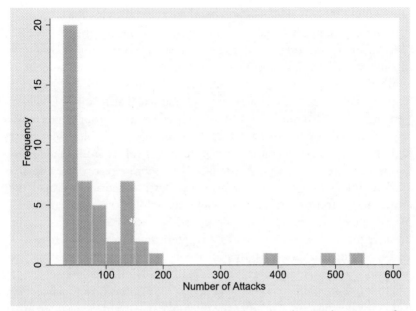

FIGURE 6.1 Country-years with one terrorist group and more than twenty-five attacks.

Lanka, including the assassination of former Indian Prime Minister Rajiv Gandhi (Schweitzer, 2000).

Sri Lanka is not an isolated case of a single group committing a large quantity of attacks. Figure 6.1 shows the frequency of country-years in which only *one* active group exists, yet there are unusually high levels of violence – more than twenty-five attacks in a year. In total, there are fifty-six observations that fit this scenario, representing countries across the world. Somalia in 2014 has the highest number of attacks in a country with a single active group, with 872. Although these are a relatively small proportion of our overall observations, they nonetheless demonstrate that a positive relationship between the number of groups and levels of violence is not always straightforward.

A common explanation for this type of behavior is a matter of centralization and legitimization (Goodhand, Hulme, and Lewer, 2000, 398). Fragmented groups, by this theory, cannot sustain themselves and do not have the resources to commit high-level attacks that yield the greatest violence. Although we do not disagree with the validity of this type of explanation, we show that competition can also drive the behavior. But, unlike previous chapters, the shadow of *potential* competition is responsible. Moreover, violence under these circumstances can be *greater* than when groups are in active competition with one another.

To demonstrate these findings, we relax a central assumption made throughout the book so far. We have mostly assumed that the number of competing groups remains fixed. A small robustness check in Chapter 2 helped justify this. If *all* groups must decide whether to form, knowing that they would compete with each other afterward, groups enter until one additional group no longer finds the enterprise profitable. This caveat highlighted a potential confounder in the empirical record: in fluid marketplaces, more groups may correlate with more violence because the market simply supports greater diversity. But competition still had the anticipated effect of causing more violence, holding the size of the competition fixed. In short, formation questions have been caveats to the broader theory and not a driver of any interesting strategic behaviors.

That said, our previous treatment of the formation problem put groups on the same footing. None already exist and all had to decide whether to enter before choosing their violence outputs. In practice, this is not always the case. Consider the dilemma an entrepreneurial terrorist faced in the Middle East in the early 2000s. At the time, a large market-share was available to capture. However, creating an organization would mean competing head to head with al-Qaeda, an established brand that had already exerted enormous effort to accumulate that marketshare. Entry might not be impossible for such an entrepreneur, but it would certainly be a challenge.

Such a strategic incentive has potential second-order consequences for an incumbent organization. Incumbents would prefer to not directly compete with anyone so as to maintain control of the entire pie. They also have a first mover advantage. An organization like al-Qaeda could produce so much violence – more than they would in a fully competitive market – just to convince potential entrants that formation is not worthwhile. Such overproduction may be costly, but deterring entry may more than compensate for the additional effort.

This intuition gives rise to our two preliminary research questions for this chapter. First, is such an overproduction strategy viable? And second, if so, does the incumbent's violence production exceed what *multiple* groups would produce in a competitive market? An affirmative answer to the first question does not imply an affirmative answer to the second. To corner the market, an existing group could, in theory, produce more than it would by itself but not as much as the two groups would combined. Nevertheless, we show that a single group may indeed produce more violence alone than two groups would in direct competition with one another. This adds another caveat to the observable relationship between the number of competing groups and violence. Although potential competition drives the massive overproduction of violence, the lack of an observable competitor makes the relationship seem otherwise.

To explore these incentives, we alter the existing contest model to occur sequentially. An incumbent group begins by choosing a violence level. A potential challenger observes this effort exerted and decides whether to pay a fixed cost to enter the market or not. If it does, the challenger then selects its own violence level. The audience splits its support according to the contest rules we have outlined previously.

As claimed, under certain circumstances, the incumbent group overexerts violence to "corner" the market. To understand why, first consider how a competitive market works. Once entered, a challenger's violence choice is *not* a function of its cost of entry – that cost is sunk, and the best the challenger can do is maximize its effort for the competition and the competition alone. If it wishes to engage in a competitive market, the incumbent recognizes this and chooses its violence level to compete with that quantity. The parties then split the market.

Imagine an extreme case where the cost of entry is high. Then the challenger may barely eke out a net profit. This represents a lost opportunity for the incumbent. By producing an amount of violence above its competitive rate, it can prevent the challenger from obtaining any net profit from entering. The challenger therefore sits out. Rather than sharing the market, the incumbent instead secures a monopoly. This is worth the cost of overproduction. The remaining question is whether the incumbent's power play results in more violence produced overall under direct competition. And, indeed, it can – the prospective gains from not having to compete with another group make incumbents willing to go to great lengths to achieve that tactical goal.

Although these results are interesting in their own right, the cornering-the-market logic also has interesting implications for counterterrorism strategies. We analyze four strategies a target state can adopt to try to stem the violence: (1) reducing grievances, in a manner similar to the previous chapter; (2) increasing barriers to entry; (3) offensive measures designed to enfeeble existing groups; and (4) defensive measures designed to harden targets against all potential attackers. Because violence can be larger when one group tries to corner the market, some of these strategies can backfire. That is, they can counterintuitively cause *more* violence than in the absence of an intervention. The negative effect is not a consequence of blowback, overreaction, miscalculation, or poor implementation. Rather, the strategies themselves are counterproductive.

First, consider reducing grievances. Smaller pies give groups less to compete over. As previous comparative statics have shown, organizations respond by lowering their outputs in competitive markets. This is not necessarily the case when an incumbent can corner the market. Indeed, fewer grievances make it more difficult for the market to support an additional organization. Observing this, the incumbent becomes more inclined to overproduce. The resulting individual output exceeds the collective output of a larger market. As such, decreasing grievances can counterintuitively *increase* violence. This may explain some empirical inconsistencies uncovered in the literature on grievances (Brancati, 2006; Dugan and Chenoweth, 2012). However, a fully committed effort to eliminate grievances will eventually cause the anticipated drop in violence.

Second, increasing the cost of group formation can also counterintuitively backfire. When the costs of formation are low, cornering the market looks unattractive for the lead group. This is because the challenger can easily enter. The lead group therefore must exert too much effort to deter that opposition from entering. When the costs of formation are high, however, the lead group finds cornering the market attractive. Thus, by increasing the barriers to entry, a target state can cause the incumbent to overproduce violence at a rate greater than the alternative. Like the grievances case, though, a full commitment to the strategy eventually makes entry so expensive that the incumbent group can produce a small amount of violence and still corner the market.

Third, offensive measures to destroy a group have weakly positive effects. Such tactics increase the amount of effort necessary for an incumbent group to produce violence. When this shifts the incumbent's preference from cornering the market to allowing competition, overall violence decreases. This strategy does not cause a spike like the previous two cases because it directly reduces the incumbent's violence output even when the market is competitive. It similarly causes lower overall violence when another group would have entered the market in the absence of an intervention. However, if the incumbent would corner the market without an intervention and still prefers to corner given the (possibly minimal) intervention, violence remains static. This is because the incumbent calculates its violence output to deter the entrant. Increasing the incumbent's marginal cost therefore makes the group work harder to produce the same amount of violence, leading to no benefit for the target.

The logic behind these offensive measures has a second key policy implication. If the target state wishes to offensively intervene against an otherwise cornering group, it must do so in a manner that leads to another group successfully competing. Critics of the "War on Terror" argue that such measures are ineffective because they resemble "Whac-a-Mole" – knock down one terrorist group and another springs up in its place. However, critics overlook how debilitating an incumbent group disincentivizes overly violent cornering behavior. Furthermore, such interventions also cripple that incumbent group in its competition with the newly formed entrant. All told, the amount of violence the target state stops the incumbent from producing exceeds the added violence from the new group. Thus, whac-a-terrorist-group can be effective despite spawning new militant groups. In fact, in our model, it is a *necessary* outcome if the target engages in any counterterrorism efforts whatsoever.

Finally, we show that defensive measures have some promise. Suppose that the vector of attack for both an incumbent and challenger group is the same, such that defensive measures stop an equal portion of both groups' violence. Because both groups face the same barriers, the incumbent's incentive to corner the market does not change. As a result, such defensive countermeasures reduce violence. Target states can implement them without much concern over the competitive balance.

However, the apparent superiority of defensive strategies is fragile. Suppose instead that a particular defensive strategy disproportionately impacts one group over another. For example, airport security would hinder a better-organized group capable of attacking planes, while stricter auditing of gun purchases would hurt a group reliant on individualistic assaults. Both of these tactics can work, but they require more thought in their implementation. Consider a countermeasure against the incumbent. If the incumbent would corner the market with or without the countermeasure, then the target wastes its implementation effort. This is because, as with offensive strategies, the incumbent chooses a level of violence designed to deter entry. Thus, insufficient defense merely causes the incumbent to work harder, without any benefit for the target. Greater defense, designed to induce the incumbent to allow the challenger's entry, can produce discontinuous benefits. And any additional defense after that monotonically decreases total violence.

Defensive countermeasures affecting the challenger require yet more thought, lest they backfire. Such strategies reduce the overall value of entry. In turn, the incumbent can more easily corner the market. Indeed, when the defensive countermeasures convince the incumbent to corner when it would not have otherwise, the market can see a disproportionate *increase* in violence. However, if the defensive countermeasures maintain the incumbent's corner versus compete decision, then defense monotonically reduces violence.

Zooming out, the model we develop is closest to Gowa and Ramsay's (2017) treatment of great power politics and the economics literature's broader analysis of entry decisions under Stackelberg competition.[3] A central mechanism recurs across these topics. A leading actor exerts great effort – terrorism, military armaments, or industrial output – to convince an opponent to renounce its claim to the market share. In short, our work is unique for two reasons. Most obviously, we take the mechanism to a new issue area. But more importantly, the extensions with government interventions break new theoretical ground.

We proceed as follows. Before developing the model, we provide some substantive descriptions of various counterterrorism policies states pursue. This allows us to think about the interesting ways we can allow a state to alter the competitive environment. We then study how potential competition operates under a different logic than the active competition models from earlier. Afterward, we extend the model according to four counterterrorism policies described earlier and explain their counterintuitive implications.

MICROFOUNDATIONS OF COUNTERTERRORISM POLICIES

Our book focuses on competition between groups. The previous two chapters have expanded that discussion to involve the target government. Both emphasized techniques to reduce the quantity of resources that competing groups could capture, either by investing in enforcement or pursuing less objectionable policies. But governments have other counterterrorism strategies at their disposal. We now highlight each of those that have interesting implications for market entry.

Reducing grievances and shrinking the pie. The last chapter discussed grievances in detail, so we only provide a quick refresher here. Some counterterrorism measures minimize what the competing groups fight over. Addressing grievances goes to the root of the problem.

---

[3] On the latter, see Dixit (1980) as an example.

Rather than trying to kill terrorists or otherwise inhibit their progress, reducing grievances makes the support base rethink their desire to join an organization or provide financial support. With the target abandoning the objectionable policies, fewer citizens want to contribute to the violence.

How a target government executes this strategy depends on the source of the issue. If foreign policy expansion angers local populations (Savun and Phillips, 2009), the solution is to scale back those endeavors. If abuse of physical integrity rights drives support, then revising laws to guarantee those rights mitigates the grievance. If government-imposed economic inequality upsets minority citizens (Piazza, 2011), then restoring equality would address the problem.

If a government prefers to stick to its objectionable policies, it can still shrink the prize at stake by increasing enforcement. These policies range from greater police presence to more careful tracking of citizen finances and movement. Thus, rather than inducing fewer individuals to participate, enforcement intercepts them as they seek membership.

As we pointed out in Chapter 4, international organizations may play significant roles here that a specific government is unable or unwilling to play. In 2018, for instance, the United Nations Development Programme (UNDP) and the UN Refugee Agency (UNHCR) launched development projects in Rohingya-dominated areas in Malaysia. The goal of such efforts is typically to "improve livelihoods, build trust and promote social-cohesion" ("UN agencies welcome green light for Rohingya projects in northern Myanmar; urge 'more effective access'," 2018). These efforts therefore serve two purposes: directly assisting populations while also mitigating grievances that may produce additional violence.

Targeting grievances would seem to be a surefire way to reduce terrorism, free from the risks of accidents and unintended consequences that come with more aggressive measures. Meanwhile, shrinking the pie through careful enforcement policies that avoid blowback would also seem effective. Yet we show that the relationship is not so clear when a group tries to deter competitors from entering the market.

Increasing barriers to entry. A second counterterrorism strategy is to increase the cost associated with forming a rival group. As Oots (1989, 142) notes, the "formation of terrorist organizations will not occur spontaneously. Group formation requires a political cause but also requires both entrepreneurial and political leadership ... to attract members and induce them to commit acts of political violence." Target states can influence those incentives in a number of ways. One major component of the US National Strategy for Combating Terrorism is to eliminate sanctuary outlets in rogue states. In the absence of a welcoming regime, would-be groups must seek asylum in less desirable and more remote locations, increasing the burden of the initial outlay to establish an organization.

The United States has also placed greater emphasis on state building in the post-September-11 world (Mallaby, 2002). Terrorist groups without a welcoming host can instead opt for the next best option: a place where they will not face active resistance. This helps explain why the United States did not immediately leave Afghanistan and Iraq after the tactical victories. A vacuum of power gives terrorist groups a foothold of operations and, indeed, chronically failed states house more terrorist organizations engaged in violence (Piazza, 2008). The United States might see an influx of more organizations in the absence of a sustained intervention.[4]

For countries with established governments, the United States has sought to create a norm against terrorism. This process began with United Nations Security Council Resolution 1373, which instructs countries to codify anti-terrorism laws and ratify anti-terrorism conventions. Political violence entrepreneurs face increased hurdles in coordinating the formation of a group under such conditions. Efforts conducted through international organizations such as the UNSC and NATO also demonstrate the important role of international organizations in increasing barriers to entry. In fact, these international mechanisms may be the only means for states to manipulate barriers to entry in other countries.

Also, on the "softer" side, a target state can manipulate the opportunity cost of entry (Blomberg, Hess, and Weerapana, 2004; Frey and Luechinger, 2003; Rosendorff and Sandler, 2010). This is a central theme of many counterterrorism campaigns (Fleck and Kilby, 2010). Russian President Dmitry Medvedev stated in 2011 that Russia "must do everything possible to influence ... the socioeconomic roots of terrorism: poverty, unemployment, illiteracy, and orphanhood" (Medvedev, 2011). Nine years earlier, President George W. Bush aimed to curb global

---

[4] Footholds are more important for groups with focused, national goals. Transnational terrorist groups with broader strategic goals have less need for a centralized base for coordination (Takeyh and Gvosdev, 2002). Combating the costs of entry for such organizations may prove more difficult.

poverty because "hope is an answer to terror" (Bush, 2002). In theory, better economic opportunities force a would-be entrepreneur to give up more to form an organization.[5]

Finally, states could simply adopt a more aggressive policy toward groups in the process of forming. Unlike the other strategies, the United States has actively resisted this path. In the words of President Obama, "not every regional terrorist organization is automatically a threat to us that would call for a major offensive. Our goal should not be to think that we can occupy every country where there's a terrorist organization."[6] Arresting or otherwise incapacitating everyone within a nascent organization before it can begin conducting operations also raises the expected cost of entry.

Given the central theme of this book, one would imagine that increasing these barriers would reduce violence. After all, more active groups seems to imply more competition and more attacks to gather support. The model we develop below qualifies that intuition.

Damaging existing groups. Offensive measures are a third strategy to reduce political violence. This has become a primary strategy for the United States and drives the cooperative relationships it shares with local governments (Pillar, 2001, 33). Here, target governments actively pursue *existing* groups, attempting to reduce their fighters, funds, and infrastructure. Many operations fit this category: demolitions of operative housing (Benmelech, Berrebi, and Klor, 2014), bombings of camps and convoys, assassinations of leadership, attacks on state sponsors, seizing financial assets held abroad, and crackdowns on black market commerce, like opiates in Afghanistan and oil in Iraq. The target government may also broaden its intelligence net – both domestic and foreign – to assist with these tasks. Going on the offense rarely eradicates an entire organization. However, proactive measures force groups to find new sources of funding, use more difficult means of attack, and operate with less capable agents.

Although offensive operations can succeed in limiting a group's ability to put together attacks, critics suggest that it is an exercise in futility. Tim

---

[5] In practice, these types of strategies might also reduce grievances. However, the mechanics here are distinct. In the grievances case, the pie that all militant groups seek to acquire shrinks. In the entry cost case, it becomes more difficult for a new group to form. To better understand the underlying mechanisms, we treat these possibilities as separate below. Nevertheless, we are cognizant that specific policies that governments adopt may influence multiple vectors, and thus policymakers need to consider all the consequences.

[6] https://nbcnews.to/2OVo1FZ.

Wirth, a State Department official and former Senator from Colorado, first compared the problem with the "Whac-a-Mole" arcade game during a Congressional hearing in the wake of the attempted World Trade Center bombing. "You put a quarter and you get so much time and you're whacking down as things pop up. You're whacking over here and they pop up over here."[7] Wirth then suggested that the United States needed to go through this runaround despite the frustration it may cause. Addressing the root problems that cause terrorism in the first place can be too costly or difficult, requiring instead heavier measures (Zakaria, 2016).

However, in the decades since Wirth's framing, Whac-a-Mole has become a rallying cry *against* offensive counterterrorism operations. President Obama frequently raised the issue during his term in office. Indeed, Obama proclaimed that "we don't approach [the problem of terrorism by] sending out armies and playing Whac-a-Mole wherever a terrorist appears because that drains our economic strength and it puts enormous burdens on our military."[8] In Northeast India, the former Leader of Opposition Conrad Sangma warned that "if [the Garo National Liberation Army] is eliminated today, another outfit will come" ("Declaring GNLA as terrorist outfit is for namesake, formality: Conrad," 2012).

President Obama's stated concern aside, the US–Afghanistan War illustrates the exact problem with offensive policies. The initial invasion and removal of the Taliban regime was largely successful. Yet, as Operation Enduring Freedom dragged on, the United States' strategy opened the door for a number of competing factions to arise in its place. The United States and its international coalition had to then pursue these separate groups, including Hezb-e Islami Gulbuddin and the Islamic Movement of Uzbekistan.

At the same time, the Taliban proved a challenging foe to completely eliminate. The group continued to grow and adjust to its new strategic challenges during the first decade of occupation. This allowed the group to reestablish an "unrivaled monopoly over Afghanistan's jihadist landscape" (Basit, 2016) as it continued to expand into the next decade. But the United States' constant pressure eventually wore out the Taliban.

---

[7] https://wapo.st/2TrLNwG.
[8] https://youtu.be/FaEoeOvbFQs. Critics of Israel's counterterrorism policy note the same concern, as decades of destruction of individual groups have only led others to spawn in their place (Catignani, 2012).

By 2015, the Islamic State – Khorasan Province entered the picture. This was the first significant competition the Taliban had faced in more than ten years and its attacks declined. Nevertheless, this did not represent an unconditional victory for the United States, as the Islamic State began filling the vacuum of violence.

Syria has witnessed a similar phenomenon. The Assad regime and the US-led international coalition prioritized the fight against ISIS. Relatively ignored by the coalition, Jabhat al-Nusra strengthened during this period ("Jabhat al Nusra and ISIS: Sources of strength," 2016). It would remain a major player until it merged with a few other organizations in 2017.

Once again, it is important to highlight the role of international institutions, whether largely informal (the coalition to defeat ISIS) or formal (the International Security Assistance Force in Afghanistan). In neither of the examples cited here did the United States pursue a sustained offensive strategy in the absence of such international institutions. A single operation in these contexts, such as the raid that killed ISIS leader Abu Bakr al-Baghdadi in 2019, often requires significant cooperation facilitated through international organizations. And in both Syria and Afghanistan, international organizational efforts frequently *supplemented* rather than *complemented* host nation efforts.

In light of these issues, a natural question to ask is whether offensive operations can ever work. That is, in the shadow of another group forming, should a state even try enfeebling an incumbent group? Or does Whac-a-Mole just make the entire operation futile? Below, we show that the replacement problem is a phantom menace. In fact, the concern obfuscates the best policy recommendation: when existing groups commit violence to deter entry, successful policies *must* induce the formation of another group.

Defensive measures and devaluing the message. Finally, a target government can opt for defensive measures. Such tactics broadly increase the likelihood that a potential attack will fail or see only limited success. Many policies fit this bill: hardening potential targets, fortifying embassies, developing vehicles resistant to improvised explosive devices, stationing extra security at large gatherings, and increasing the scope of searches at airports (Pillar, 2001, 37–40). Even efforts to increase public health and mitigate the effectiveness of biological attacks fall under this category (Chyba, 2001).

The United States invests heavily in defense each year, with the Department of Homeland Security operating on a $40.6 billion budget

in 2017 alone.[9] Indeed, the United States spends about half of all counterterrorism funds on target hardening (Rosendorff and Sandler, 2004,
658). Modern building designs increasingly incorporate defensive security considerations. The growing integration of landscape architecture
with vehicle and pedestrian barriers means that these security considerations are becoming a ubiquitous feature of modern life, particularly
in developed countries (*National Institute of Building Sciences Whole
Building Design Guide*, 2016).

Of course, defensive measures are not perfect. Holding fixed a level
of effort, terrorist groups can still cause harm to their targets. But the
purpose is to limit the damage, foil some percentage of the operations
outright, or substitute one type of attack with another (Enders and
Sandler, 2002).

Take the United States' efforts to secure its embassies. In 1976, 1985,
and 1986, the United States earmarked major resource allocations to for-
tify its diplomatic missions from attacks abroad. These efforts appear to
have been successful: attacks on embassies declined by thirteen incidents
per quarter (Enders and Sandler, 1993). The best defensive measures
may not make the target invulnerable, but it can force organizations
to divert to other targets (Lum, Kennedy, and Sherley, 2006). Indeed,
recognizing the new strategic problem with embassies, terrorist assassinations of US diplomatic personnel *outside* of embassies increased.
Such attacks require more luck to execute successfully, as the perpetrator cannot rely on the fixed target an embassy provides. Thus, despite
the substitution effect, the additional embassy security succeeded in its
goal.

In fact, the substitution effect is a general property of counterterrorism strategies (Powell, 2007). States should secure their most sensitive
targets until the potential damage is on par with less sensitive targets.
This is most apparent at airports. Consider how the US mandate that
metal detectors be installed in all airports after 1973 altered a terrorist's incentives. The risk of passing a weapon through security massively
increased. The terrorist either needed some luck to hijack the plane while
armed or had to roll the dice that the hijacking would succeed without
a real weapon. Unsurprisingly, one study concluded that the installation
of metal detectors resulted in up to fifty fewer skyjackings through 1976
(Landes, 1978).

---

[9] www.dhs.gov/sites/default/files/publications/FY2017_BIB-MASTER.pdf.

Following the September 11 attacks, new security measures have vastly reduced the ability to use airplanes in terrorist attacks. Before, ten individuals could kill thousands and demolish two of the tallest buildings in the world. Today, if a terrorist group wanted to send ten individuals on a well-coordinated suicide mission, the damage they could inflict would likely be substantially smaller – that vector of attack is no longer readily available.

For competing groups that each rely on the same vectors of attack, defensive strategies do not discriminate. Additional security at a US stadium will more quickly subdue a terrorist attack whether the perpetrator proclaims allegiance to al-Qaeda, Islamic State, or any other group. This is in contrast to increasing the barriers of entry and offensive measures, which impact entrants and incumbents respectively.[10] The implications are accordingly different, with symmetric defensive tactics proving generally effective.

Of course, not all groups use the same vectors and strategies to attack their targets. To illustrate, well-organized groups can leverage sophisticated bombs to strike targets that are out of reach for groups that must rely on crude vehicle or small arms attacks. In these cases, defensive measures have asymmetric effects. For example, erecting barriers in front of large crowds can stop trucks from entering but will not prevent explosives from doing the job. Such measures have the effect of reducing one organization's recruitment value for any attack while having little to no effect on the other.

Casting asymmetric defensive measures in this light makes them similar to the use of counterpropaganda. The group may still benefit to some degree by using violence to attract publicity. But if the counterpropaganda is effective, would-be supporters become more inclined to support a different organization, if such an alternative exists.[11]

Most recently, the United States and other countries have demonstrated this as an effective mechanism to damage ISIS's ability to recruit. This is particularly significant because ISIS has benefited from a large pool of recruits, ranging from Finland to Pakistan. A central component of the strategy against ISIS has been broad communications and counter-messaging strategies aimed at diminishing the perception of the organization. Further, governments have coordinated their strategies

---

[10] It is similar to grievances in that reducing the size of the pie also affects both parties.

[11] This contrasts with propaganda designed to turn off supporters from helping any organization at all, which would fall under the reducing grievances framework.

cross-nationally at the highest levels. The global coalition to defeat ISIS, for instance, established a Communications Working Group to wage a "PR" campaign against the organization (Quanrud, 2017). Led by the United States, the United Kingdom, and the United Arab Emirates, the group "regularly convenes meetings between member countries and academics, civil society, media, and tech companies to share information and strategies to counter terrorist messages online and offline, and present positive alternative narratives" (US Department of State, 2019). As part of this initiative, the group established "messaging centers" around the world that assisted countries in countering the "falsehoods" of ISIS (Quanrud, 2017). Much of this work involved fighting back against the dominant ISIS narrative that they are champions of Sunni Muslims. By disseminating evidence that Sunni Muslims had, in fact, suffered greatly under ISIS's rule, these efforts have contributed to creating a more challenging recruitment environment for the organization.

Likewise, information emphasizing the weaknesses of the group has helped shatter the perception of invincibility that the organization peddles. The communications efforts of the global coalition, for instance, adroitly capitalized on the group's 2016 abandonment of Dabiq, largely without a fight (Berger, 2017). Since Dabiq was central to the apocalyptic narrative of the organization, this defeat and its subsequent publicity likely dealt a critical blow to their recruitment. As further evidence, when the coalition began recognizing the value of the communications strategy and flooded online forums and social media with anti-ISIS content, pro-ISIS content notably went into a steep decline (US Department of State, 2017; "ISIS' American recruitment on decline, FBI director says," 2016). The combined efforts apparently helped to destroy the notion that ISIS was somehow building a Sunni utopia in the Middle East, as the group's moral intentions, capabilities, and resolve were increasingly called into question. A variety of strategies may therefore serve the same purpose: to lessen the appeal of an organization among potential supporters and recruits. No matter the particular strategy used, if there are fewer potential supporters and recruits, then groups have reduced incentives to use violence to compete against one another for their attention.

As with other US strategies to counter ISIS, these efforts were not unilateral, but were in many ways conducted through informal international institutions that developed in the context of the Syrian Civil War. Formal international institutions can play a similar role, such as the UN's Office of Counter-Terrorism. And defensive standards are often coordinated internationally through organizations such as the International

Civil Aviation Organization (ICAO). Like the other strategies discussed in this chapter, defensive measures are not always a unilateral consideration and, indeed, the effectiveness of any strategy may be augmented through multilateral coordination.

MODELING ENTRY INTO THE MARKET FOR VIOLENCE

In past chapters, the competition decision featured pre-formed organizations choosing how to compete with one another. We begin this chapter's formal analysis by revising the model in two ways. First, organizations make violence decisions sequentially. Second, only an incumbent group begins the game in existence. A challenging group can enter after it observes the incumbent's decision if it pays a cost to do so. After we have established how incentives differ in this environment, we extend the model to allow for the various government interventions we outlined in the previous section.

The Game

Players. Consider a baseline model featuring a pair of violent non-state actors. Group 1 is an existing producer of violence seeking to keep its support flowing. Group 2 is a potential entrant into the market that might compete for Group 1's resources.[12]

We feature only one existing group and one potential entrant to increase the transparency of the mechanisms coming out of the incentive structure. Nevertheless, it is worth stressing that the fundamental theoretical results we present are robust to interactions with multiple existing groups and multiple potential entrants into the market. This is because cornering the market to deny competitors entry allows all existing groups to share a larger pie, potentially making the existing groups willing to overproduce violence.

Actions and timing. As Figure 6.2 illustrates, play begins with Group 1 choosing a violence level $v_1 \geq 0$. As in previous chapters, larger values represent greater effort exerted. This effort translates into greater violence against the target government, which we introduce later.

---

[12] Although we refer to these groups as distinct organizations, one may conceive of the potential entrant as an entrepreneurial individual within the existing group who is considering whether to splinter off.

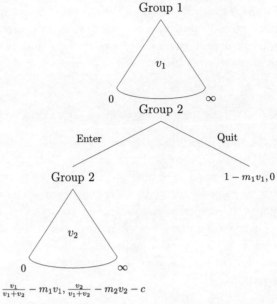

$$\frac{v_1}{v_1+v_2} - m_1v_1, \frac{v_2}{v_1+v_2} - m_2v_2 - c$$

FIGURE 6.2 The two-player extensive form game.

Group 2 observes Group 1's selection and decides whether to enter the market or not. We call a market that Group 2 enters "competitive" and a market that Group 2 does not enter "cornered." Entering the market costs $c > 0$, which represents the fixed costs of creating the organization. It also captures any civilian support Group 2 might receive if and only if it stays as a non-militant organization. If Group 2 enters, it then selects a violence level $v_2 \geq 0$. The game then ends.

Preferences and payoffs. As before, we use the proportional contest success function to map group effort into a division of audience resources. To reduce notational clutter, we standardize the pie the groups compete over worth 1 until the extension that takes a comparative static on that parameter.[13] Meanwhile, due to the entry wrinkle, some minor modifications are necessary. Recall that Group 1 earns $\frac{v_1}{v_1+v_2} - m_1v_1$ in the contest framework, where m_i represents i's marginal cost of effort. If Group 2 does not enter, then $v_2 = 0$ and Group 1's payoff simplifies

---

[13] Thus, because games are identical across positive affine utility transformations, the notationally simplified model implicitly accounts for differential market sizes. However, taking comparative statics on standardized models presents a barrier to inference, so we reintroduce a market size parameter later.

to $1 - m_1v_1$ if $v_1 > 0$. To preserve continuous utility functions, we also assume that Group 1 captures the entire value if neither exerts effort. Meanwhile, Group 2 payoff earns 0 if it does not enter. If it does enter, it earns $\frac{v_2}{v_1+v_2} - m_2v_2 - c$.

Given this setup, if $c > 1$, then Group 2 has a strictly dominant strategy to not enter. This is because the entry cost exceeds the most Group 2 could possibly earn from the competition subgame, even under the rosy assumption that Group 1 had not produced any violence. This leads to a trivial outcome: Group 1 exerts no effort and Group 2 does not enter. We therefore focus our attention on cases where $c \in (0, 1)$.

Optimal Levels of Violence

Because this is a sequential game of complete information, we search for its subgame perfect equilibrium. Although the interaction has few moves, it is complex to fully solve because of the lack of restrictions on quantities of violence that the actors can produce. We therefore discuss each decision one step at a time. Moreover, we emphasize the intuition for these choices; the appendix contains full proof of the central subgame wherever applicable.

Group 2's violence decision. This choice is straightforward. Once Group 2 has entered, Group 1 has already selected its violence level and Group 2 has already paid the cost of entry. Group 2 therefore only needs to optimize its payoff for the contest. Group 2's objective function for that contest is $\frac{v_2}{v_1+v_2} - m_2v_2$. Optimizing this yields $v_2^* \equiv \sqrt{\frac{v_1}{m_2}} - v_1$.

Note that this optimal violence level decreases in Group 2's marginal cost m_2; the more expensive violence is for Group 2, the less inclined it is to commit violence. In addition, if Group 1's allocation is sufficiently large, Group 2's marginal utility for each unit of violence begins to decline. Intuitively, producing one unit of violence produces a greater return for Group 2 when Group 1 has produced one unit of violence than when Group 1 has produced one million units. In fact, if Group 2's marginal cost and Group 1's violence level are too high (i.e., $m_2v_1 > 1$), v_2^* turns negative. In this case, Group 2 produces no violence at all.

Group 2's entry decision. There are two cases to consider here. First, suppose that the combination of Group 1's violence and Group 2's marginal cost is sufficiently high. Then Group 2 optimally produces $v_2 = 0$ and receives a payoff of 0 from the contest. If it enters under these circumstances, its payoff is $-c$. If it quits, it receives 0 instead. Group 2 therefore quits. Intuitively, it makes no sense to pay the fixed costs of entry and then not exert any effort.

Second, suppose that the combination of Group 1's violence and Group 2's marginal cost is sufficiently low. Now Group 2 will optimally produce a positive amount of effort, namely v_2^*. It may nevertheless not wish to compete with Group 1 if the cost of entry is too great. This could be because, while the contest itself may be profitable, those profits do not counterbalance the cost of entering.

More concretely, recall that Group 2's overall utility for entering and then choosing v_2^* equals $\frac{v_2^*}{v_1 + v_2^*} - m_2 v_2^* - c$. Group 2 therefore enters if this amount is greater than 0, its payoff for quitting. Setting up this inequality, substituting $v_2^* \equiv \sqrt{\frac{v_1}{m_2}} - v_1$, and solving for v_1 yields:

$$v_1 > v_1^* \equiv \frac{(1 - \sqrt{c})^2}{m_2} \qquad (6.1)$$

Thus, Group 2 quits if $v_1 > v_1^*$, enters if $v_1 < v_1^*$, and is indifferent between the two when $v_1 = v_1^*$. As Group 1 produces more violence, Group 2's payoff for competition declines. In turn, if Group 1's production is sufficiently high, Group 2 prefers quitting to paying a cost to enter a competition that will not end well. But if Group 1's production is sufficiently low, it is worth paying the entry cost to obtain the benefits from the contest.[14] Also note that Group 2 is less likely to enter when the cost of entry or its marginal cost is high.

Group 1's violence decision: to corner or compete? Now consider Group 1's decision. As a starting point, the lead group can do *no worse* under the sequential game than under the simultaneous move model that the other chapters explored. This might come as a surprise given that Group 2 has an apparent advantage of seeing what Group 1 has done and optimally responding to that. However, if Group 1 wants to mimic the equilibrium of the simultaneous move game, it can always choose the violence output that matches its equilibrium production with simultaneous moves.

[14] The critical value of v_1 from Line 6.1 provides insight into situations with multiple potential entrants. Suppose those entrants have differing costs of entry c_i and m_i. Then the maximum of $\frac{(1 - \sqrt{c_i})^2}{m_i}$ is sufficient to corner the market. This is because if the group with the highest expected utility for competing is unwilling to enter the market, all others would stay out as well. It is also true that violence spikes when Group 1 produces that amount instead of the optimal quantity to compete with the best opposing group, and this spike drives all the key results in the extensions we develop below.

By construction of Nash equilibrium, Group 2's best response is to produce what it would under the simultaneous move game. As a result, Group 1 can always duplicate that outcome. In turn, the game has a first-mover advantage. If Group 1 chooses anything other than its normal quantity, it does so because that quantity yields a greater payoff.[15]

Indeed, Group 1 can use two elements of the game to secure a better outcome for itself. Structurally, the first-mover decision means it can credibly commit to a larger quantity of violence than it could otherwise. Beyond that, Group 1 controls Group 2's entry. After all, Group 2 only enters if v_1 is small enough. Producing large amounts of violence corners the market, while choosing a smaller value of v_1 induces competition.

Taking stock, Group 1's decision-making process goes through the steps outlined below:[16]

1. Calculate the minimum amount of violence production (v_1) such that Group 2 would want to quit. This is v_1^*.[17]
2. Calculate Group 1's payoff for cornering the market in the manner described in (1).
3. Calculate the optimal value of v_1 conditional on Group 2 entering, which is $\frac{m_2}{4m_1^2}$.
4. Calculate Group 1's payoff for choosing the strategy in (3).
5. Compare the payoffs from (2) and (4). If (2) is larger, play (1); if (4) is larger, play (3).

Whether the payoff for cornering is larger than the payoff from competing depends on c. Specifically, if

$$c > c^* \equiv \left(1 - \sqrt{\frac{m_2}{m_1} - \frac{m_2^2}{4m_1^2}}\right)^2 \qquad (6.2)$$

Group 1 prefers to corner the market. This is because higher costs of entry mean that Group 1 can produce less violence and still deter Group

---

[15] The first-mover advantage does not imply that Group 2's welfare is worse under the sequential game than under the simultaneous move game. Because players expend effort, it is possible that both can improve their payoffs with a reordering of the moves. See Konrad (2009, 69–71) for a discussion on this.

[16] The precise details of its strategy are more complicated. See the appendix for a full discussion.

[17] This assumes that Group 2 quits when indifferent between that and entering. The appendix shows that equilibrium conditions require this.

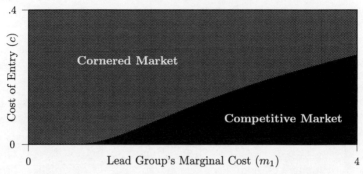

FIGURE 6.3 Substantive outcome of the game's equilibrium.

2 from entering. Cornering the market in turn looks more attractive, causing Group 1 to be more likely to pursue that strategy.

Meanwhile, if $c < c^*$, Group 1 finds cornering the market to be too expensive. In turn, Group 1 produces the optimal amount of violence as if it were expecting Group 2 to enter, and Group 2 indeed enters.[18]

Figure 6.3 plots Line 6.2's cutpoint, setting $m_2 = 1$. Note that the model produces two intuitive results. The incumbent group is more likely to corner the market when its own marginal cost of violence is low and its potential opponent's cost of entry is high. This is because it is cheap for the group to overproduce violence and the overproduction does not need to be too extreme to convince the would-be challenger to stay out of the market. More substantively, the result on marginal costs indicates that existing groups with poor organizational operations and resistance from the non-contributing population are more likely to see challengers arise.

A more subtle result that Figure 6.3 captures is how m_1 must be sufficiently large relative to m_2 for competition to be possible at any entry cost level. In particular, the appendix derives this as $m_1 > \frac{m_2}{2}$. When m_1 falls below that threshold, Group 1 has such a strong advantage in violence that it would overwhelm Group 2 in a competitive market – so

---

[18] This discussion provides insight into what happens if Group 1 faced an upper limit on how much violence it could produce. Under circumstances where Group 1 would want to corner, if the upper limit is below the minimum necessary cornering violence, then constraint is not binding. Group 1 corners as normal. Otherwise, Group 1 must select its violence level conditional on Group 2 entering. All of the key comparative statics examine what happens as the game transitions from a cornering outcome to a competitive outcome, so a non-binding constraint is necessary for the counterintuitive results.

much so that it can scale back and still deter entry. This is true even if Group 2 could enter for free.

These properties of the equilibrium may seem straightforward, but they conceal some unexpected relationships regarding when we observe the most violence. This is the next question we address.

When Is Violence Most Prevalent?

Throughout this book, we have seen outbidding make a consistent prediction regarding group competition and violence. Holding fixed the size of the audience receptive to such actions, overall violence increases in the number of groups competing. This chapter's model provides an additional caveat to that result: violence may be higher when *fewer* groups exist. This happens because a single group may wish to overproduce violence to deter others from entering the market.

To demonstrate this, consider the two equilibrium outcomes to compare: cornered versus competitive markets. When Group 1 corners, it produces $v_1^* = \frac{(1-\sqrt{c})^2}{m_2}$; this convinces Group 2 not to enter and thus it produces no violence. In contrast, in a competitive market, Group 1 produces $\frac{m_2}{4m_1^2}$ and Group 2 responds with $\sqrt{\frac{m_2}{4m_1^2}} - \frac{m_2}{4m_1^2}$. Violence is greater in the first case if:

$$\frac{(1-\sqrt{c})^2}{m_2} > \frac{m_2}{4m_1^2} + \sqrt{\frac{\frac{m_2}{4m_1^2}}{m_2} - \frac{m_2}{4m_1^2}}$$

$$m_1 > \frac{m_2}{2(1-\sqrt{c})^2} \qquad (6.3)$$

Where the overall rate of violence maximizes as a function of each parameter is complicated. In fact, those complicated relationships drive the unexpected findings that are underlying government interventions. However, as those extensions later visualize, Line 6.3 holds at Line 6.2's boundary: when Group 1 just barely prefers cornering the market, overall violence is greater than when Group 1 just barely prefers inducing competition. The transition point results in a discontinuous increase in violence going from cornered violence to competitive violence. That discontinuity increases as Group 2's marginal cost of violence decreases. Group 2 finds entry more profitable under those circumstances – if it enters, it will produce more violence at a lower price and capture more of the marketshare. Thus, Group 1 must flood the market with violence to deter Group 2's entry.

Why does violence spike with only one group? A numerical example illustrates the logic. Suppose that $m_1 = m_2 = 1$ and that Group 2 would assuredly enter. Then Group 1 optimally selects $\frac{m_2}{4m_1^2} = \frac{1}{4}$. Group 2 responds by selecting $\sqrt{\frac{v_1}{m_2}} - v_1 = \frac{1}{4}$.[19] Because both select the same amount of violence for these parameters, they split the contest and each receives $\frac{1}{2}$ of the resources. After subtracting out their costs, each receives a final payoff of $\frac{1}{4}$ for the contest, with Group 2 also subtracting out its cost of entry. The sum of violence equals $\frac{1}{2}$.

Note that out of the whole standardized value of 1, Group 1 only nets a payoff of $\frac{1}{4}$. Consequently, Group 1 is willing to commit up to $\frac{3}{4}$ in violence to exclude Group 2 from the market. This would give Group 1 the entire pie and leave it with more left over than if it had competed. Put differently, it is willing to use more violence by itself to corner the market than the groups would combine to produce in a competitive market.

Indeed, this is exactly what happens for some parameter spaces. For example, if $c = \frac{1}{25}$, then Line 6.1 says that Group 1 can produce $v_1 = \frac{(1-\sqrt{c})^2}{m_2} = \frac{16}{25}$ in violence to deter Group 2's entry. This leaves Group 1 with a payoff of $1 - \frac{16}{25} = \frac{9}{25}$, which is better than its payoff if it induces Group 2's entry. As such, Group 1 corners the market by choosing that level, which is well above the $\frac{1}{2}$ the two would combine to produce together when in competition.

To be clear, violence is not always greater when only one group commits it. Indeed, under conditions of tough entry for Group 2 – e.g., a high cost c – Group 1 can corner the market with only a small quantity of violence. Violence is lower here than a counterfactual world where Group 2 entered and competed fully with Group 1. Rather, the point is that violence is higher for parameters where Group 1 just slightly prefers to corner than parameters where Group 1 just slightly prefers to permit entry.

Regardless, there is a stark contrast between this result and Chapter 2's robustness check on destroying groups. In the original model, the target state would always benefit by removing a group from competition. But this logic falls apart with sequential entry. Now having one less group

---

[19] The fact that both produce the same violence quantity here is a quirk of these particular parameters and does not generally occur.

seems to cause problems. This forms the basic logic of the extensions below. Any action that makes group entry more likely could backfire.

Meanwhile, like the central empirical claim from Chapter 5, the results here suggest caution in generalizing Chapter 3's empirical relationships. Our book's central narrative is that competition normally yields more violence, as additional groups try to capture some of the marketshare. Much of our empirical evidence is consistent with that. But consistent with the previous chapter's theme, broad trends do not reveal universal truths. Some cases may have a different data-generating process that yields the opposite causal connection despite the average tending toward a positive relationship.

The partial equilibrium analysis also suggests a need to think more holistically about competition. Kydd and Walter (2006, 78), for example, argue that "one solution to the problem of outbidding would be to eliminate the struggle for power by encouraging competing groups to consolidate into a unified opposition." The model demonstrates an important hidden assumption underlying that claim: if consolidation creates new opportunities for other groups to enter the market, unification may backfire if the expanded group uses its resources to drive out those potential competitors.

Indeed, these types of manipulations can have strange effects on the market for violence. We therefore formalize some key strategies below in the complete models.

MANIPULATING THE MARKET

The previous chapter highlighted how the targets of violence may wish to manipulate the incentives that competing groups face. That earlier discussion emphasized a government's ability to shrink the number of potential supporters within the marketplace for political violence. Although we continue that discussion in this chapter, those target states have other options. They may increase the barriers to entry for groups considering whether to form. They can also increase the marginal cost of violence for existing groups by gutting their infrastructure. Or they could implement defensive measures to mitigate violence from all potential attackers.

To understand how these tactics alter the strategic environment, we now introduce a third player to the game: the target state. The state begins the new interaction by choosing to pay a cost to shift these parameters in ways that would apparently handicap the groups in some way. In the main text, we give a qualitative description of those actions with some light notation; in the appendix, we fully formalize the utility functions and derive the state's optimal strategy. Regardless, the choices share a common theme. The more effort the state exerts, the greater the direct effectiveness of the intervention. Nevertheless, the state must exercise caution. The results below indicate that some of these strategies can backfire, causing *more* violence, not less. This is because the new barriers can shift a competitive market into a cornered market. And as we emphasized above, cornered markets can be more violent that competitive ones.

From a research design perspective, we tackle each of the four types of interventions individually. In practice, certain counterterrorism tactics may affect multiple components simultaneously. For example, broad-scope domestic surveillance can increase the difficulty of both planning an attack and coordinating the formation of an organization. Alternatively, governments may repress large swaths of their populations to increase the difficulty of conducting an attack. But higher levels of repression create proportionate levels of grievances among the population (Lichbach, 1987; Lichbach and Gurr, 1981).

Despite potential crossovers, modeling each component on its own increases the transparency of each mechanism. This is a key goal of the modeling enterprise (Paine and Tyson, 2020). To wit, if we modeled both effects of broad-scope domestic surveillance and the result produced greater violence, it would be unclear whether this was due to the added difficulty of attack planning or the more challenging path to group formation. In contrast, modeling those factors one at a time reveals a clear answer.[20]

For the two measures that involve active intervention, we also assume that states can implement them flawlessly.[21] We are well aware that this is often not the case in practice and is a central part of the provocation literature (Carter, 2016; Crenshaw, 1981; Rosendorff and Sandler,

---

[20] Adopting policies in light of our results also requires substantive verification that a measure actually alters the environment in the manner described. This is not always straightforward. Anti-IED technology provides a good illustration of this (Trebbi et al., 2017). In Afghanistan and Iraq, first-generation IEDs would detonate after a vehicle activated a weight sensor. The United States fitted its vehicles with forward pressure plates to trigger the detonation before vehicle occupants were above the explosion. Insurgents countered by placing the triggers on a delay. Thus, the defensive tactic ultimately caused a change in the marginal cost of production, as insurgents had to add an extra component to the device.

[21] Pork barrel politics can also interfere with optimal defensive allocations (Powell, 2007, 528), but that is more of a problem with inefficiency and less about counterproductive behavior.

2004; Spaniel, 2019). Without exercising caution and discipline, states can execute messy operations that cause blowback, a larger market, and increased incentives for groups to capture the larger prize. Principal–agent problems can also lead to issues, where uniformed soldiers take actions that their superiors know will wreak havoc. Such imperfections would seem to result in bad outcomes for the state.[22] But a natural question to study is whether shoddy implementation is at fault or the strategy itself cannot obtain the desired outcome (Myerson, 1999, 1069). Put differently, we can conduct a theoretical "experiment" (Paine and Tyson, 2020) to investigate whether policy adjustments can function as intended. Unfortunately, this method of isolation shows that the apparent "solutions" sometimes do not work even if policymakers implement them as intended.

Of course, sometimes those tactics succeed. With that in mind, we urge practitioners to exercise caution in translating our results into specific policy recommendations. For programs that manipulate multiple parameters simultaneously, there is no substitute for comparing the status quo outcome with what would happen if a state altered multiple parameters.

Does Resolving Grievances or Enhancing Enforcement Reduce Violence?

A soft power approach to counterterrorism involves reducing grievances among those who would otherwise wish to lend support to an organization. The previous chapter indicated that this is an effective strategy to reduce competitive incentives and thus minimize outbidding violence. Likewise, Chapter 4 showed that government enforcement to intercept contributions also reduced outbidding incentives. Nevertheless, in this section we show that grievance reduction comes with an important caveat. If a group produces violence to keep others out, insufficient concessions or enforcement may cause more damage.

To explore the counterintuitive effect, recall that this chapter's initial model standardized the pool of support to 1. Here, let the size of that pie equal $\pi \in [0, 1]$. The target state begins the game by selecting π. Lower choices correspond to softer, more conciliatory policies that reduce the aggrieved population's desire to contribute to an organization.[23] Meanwhile, the value of the contest for Group i given

---

[22] In fact, as our result on grievance indicates, such blowback may be beneficial in the setting we study.

[23] For pure grievance reduction, the state's utility function only needs a scalar for how much the government values the objectionable π value it takes and the negative of the

j's violence is now $\pi \left(\frac{v_i}{v_i + v_j} \right) - m_i v_i$; this is in line with this book's earlier models with explicit terms for market size. Group 2 still pays c if it enters. The state's payoff has two components: the negative sum of violence and the quantity of the pie it consumes. We weigh the quantity of the pie by a scalar to reflect how much the state cares about capturing the good versus suffering violence.

As before, the appendix contains a detailed explanation of this game's equilibrium behavior. However, the following proposition explains the key finding:

Proposition 6.1 *Decreasing grievances or increasing enforcement (i.e., decreasing π) can lead to an increase in violence.*

Figure 6.4 illustrates the central intuition. When the size of the pie is small, too few resources exist to justify Group 2's entry. Even as the pie increases to where it could support both groups, Group 1 can corner the market at a relatively low price. It therefore does so. Only after sufficient support exists (i.e., $\pi > \pi^* \equiv c \left(1 - \sqrt{\frac{m_2}{m_1} - \frac{m_2^2}{4m_1^2}} \right)^{-2}$) is Group 2 willing enough to enter that Group 1 no longer wishes to overproduce to corner the market.

But this puts the target state in a dilemma. If it reduces grievances among the groups' audience (that is, it moves from right to left on

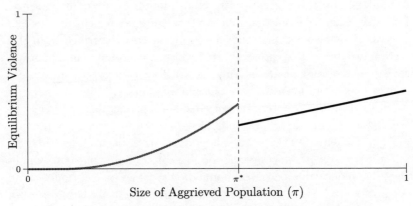

FIGURE 6.4 Violence as a function of market size.

total violence production. This is similar to the last chapter. For enforcement, the state's utility function can hold the value of the demand constant but must include an effort function. This is similar to Chapter 4.

Figure 6.4), it switches from a competitive market to a cornered market. And because cornering the market near the cutpoint π^* requires Group 1 to produce more violence than the sum of their violence in a competitive market, reducing grievances can backfire.

That said, outside the discontinuity, equilibrium violence increases within the segregated parameter spaces as the total resources available increase. For example, in the right region where the groups compete, the amount of violence produced decreases as π decreases. Thus, the groups do internalize the state's decision to reduce the size of the pie. As such, the state may wish to alter grievances or enforcement in a manner that does not change a competitive market to a cornered market. However, if it wishes to alter a potentially competitive market to a cornered market, half measures will fail. This is because the state must place π well below π^* to actually observe a net decline in the rate of violence.[24]

Indeed, many substantive examples illustrate how organizations sometimes increase violence following concessions. Dugan and Chenoweth (2012), for instance, find that Israel experienced an uptick in violence following the first Intifada and the Oslo Lull following minor concessions. Meanwhile, Brancati (2006) reports that offering decentralization in ethnic conflicts has an inconsistent track record. Bueno de Mesquita (2005a) explains the counterintuitive relationship as the result of moderates pulling out of the organizational hierarchy; the remaining extremists correspondingly push the agenda harder than before. Alternatively, the conciliator may expect this as the cost of doing business, knowing that some individuals may wish to spoil the peaceful path forward (Findley and Young, 2015; Kydd and Walter, 2002; Stedman, 1997).[25]

In sum, drawing on the Lucas (1976) critique, Proposition 6.1 urges caution in using observational relationships to make policy recommendations. Consider the vast literature that shows a negative correlation between generosity and terrorism. This chapter, the previous chapter, and the arguments made in these respective papers give theoretical reasoning to believe that the relationship is causal. Many of these papers therefore go a step further, suggesting that governments alter their policies to further take advantage of the benefits. Walsh and Piazza (2010, 571–572),

---

[24] As in the previous chapter, equilibrium violence goes to 0 as π goes to 0. If instead some segment of the population would want to contribute even if $\pi = 0$, equilibrium violence would remain strictly positive. This does not affect the main result on the discontinuity at π^*, however.

[25] A reputation mechanism (Walter, 2006) can also explain a spike in violence from outside parties.

for example, recommend that "governments that prioritize counterterrorism should carefully protect physical integrity rights." Burgoon (2006, 197) echoes this sentiment, stating that "the development and maintenance of social safety nets should perhaps be a part of national strategies to fight terrorism on one's own soil or elsewhere."

For data-generating processes like our own, these claims can be true *some* of the time. Strategic states only implement the policy in those cases. But extending the recommendation to other cases can yield *more* violence, which a strategic government would otherwise avoid. Thus, blanket policy recommendations are inadvisable here.

Correspondingly, Savun and Phillips (2009, 896–897) make a more cautious recommendation. Just because more expansive foreign policies correlate with more terrorism, "this does not necessarily imply that states should refrain from establishing or maintaining alliance ties with the United States or intervening in civil wars," they write. Instead, their findings suggest "that states should be wary of the consequences of their actions with other states [access] how their actions can cause frustration and discontent in other parts of the world." This is the type of policy recommendation that fits with our theoretical findings.

As a final note, we can rewrite Proposition 6.1 to say that an increase in grievances can lead to a *decrease* in violence. This has an interesting implication for theories of provocation, which assume that operations intending to kill terrorists or dismantle a network can inspire more individuals to join an organization. Under existing explanations, states choose to do this because the benefits of a neutered opponent outweigh the recruitment aspect, astrategic behavior from policymakers (Kydd and Walter, 2006, 69–72), or information problems (Spaniel, 2019). Proposition 6.1 suggests another mechanism: when a group may wish to corner a smaller market, expanding grievances through military interventions can yield less violence even without any tactical advantages from those interventions.

Increasing the Barriers to Entry

A second counterterrorism strategy states pursue is to raise the barriers of entry. In terms of our model, this means increasing c. With that in mind, suppose the game now begins with the state choosing $c \in [\underline{c}, \infty]$. The value $\underline{c} > 0$ represents the cost of entering without any intervention by the state; progressively higher values represent more effective but more expensive state operations. Afterward, the groups play the baseline game, with the state having endogenously determined c.

Let the state's payoff have two components. First, as with the previous case, it suffers the sum of the violence produced. Second, it pays a cost that is a function of how much effort the target expends to increase the barrier of entry.

Broadly, the state's optimal strategy can take one of two forms. Recall that the cost of entry c partially determines whether Group 1 corners the market. If c is great, Group 1 deters Group 2 from entering because doing so only requires a modest amount of violence; if c is small, on the other hand, Group 1 prefers competing with Group 2 because cornering requires too much violence. The value c^* from Line 6.2 reflects this cut-point. Thus, if $\underline{c} < c^*$, the state's decision determines whether Group 1 will corner or compete. If not, then the cost of entry is already so expensive that Group 2 will naturally stay out of the market. Increases to c only reinforce that decision.

The fact that the state can turn a competitive market into a cornered market in the first case leads to the following result:

Proposition 6.2 *Increasing the fixed costs of entry (c) can lead to an increase in violence.*

Figure 6.5 helps communicate the logic. When $c < c^*$, the parties commit a fixed amount of violence in a competitive market. The precise value of c does not impact the groups' production choices because, conditional on entering the market, the cost c is sunk for Group 2 and therefore does

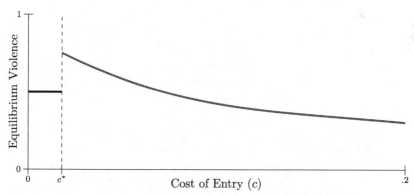

FIGURE 6.5 Violence as a function of entry cost.

not affect its violence decision.[26] Pushing past c^*, however, spikes the violence because the market shifts from competitive to cornered. Group 1 correspondingly overproduces violence to exclude Group 2. Further increases to c decrease equilibrium violence on this range because Group 1 can produce less violence to convince Group 2 to stay out as the cost of entry increases.

The shape of the violence levels has a number of important implications for counterterrorism and counterinsurgency. First, and most apparent, increasing barriers to entry can backfire. Starting in a world where a competitive market would result and shifting to a cornered market may spike violence. To make matters worse, the state would also waste resources to shift c in the process. Consequently, strategic states do not choose such c values.

Second, if a competitive market is the result of inaction and the state chooses to increase the cost of entry, it *must* create a cornered market. This is because a shift from $\underline{c}$ to another value still below c^* does not alter equilibrium violence, as the left portion of Figure 6.5 illustrates.[27] Meaningful change requires moving to a cornered market, with the caveat from above that this can do more harm than good.

These incentives cause the state to play a "go big or go home" strategy in equilibrium. In particular, the state calculates the optimal tradeoff between its effort to change c and the violence *conditional* on inducing a cornered market. If its utility for that is less than maintaining $\underline{c}$, it choses $\underline{c}$. If it is greater, then it picks that optimal c. But note from Figure 6.5 that this optimal c must be well above c^*. That is because the equilibrium violence in the optimal cornered market must be below the amount of violence from a competitive market. Due to the discontinuous jump in violence at c^*, the state must place c well above c^* to see any net decrease in violence.

Consequently, the Lucas (1976) critique urges caution when considering empirical implications here as well. Suppose that the full empirical record reveals a monotonic decrease in violence as targets increase the barriers of entry for groups. It would be tempting to then conclude that

---

[26] This may not always be substantively accurate. For example, spending more on entry might strain a new group's resources, which affect its marginal cost of violence production. Nevertheless, Proposition 6.2's result does not depend on this. The key insight is the discontinuity in violence at the c^* cutpoint. A connection between c and m_2 would only alter the extent of the discontinuity and where the discontinuity occurs.

[27] Unlike the central discontinuity result, the implication is sensitive to the cost of entry not straining Group 2's marginal cost.

governments seeking to reduce violence should increase the costs of entry. However, the state never chooses a value of c that increases equilibrium violence. The strategic decision therefore obscures the overall effects.

In fact, this critique applies to our understanding of economic aid. The empirical literature shows a negative relationship between aid and terrorism violence (Azam and Thelen, 2008; Burgoon, 2006). This leads Azam and Thelen (2008, 375) to conclude that "Western democracies, which are the main targets of terrorist attacks, should invest more funds in foreign aid." However, economic aid also increases the opportunity costs for creating a group.[28] Strategic donors only give aid when it will force violence rates to decline. A blanket recommendation to increase aid would result in some states shifting the parameters of a competitive market with less violence to cornered markets with *more* violence. Without a theoretical understanding of the data-generating process, the policy recommendation could backfire.[29]

Figure 6.5 also helps explain the empirical relationship between violence and economic opportunities in general. Many studies show that terrorism maximizes for middling levels of a country's gross domestic product (Freytag et al., 2011; Lai, 2007). As before, standard explanations point to economic opportunities for why terrorism declines at high levels of GDP. On the lower end, existing theories give three reasons why terrorism is infrequent: agents need to simply survive, agents have low skill (Bueno de Mesquita, 2005b), and extremists cannot signal their preferences (Spaniel, 2018b). However, opportunity costs and entry deterrence also predict such a relationship. Violence maximizes under our mechanism when opportunity costs for entry are large enough that the

---

[28] It may also decrease grievances by lowering collective animosity toward the donor. As we discussed before, though, decreasing grievances has the same counterintuitive effect. Thus, we would still expect the same relationship if we modeled economic aid as doing both. That said, economic aid does not unambiguously decrease π in our model. Although we described that parameter as grievances, it more accurately represents the total quantity of resources the groups can capture. If economic aid removes some donors from the pool but raises the donation size of those who remain, then the net effect is nebulous.

[29] Spaniel (2018b) makes a similar criticism of the aid literature. However, the mechanisms are distinct. In Spaniel's (2018b) model, aid resolves principal–agent problems by allowing more committed operatives to signal their ideology. Thus, by his mechanism, aid exacerbates violence in places where terrorist groups cannot monitor their agents. In contrast, our mechanism operates in cases where groups could enter the political violence marketplace.

incumbent group wishes to corner the market but not so enormous that it can deter entry with small quantities of violence.

For policymakers, it is worth reemphasizing the warning from this section's introduction in light of Figure 6.5 and Proposition 6.1. The model assumes frictionless implementation of these countermeasures. This seems reasonable for bureaucratic options like adoption of anti-terrorism conventions in the United Nations. In contrast, more aggressive tactics like repression would seem to expand grievances; softer approaches like economic redistribution would have the opposite effect. The previous case showed that decreasing grievances reduces violence if the size of the market remains static but can also shift a cornered market to a competitive one.

Nevertheless, separating out these two mechanisms is useful. Suppose a state increases the barriers to entry and simultaneously increases grievances in the process. If such strategies maintained a competitive market, then the combined results of Propositions 6.1 and 6.2 indicate that the net effect is more violence. Separating the propositions shows that this is because increasing the barriers has no impact while increasing grievances harms the situation, not because the effect of raising c does not do enough to overcome the increased anger. The state instead should not exert any effort here.

Now suppose that such strategies turned a competitive market into a cornered market. Under these conditions, it is possible for violence to increase over the alternative. In a model that featured both increased grievances and greater barriers to entry, one might jump to the conclusion that the grievances must be responsible. Again, though, separating the mechanisms reveals a different story. The greater barriers convince Group 1 to overexert effort to corner the market and that causes the spike. Grievances may exacerbate the necessary cornering violence, but they can also incentivize Group 1 to allow entry and reduce violence overall.

Thinking beyond the tools a target state has to manipulate the market, recall Chapter 2's extension that conceptualized the price of entry as the opportunity cost for sacrificing support from individuals who only want to help nonviolent groups. Figure 6.5 also has a counterintuitive implication on this front. One would imagine that environments with larger audiences committed to peaceful resistance would disincentivize violence. This is true if such audiences are enormous, enough to dominate whatever small benefits could arise from monopolizing a very small set of proviolence supporters. However, if the number of pacifist supporters falls in a moderately low range, the opposite effect rises. By committing to excess violence, an existing group can convince the potential entrant to stay out. This looks relatively attractive compared with competing precisely because the number of pacifist supporters is large enough to be worth maintaining.

Does Whac-a-Mole Work?

Offensive measures are a third strategy to reduce political violence. The "Whac-a-Mole" theory of counterterrorism suggests that these results could backfire. Ostensibly, destroying one group is not helpful because another group can arise to take its place and capture that marketshare. Policymakers might find this especially concerning if a strong group replaces an otherwise enfeebled one. Nevertheless, we demonstrate the opposite in the context of group competition with endogenous strategy. Whac-a-Mole can work, but a challenger entering the market is *required* for success.

To demonstrate that claim, suppose that the target state begins the game by choosing $m_1 \in [\underline{m}_1, \infty)$, where $\underline{m}_1 > 0$ represents Group 1's marginal cost of violence if the state takes no action. The state pays a cost that grows as it makes Group 1's marginal cost larger. The groups then play the baseline subgame.

It turns out that the state's decision hinges on whether to choose a marginal cost above or below a particular cutpoint. Recall that m_1 partially determines whether Group 1 corners the market. In terms of c, Group 1 cornered if $c > \left(1 - \sqrt{\frac{m_2}{m_1} - \frac{m_2^2}{4m_1^2}}\right)^2$. Solving for m_1 yields:

$$m_1 < m_1^* \equiv \frac{m_2 + m_2\sqrt{2\sqrt{c} - c}}{2(1 - \sqrt{c})^2} \tag{6.4}$$

Thus, Line 6.4 holds, Group 1 corners because the necessary overproduction of violence to deter entry appears relatively cheap.[30] But if Line 6.4 fails, cornering is too expensive, and thus Group 1 chooses to compete with Group 2.[31]

---

[30] Solving for m_1 requires using the quadratic formula, which generates two solutions. The requirements of this parameter space rule out the smaller of the two solutions, thereby generating a single relevant cutpoint.

[31] If $\underline{m}_1 > m_1^*$, the state can only select a value that leads to a competitive market.

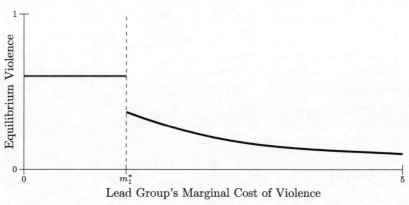

FIGURE 6.6 Violence as a function of the incumbent's marginal cost.

Because increasing the marginal cost cannot turn an otherwise competitive market into a cornered one, the following proposition states that offensive measures are mostly effective:

Proposition 6.3 *Increasing the lead group's marginal cost of violence* (m_1) *weakly decreases violence.*

Figure 6.6 explains the relationship. Setting $m_1 < m_1^*$ induces Group 1 to corner the market. This yields a constant violence level that is *not* a function of m_1. Given the logic of cornering the market, the reason is straightforward. To deter entry, Group 1 must produce sufficient violence that Group 2 cannot profitably enter. As Line 6.1 shows, that quantity is a function of c and m_2, which represent Group 2's payoff parameters. That is, Group 1's marginal cost has no direct impact on whether Group 2 finds entry profitable. Instead, m_1 only affects how much Group 1 internalizes that necessary violence level. Changing m_1 therefore has no effect on total violence output conditional on Group 1 maintaining its corner decision, as the left side of the figure illustrates.[32] That level is generally high because Group 1 overproduces violence to deter entry.

However, setting $m_1 \geq m_1^*$ triggers a discontinuous decrease in violence. Because Group 1's marginal cost is so large here, Group 1 dislikes

---

[32] In practice, if violence provided some ancillary benefits beyond the competition with Group 2, then violence would decrease within the region. As such, the target may benefit from decreasing Group 1's marginal cost within the region. However, this does not change the existence of a discontinuity, which is what drives our central theoretical claims about the potential benefits of offensive operations.

overproducing violence to corner the market. Group 2 enters the market, but the active competition yields less violence overall. Furthermore, equilibrium violence output declines as m_1 further grows because Group 1 prefers to produce less in a competitive contest as its per unit cost increases.[33]

In turn, if $\underline{m}_1 < m_1^*$, the state's optimization decision works as follows.[34] It begins by calculating its overall payoff for maintaining a cornered market by selecting $\underline{m}_1$. The state will not choose a value between $\underline{m}_1$ and m_1^* because doing so requires costly effort but maintains an identical amount of violence as $\underline{m}_1$.[35] It then calculates the optimal tradeoff between increasing m_1 and the state's own marginal cost of effort, assuming that the market will be competitive. Suppose first that the optimal m_1 in this calculation is greater than m_1^*. This means Group 1's optimal tradeoff between effort and violence suffered naturally creates a competitive market. Then Group 1 compares its utility for selecting that with its utility for keeping $\underline{m}_1$. It chooses the value associated with the greater payoff.

Now suppose the optimal m_1 in this calculation is less than m_1^*. This means that Group 1's optimal tradeoff between effort and violence naturally does not make a market competitive. One might imagine then that the state should not engage in any offensive counterterrorism operations. After all, when cornering the market, Group 1 produces a fixed quantity of violence no matter its marginal cost. But this is a hasty conclusion. Because switching a cornered market to a competitive one results in a discontinuous decrease in violence, the state may wish to overexert effort to obtain that benefit. To make that decision, it compares its payoff for $\underline{m}_1$

---

[33] Increasing m_1 can increase Group 2's production. However, overall violence production

equals $\frac{m_2}{4m_1^2} + \left(\sqrt{\frac{\frac{m_2}{4m_1^2}}{m_2}} - \frac{1}{2m_1} \right) = \frac{1}{2m_1}$, which decreases in m_1.

[34] If $\underline{m}_1 > m_1^*$, the target can only induce a competitive market. It therefore chooses the value of m_1 that maximizes the reduction in violence versus its marginal cost of effort.

[35] Long (2014) describes an empirical trend that is consistent with this logic. Leadership targeting in Afghanistan and Iraq had limited change in violence rates for better institutionalized groups. Such organizations do not rely on leadership as the exclusive coordinator of activities and thus would see only a small change to their marginal costs. The model predicts that such changes – conditional on cornering behavior – are insufficient to alter violence outputs. In contrast, Long shows that leadership targeting reduced violence for poorly institutionalized groups. Such groups are more reliant on leadership to coordinate activities and would thus see a larger increase in their marginal cost of production. The model predicts that such changes are sufficient to see sizable decreases in cornering violence.

with that of m_1^*.[36] It picks the strategy that produces the greater payoff between these two. Note that the state does not go past m_1^* here because the marginal reduction in violence is not worth the marginal cost of effort at that point. Only the discontinuity is worth obtaining.

Consequently, increasing the incumbent group's marginal cost has mostly positive effects. The lone issue is that exerting effort but choosing a value less than m_1^* (rather than sticking with $\underline{m}_1$) has no impact on violence. Thus, if the state wishes to manipulate Group 1's marginal cost in an otherwise cornered market, it *must* shift m_1 to a value that produces a competitive market.[37]

What do the Whac-a-Mole critics miss? Their main concern is that destroying one group merely allows another organization to arise to capture the marketshare. The equilibrium results sympathize with this – increasing m_1 across the m_1^* threshold indeed produces another group. But the introduction of another group is *exactly* what the state wishes to induce – if no intervention would result in a single group cornering the market, the state's manipulation must cause an additional group to form. Despite making the world seem more chaotic, this pleases the target. The outcome switches from a cornered market with an overproduction of violence to a competitive market with a smaller violence level.

These results provide theoretical support for how the United States responded to al-Qaeda following September 11, 2001. More than a decade of the War on Terror left al-Qaeda a shell of its former monolithic self. A large number of groups rose from the ashes. However, using President Obama's phrasing, many of these mimicked a "JV team" of al-Qaeda – groups whose crosshairs were not "focused on the homeland" and not of the "Osama bin Laden and 9/11" mold.[38] Although Obama's characterization of Islamic State as a JV team was a major underestimation, the general principle still applies. Even organizations similar to Islamic State do not have the capacity to strike the United States in the same manner as al-Qaeda once did. Indeed, Islamic State has replaced al-Qaeda's coordinated attacks against American infrastructure with disorganized assaults on the homeland by loosely affiliated confederates.

---

[36] The state assumes that Group 1 will create a competitive market when indifferent here, which is a required condition for equilibrium.

[37] Unlike the manipulation of c, though, the state might not want to go deep past m_1^*. Rather, Group 1 might wish to go exactly to m_1^* to experience the discontinuous dropoff and leave it at that.

[38] https://nbcnews.to/2oVo1FZ.

Still, Whac-a-Mole correctly cautions against the general efficacy of large-scale offensive operations. Because another organization waits in the wings, enfeebling the incumbent group has diminishing marginal returns. Although the state may wish to intervene in a competitive market, that competition nonetheless limits the effectiveness of that intervention. For example, despite al-Qaeda's reduced capacity, the United States does not enjoy full benefits because Islamic State has entered the market. Policymakers therefore must weigh this possibility in their decision to allocate effort toward the destruction of an existing group.

Zooming out, offensive operations interact with the previously described manipulations in interesting ways. To begin, the critical value c^* in Figure 6.5 drifts to the right as m_1 increases. Thus, enfeebling Group 1 means that the state has to increase the cost of entry at a higher level than before to cause a decline in violence. Second, grievances here can *compound* the positive effect. If increasing marginal costs also increases the market size, the state can reach the discontinuous decrease in Figures 6.4 and 6.6 faster.[39]

The discontinuity in violence at m_1^* also has an important implication for collective counterterrorism. Throughout, we have described the target state as a single entity. Arce and Sandler (2005), however, note that transnational terrorism often strikes multiple entities. Further, they show that counterterrorism under these circumstances can form a collective action problem. Individual incentives encourage states to bolster their own defense. But this imposes negative externalities on other states, as those less-defended countries are more tempting terrorist targets. This leaves all states worse off than if they offensively attacked the organization. Proactive measures, after all, generate positive externalities.

Despite the temptation to free ride, a state may wish to engage in a proactive effort to enjoy the discontinuity. Even a minor intervention could cause a major decline in violence, inconsistent with a collective action problem. Of course, such an incentive structure can create a volunteer's dilemma. It may not be clear *which* state should take the action, but each individual state would prefer to do it if they knew the others would not. The key here is that, unlike with traditional collective action problems, efficient equilibria exist.

On the other hand, the model also gives an alternative explanation for a lack of counterterrorism. When an incumbent group's marginal cost

---

[39] Of course, grievances also decrease the value of raising the marginal cost once in the competitive equilibrium, disincentivizing further investment.

of violence is very low, the counterterrorist must exert a great deal of effort to reach the nonmonotonic decline in violence. As such, rather than contributions failing due to a collective action problem, moving the needle may simply be too expensive.

The Effectiveness of Defensive Measures

Our final strategy is defensive measures. Unlike the other tactics, for groups committing the same form of attacks, defensive measures do not discriminate. Airport security, for example, stops hijackers whether they are members of al-Qaeda or ISIS. Thus, in contrast to the offensive and proactive measures described above, reinforcing security impacts all organizations, formed or unformed.

To model the consequences of defense, we begin with this ideal case where both groups must overcome the measure. Suppose the game begins with the target state choosing $\gamma \in [0, 1]$, where γ represents the portion of violence that is successful. Thus, the original game is the special case where $\gamma = 1$. A value of $\gamma = \frac{2}{3}$ means that only two-thirds of the groups' effort turns into punishing violence, with defensive measures absorbing the remaining third. The state pays a cost that increases as the extent of defensive measures increases. This captures the extra direct expenses from hiring extra security and the redesigning of buildings and event spaces. It also includes the costs of coordination across different categories (e.g., law enforcement, intelligence, private businesses).[40] From there, the game proceeds as usual except that Group i's contribution to the contest is now γv_i instead of v_i.

A surprising result follows immediately from the groups' utility functions. For example, Group 1's function equals $\frac{\gamma v_1}{\gamma v_1 + \gamma v_2} - m_1 v_1$. The γ values immediately cancel. The same is true for Group 2's utility function. Therefore, γ *has no impact on the remaining subgame*.[41] Group 2 still uses the same decision rule for entry, and both groups choose their violence levels exactly as before. This is because the defensive measures impact both groups equally and they choose their violence levels where their marginal gain equals their marginal cost. The violence strategies of

---

[40] The coordination costs are an unappreciated disutility of defensive measures. Even though counterterrorism policy is largely a state-driven process, defensive measures are most often placed under direct control of local actors (Perliger, Pedahzur, and Zalmanovitch, 2005).

[41] The same canceling occurs for Chapter 2's original model. As such, the implications for the ideal case apply equally there.

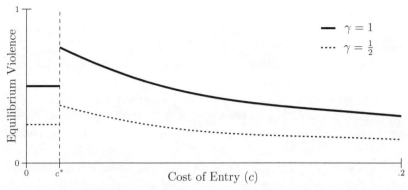

FIGURE 6.7 Violence for two levels of defensive efforts.

the original game hit this point for the extension precisely because γ has no effect on the contest.[42]

Nevertheless, the state benefits. Violence efforts remain the same, but the net damage declines because only γ portion gets through. In turn, the state needs to optimize a straightforward tradeoff between the sum of violence realized $\gamma(v_1 + v_2)$ and its cost of effort. The following proposition summarizes how the state can think about the benefits of defensive actions:

Proposition 6.4 *Increasing defensive measures (i.e., decreasing γ) strictly decreases equilibrium violence.*

Figure 6.7 illustrates the relationship, showing how equilibrium violence changes as a function of c for two levels of γ. The solid line charts the baseline $\gamma = 1$ case, which is a duplicate plot of Figure 6.5. The dotted line tracks $\gamma = \frac{1}{2}$. The cutpoint for c remains constant, and the violence decreases by exactly half across the board. Generalizing from this, decreasing γ further will only force equilibrium violence to decline. The figure also shows that defense is most useful in just-barely cornered markets. Violence peaks under those circumstances, making the marginal cost of defense look less onerous. But, regardless of the situation, the state has a straightforward optimization problem: it simply chooses the γ level

---

[42] This also provides insight into a model where supporters assign value based on a group's effort rather than its net output. The contest function remains $\frac{v_1}{v_1 + v_2}$ and thus the groups' objective functions are identical to the main model. However, the government only suffers γ portion in damage. It therefore maximizes the tradeoff between the cost of defensive measures and reduction.

that maximizes the cost of implementing defensive measures. It does not have to consider any deeper, second-order problems that its manipulation may cause.

The monotonic reduction in violence here means that defensive measures have an attractive quality that the others lack: non-strategic increases to defense always pay off for the target state. This ease of implementation may help explain why defensive measures have become pervasive. However, the takeaway here is not that governments should exclusively rely on defense. Other strategies can also work and their marginal utility may be superior due to the beneficial nonmonotonic declines in violence. Policymakers must exert more effort to properly calibrate those strategies to ensure the benefits though.

That said, not all defensive strategies affect the groups in the same manner. Competing groups are not always uniform in their tactics (Conrad and Greene, 2015). For example, if the incumbent group specializes in improvised explosive devices but a potential challenger could only muster mass shootings, then IED protection would mitigate the first source of damage but do nothing to stop the second. Likewise, signals intelligence is more effective at stopping organizations planning to carry out coordinated attacks than groups focused on isolated operations from disconnected individuals.[43] Insofar as a government's counterpropaganda both reduces the messaging value of an attack (by undermining the group's credibility) and increasing the cost of conducting attacks (by making the civilian population more hostile to the group), this setup also maps onto such counterpropaganda campaigns. One may then wonder whether these measures still guarantee an overall reduction in violence if they only affect one group.

Fortunately, this is straightforward to answer by considering two altered versions of the model. We briefly describe their key implications here. First, suppose that the state begins by choosing $\gamma_1 \in [0, 1]$. This changes the contest so that Group 1's share equals $\frac{\gamma_1 v_1}{\gamma_1 v_1 + v_2}$. That is, it reduces the effectiveness of Group 1's output while leaving Group 2's identical. The game continues as normal.

This extension most closely matches manipulations to Group 1's marginal cost. Mitigating v_1 disincentivizes Group 1 from cornering the market. This is because overproducing to deter entry requires even

---

[43] These counter-strategies are popular among high-capacity states. Because coordinated operations represent a greater threat, lone-wolf attacks are more deadly in those countries (Phillips, 2017).

more overproduction to compensate for the defensive measures. Thus, sufficient defense against Group 1 can turn a cornered market into a competitive market. Smaller effort keeps a cornered market cornered. And any effort in an already competitive market will keep it competitive. It is not possible for such measures to turn a competitive market into a cornered one.

Because going from a cornered market to a competitive market yields a discontinuous decrease in violence, these measures are also attractive. Defensive levels that keep a competitive market competitive also decrease violence for the intuitive reason that defensive measures should mitigate the problem. However, defensive levels that keep a cornered market cornered generate no such benefit. The consequence is similar to what the left side of Figure 6.6 showed. When Group 1 wants to corner, it must choose a quantity of *realized* violence that makes entry from Group 2 unprofitable. Because defense against Group 1 does not alter Group 2's violence here, that realized output remains identical across those defensive values. The state must therefore adopt another "go big or go home" strategy. If Group 1 would corner the market in the absence of any policy interventions, then the state should either force Group 1 to compete or do nothing at all.

Second, suppose that the state instead chooses $\gamma_2 \in [0, 1]$. Now Group 1's share equals $\frac{v_1}{v_1 + \gamma_2 v_2}$. As such, the defensive measures absorb some of Group 2's output while leaving Group 1's identical. The violence decisions then unfold in the same manner as before.

This extension most closely matches the manipulations to grievances. Absorbing more of Group 2's potential damage incentivizes Group 1 to corner the market. This is because Group 2 finds competition more difficult in general. With a lower possible payoff for entry, Group 1 can deter the challenger with a smaller overpayment. But a smaller overpayment can still exceed the sum of violence in a competitive market. Thus, if the state wants to transition an otherwise competitive market to a cornered one, it must also adopt a "go big or go home" strategy here. Just barely pushing Group 1 into cornering results in a violence level higher than the damage it would suffer by instead just barely maintaining a competitive market.

The state's choice is simpler when the defensive strategy maintains the entry decision. If Group 1 would naturally corner the market, greater defense against Group 2 will not change that outcome. But it does monotonically reduce the total violence, and so the state can exert effort until its marginal cost is no longer worthwhile. This leads to an odd policy recommendation. In such a case, the mode of attack the state defends against is one that Group 1 never engages in. Yet it may still prove fruitful to guard against the other vector despite knowing that Group 2 will never enter. The state benefits indirectly by addressing the competition that drives Group 1's violent behavior.

Finally, if Group 1 would naturally allow competition, sufficiently small defensive measures against Group 2 will not change that. Those measures, however, result in less violence through a direct effect. As such, the state may wish to invest in defense for that purpose. But the above caveat still applies: too much defense may induce Group 1 to corner. If the defensive measures are not sufficiently pervasive, then the state finishes in a worse position than if it had maintained the status quo.

CONCLUSION

This chapter studied the effect of potential group entry on competitive political violence. Two key results emerged. First, the incentives for an existing group to try to corner the market are strong. Successful monopolization means capturing all of the support for itself. Thus, incumbent groups are willing to commit more violence on their own than both groups would in competition if it means deterring the potential entrant. We found just that sort of behavior in equilibrium. In turn, the empirical implication that *observed* competition results in higher predicted violence levels requires a critical caveat. It may not apply to cases where *potential* competition is the primary driver of a group's decision-making process.

Second, the fact that cornering violence exceeds competitive violence yields many counterintuitive policy implications for states wishing to minimize the damage. Minimizing grievances and increasing the barriers to entry appear to disincentivize terrorism in general. But they also increase an incumbent group's incentive to corner the market, and the latter effect dominates under weak interventions. In contrast, attacking an incumbent group's ability to produce violence both reduces the incentives to commit terrorism and that group's ability to corner the market. Such a policy is effective, but the optimal intervention requires that a challenging group enter the marketplace to compete with the enfeebled incumbent. Defensive tactics can also prove successful. But even then the target may not want to put its effort toward defending against vectors that an entering group would choose, lest it incentivize the incumbent group to corner the market. In short, policymakers must exercise caution to ensure that their adjustments improve the situation and do not exacerbate violence.

Following best practices of modeling to understand mechanisms (Paine and Tyson, 2020), we examined each intervention option in isolation. In practice, implementation often has multiple effects no matter how targeted the policy may be. Offensive operations against existing groups, for example, might also create grievances that did not exist previously. Reducing grievances by vacating a region could increase the cost of launching a new group without the same narrative of oppression to expound. Thus, a natural question to ask is how policymakers should think about such interventions. In short, the answer is to treat the problems as a combination of the propositions discussed earlier. If each effect pushes in the same direction, then the result is only reinforced. If they run in opposite directions, then policymakers should spend more time thinking about which effect is stronger. Even if the positive effect dominates, policymakers should recognize that the net benefit is smaller than it may otherwise appear.

Looking forward, throughout this chapter we have focused on the incentives of the target state in the shadow of group entry. However, future work could consider how existing groups manipulate the market for entry. An interesting twist to our setup is to conceptualize the challenger as a potential splinter group rather than a separate entity. Leadership in an incumbent group benefits from higher costs of entry, as they must exert less effort to convince would-be entrepreneurs that entry is not worthwhile. Target governments are not the only entities that can influence entry decisions though. How terrorist groups govern themselves also affects incentives to deviate from the broader organizational mission (Shapiro, 2013).

One issue pertinent to splintering and our competition framework is credit claiming. Leadership often needs to delegate entire attacks to semi-autonomous cells within the organizational umbrella. Imagine such a cell commits a spectacular attack. Its parent organization would like to use the corresponding publicity to attract support to its ranks. But consider the incentives of the lieutenants within the cell. If they broke away from the group, they could use the attack as a rallying call to the new organization. This chapter's same central mechanism applies: an incumbent group has incentive to commit great violence – from a variety of sources – to discourage its operatives from breaking away. But it also faces a hold up problem. Anticipating that a cell could break off, the organization might not want to endow it with the resources to commit the spectacular attack in the first place.

APPENDIX

This appendix has two phases. First, we solve for the two-player entry game featuring only the militant groups. This proves everything up until the chapter's propositions. We then fully define the state's utility function for the extensions and give full descriptions of the equilibrium strategies pursued. The process of proving these strategies imply the results claimed by the chapter's more substantively descriptive propositions.

Group 2's Violence Decision

Lemma 6.1 *Let $v_2^* \equiv \sqrt{\frac{v_1}{m_2}} - v_1$. In all SPE, Group 2 selects $max\{0, v_2^*\}$.*

Proof: Group 2's decision comes at the end of the game, so it optimizes its payoff by choosing the value of v_2 that maximizes:

$$\frac{v_2}{v_1 + v_2} - m_2 v_2$$

The first-order condition is:

$$\frac{v_1 + v_2 - v_2}{(v_1 + v_2)^2} - m_2 = 0$$

$$m_2 v_2^2 + 2m_2 v_1 v_2 + v_1(m_2 v_1 - 1) = 0$$

Applying the quadratic formula to obtain the roots yields:

$$\frac{-2m_2 v_1 \pm \sqrt{4m_2^2 v_1^2 - 4m_2 v_1(m_2 v_1 - 1)}}{2m_2}$$

$$\pm \sqrt{\frac{v_1}{m_2}} - v_1$$

Because $v_2 \geq 0$, $-\sqrt{\frac{v_1}{m_2}} - v_1$ is not the solution – it is always negative. This leaves $\sqrt{\frac{v_1}{m_2}} - v_1$, which itself may be negative if $v_1 > \frac{1}{m_2}$.[44] Consequently, Group 2 selects the maximum of 0 and v_2^*.

Group 2's Entry Decision

Now to the entry decision. We base the cutpoint on Group 1's chosen violence level v_1 because Group 1 selects v_1 in the next move that we

---

[44] This is a maximum because the second derivative of the objective function is $-\frac{2}{(v_1 + v_2)^3}$.

need to solve for. As the following lemma shows, that level of violence determines Group 2's entry decision:

Lemma 6.2 *Let* $v_1^* \equiv \frac{(1-\sqrt{c})^2}{m_2}$. *Group 2 enters if* $v_1 < v_1^*$, *stays out if* $v_1 > v_1^*$, *and is indifferent between the two choices if* $v_1 = v_1^*$.

Proof: Consider four cases. First, suppose $v_1 \geq \frac{1}{m_2}$. By Lemma 6.1, Group 2 would select $v_2 = 0$ if it were to enter, giving it a payoff of 0 for the competition phase. However, to reach that point, it would have to pay a cost of c. Because not entering generates a payoff of 0, Group 2 must not enter.

Second, suppose $v_1 \in (v_1^*, \frac{1}{m_2})$. If Group 2 enters, it selects $v_2 = v_2^*$. Working through the contest success function, Group 2's payoff for the competition phase equals:

$$\frac{\sqrt{\frac{v_1}{m_2}} - v_1}{v_1 + \sqrt{\frac{v_1}{m_2}} - v_1} - \left(\sqrt{\frac{v_1}{m_2}} - v_1 \right)$$

$$(1 - \sqrt{m_2 v_1})^2$$

Therefore, Group 2 stays out if:

$$(1 - \sqrt{m_2 v_1})^2 - c < 0$$

$$v_1 > \frac{(1 - \sqrt{c})^2}{m_2}$$

This is true because the first condition requires this exact inequality.

Third, suppose $v_1 < v_1^*$. By analogous argument, Group 2 enters if $v_1 < \frac{(1-\sqrt{c})^2}{m_2}$. This holds here, so Group 2 enters.

Finally, suppose $v_1 = v_1^*$. By analogous argument, Group 2 is indifferent between entering and not entering, so it may mix freely between the two strategies. For the rest of the proof, we assume that Group 2 does not enter as a pure strategy in this case. No equilibria exist where this is not true.[45]

---

[45] This is because Group 1's payoff is continuous and strictly decreasing for all $v_1 > v_1^*$. If Group 2 mixed when indifferent, Group 1 has a profitable deviation to some $v_1 = v_1^* - \epsilon$. But those values cannot be optimal because Group 1's payoff strictly decreases in v_1 on that interval. This is the same logic that causes the ultimatum game to have a unique equilibrium.

Group 1's Violence Decision

We solve for this over two subcases:

Lemma 6.3 *Suppose* $m_1 > \frac{m_2}{2}$. *Let* $c^* \equiv \left(1 - \sqrt{\frac{m_2}{m_1} - \frac{m_2^2}{4m_1^2}}\right)^2$. *In the unique SPE, Group 1 chooses* $v_1 = v_1^*$ *if* $c \geq c^*$ *and* $v_1 = \frac{m_2}{4m_1^2}$ *if* $c < c^*$. *Group 2 quits in the first case; it enters and produces* v_2^* *in the second case.*

Proof: Broadly, Group 1 can select from two categories of violence: an amount at least as great as the cutpoint v_1^* or an amount below. If Group 1 picks from the larger set, Group 2 quits. Group 1's payoff is therefore $\frac{v_1}{v_1 + 0} - m_1 v_1 = 1 - m_1 v_1$. Note that this amount is strictly decreasing in v_1 – that is, any extra violence here serves no purpose to Group 1 but is costly. Consequently, no equilibria exist in which Group 1 picks a $v_1 > v_1^*$.

Now consider an amount from the smaller set. Group 2 enters and (by Lemma 6.1) produces $v_2 = max\left\{0, \sqrt{\frac{v_1}{m_2}} - v_1\right\}$ in violence. Using the contest success function, provided that $\sqrt{\frac{v_1}{m_2}} - v_1 > 0$, Group 1's payoff equals:

$$\frac{v_1}{v_1 + \sqrt{\frac{v_1}{m_2}} - v_1} - m_1 v_1$$

$$\sqrt{m_2 v_1} - m_1 v_1$$

The first-order condition of that objective function is:

$$\frac{\sqrt{m_2}}{2\sqrt{v_1}} - m_1 = 0$$

$$v_1 = \frac{m_2}{4m_1^2}$$

This a maximum because the second derivative of the objective function is $-\frac{m_2^{\frac{1}{2}} v_1^{-\frac{3}{2}}}{4}$, which is negative. Further, note that $v_1 = \frac{m_2}{4m_1^2}$ implies that $\sqrt{\frac{v_1}{m_2}} - v_1 > 0$ because the lemma assumes $m_1 > \frac{m_2}{2}$. This in turn means that Group 1 maximizes its payoff with Group 2 still playing a violence strategy on the interior.

Now compare Group 1's utility for the minimum amount of violence necessary to drive out Group 2 versus Group 1's optimal competitive quantity. If Group 1 drives Group 2 out at the lowest price, it earns $1 - m_1 v_1^*$. Meanwhile, choosing the optimal competitive amount produces a payoff of $\frac{\frac{m_2}{4m_1^2}}{\frac{m_2}{4m_1^2} + v_2^*} - m_1 \frac{m_2}{4m_1^2} = \frac{m_2}{4m_1}$. Thus, Group 1 induces entry if:

$$\frac{m_2}{4m_1} > 1 - m_1 \frac{(1 - \sqrt{c})^2}{m_2}$$

$$c < \left(1 - \sqrt{\frac{m_2}{m_1} - \frac{m_2^2}{4m_1^2}}\right)^2$$

This is the cutpoint given in the lemma.[46]

By analogous argument, Group 1 chooses v_1^* to corner the market if $c > \left(1 - \sqrt{\frac{m_2}{m_1} - \frac{m_2^2}{4m_1^2}}\right)^2$. The argument also shows that it is an equilibrium to corner the market if $c = \left(1 - \sqrt{\frac{m_2}{m_1} - \frac{m_2^2}{4m_1^2}}\right)^2$.

Lemma 6.4 *Suppose $m_1 \leq \frac{m_2}{2}$. In the unique SPE, Group 1 chooses $v_1 = v_1^*$ and Group 2 quits.*

Proof: By Lemma 6.2, if Group 1 selects $v_1 > v_1^*$, Group 2 quits. No equilibria exist for $v_1 > v_1^*$ because Group 1 can profitably deviate to a slightly smaller level of violence still greater than v_1^*.

If Group 1 selects $v_1 \in (0, v_1^*)$, Group 2 enters and produces v_2^* violence. Group 1's utility equals $\frac{v_1}{v_1 + v_2^*} - m_1 v_1$. The first-order condition from Proposition 1 demonstrates that this function strictly increases until $v_1 = \frac{m_2}{4m_1^2}$. Note that for this proposition's parameter space ($m_1 \leq \frac{m_2}{2}$), $\frac{m_2}{4m_1^2}$ is greater than v_1^*. Thus, Group 1's utility strictly increases on the interval $v_1 \in (0, v_1^*)$. In turn, no equilibrium can exist on that range

---

[46] Note that the value inside of the radical is positive if $m_1 > \frac{m_2}{4}$. This must be true because the parameter space has the more stringent requirement that $m_1 > \frac{m_2}{2}$. Thus, although the causes of terrorism are complex, the cutpoint is not. One might also be concerned that the optimal competitive level of violence is greater than the minimum necessary to exclude Group 2. (This could be the case if c is high.) However, the inequality still produces the correct result because the left-hand side represents a value that gives less than the whole prize and at a greater cost than the right-hand side. Thus, the inequality would tell us that Group 1 would pick the quantity to keep out Group 2.

because Group 1 could profitably deviate to a level of violence slightly greater while still below v_1^*.

The only case left to check is when Group 1 produces exactly v_1^*. Group 2 is indifferent between entering and quitting. The proof for Proposition 6.3 showed that Group 1 receives strictly more when Group 2 quits under these circumstances. As such, this is an equilibrium.[47]

Violence at the Corner/Compete Cutpoint

The central comparative statics on the various inputs relied on the fact that violence is strictly greater at the cutpoint when Group 1 corners than when it competes. As the main text described, violence is greater in the corner case if $m_1 > \frac{m_2}{2(1-\sqrt{c})^2}$. Substituting $c = c^*$ yields $m_1 > \frac{m_2}{2}$. As with Lemmas 6.3 and 6.4, this is the necessary condition for a cutpoint c to exist such that Group 1 prefers to corner for values above the cutpoint and prefers to compete for values below the cutpoint. Thus, the claim holds.

Endogenous Grievances

We begin by solving the extensions with endogenous grievances. To define the game, let the state begin by choosing $\pi \in [0, 1]$. Regardless of the choice, the game proceeds to the competition stage. The only difference is that, instead of competing over a unit value, they fight over a pie the size of π. The state's utility equals $\alpha\pi - (v_1 + v_2)$, where $\alpha > 0$ is a scalar capturing how much the state weighs the value of the policy versus the costs of violence.

Solving the two-player interaction with Group 1 and Group 2, the proof strategy follows the strategy of the original game, as it is a special case of this version with $\pi = 1$.

Group 2's violence decision. At the end of the game, if Group 2 has entered, its objective function is:

$$\frac{v_2}{v_1 + v_2}(\pi) - m_2 v_2$$

The first-order condition is:

$$\frac{v_1}{(v_1 + v_2)^2}(\pi) - m_2 = 0$$

---

[47] The equilibrium is also unique for reasons similar to the last case.

$$v_2 \equiv \sqrt{\frac{\pi v_1}{m_2}} - v_1$$

This is negative if $v_1 > \frac{\pi}{m_2}$, so Group 2 chooses $max\{\sqrt{\frac{\pi v_1}{m_2}} - v_1, 0\}$.[48]

Group 2's entry decision. If $v_1 \geq \frac{\pi}{m_2}$, Group 2 produces 0 for the contest and thus receives 0 as its payoff for the contest. Since entering costs c, Group 2 will not enter if $v_1 > \frac{\pi}{m_2}$.

If $v_1 < \frac{\pi}{m_2}$, Group 2 produces $\sqrt{\frac{\pi v_1}{m_2}} - v_1$. Routing this through its utility function for the contest, entering produces $\frac{\sqrt{\frac{\pi v_1}{m_2}} - v_1}{v_1 + \sqrt{\frac{\pi v_1}{m_2}} - v_1}(\pi) -$ $m_2\left(\sqrt{\frac{\pi v_1}{m_2}} - v_1\right)$ at cost c. Quitting generates 0. Group 2 therefore enters if:

$$\frac{\sqrt{\frac{\pi v_1}{m_2}} - v_1}{v_1 + \sqrt{\frac{\pi v_1}{m_2}} - v_1}(\pi) - m_2\left(\sqrt{\frac{\pi v_1}{m_2}} - v_1\right) - c > 0$$

$$c < (\sqrt{\pi} - \sqrt{m_2 v_1})^2$$

Analogously, Group 2 quits if $c > (\sqrt{\pi} - \sqrt{m_2 v_1})^2$ and is indifferent when $c = (\sqrt{\pi} - \sqrt{m_2 v_1})^2$.

Group 1's violence decision. The minimum cost necessary to drive out Group 2 is $c = (\sqrt{\pi} - \sqrt{m_2 v_1})^2$.[49] Solving for v_1 yields $\frac{(\sqrt{\pi} - \sqrt{c})^2}{m_2}$. Thus, Group 2 enters if Group 1 selects $v_1 < \frac{(\sqrt{\pi} - \sqrt{c})^2}{m_2}$ and stays out if $v_1 \geq \frac{(\sqrt{\pi} - \sqrt{c})^2}{m_2}$.[50] In turn, Group 1's optimal level of violence to exclude Group 2 equals $\frac{(\sqrt{\pi} - \sqrt{c})^2}{m_2}$.

If Group 1 wishes to induce Group 2's entry, its objective function is:

$$\frac{v_1}{v_1 + \sqrt{\frac{\pi v_1}{m_2}} - v_1}(\pi) - m_1 v_1$$

---

[48] This is maximum because the second derivative is $-\frac{2\pi}{(v_1 + v_2)^3}$.

[49] We assume that Group 2 stays out when indifferent, but this must be true in equilibrium as before.

[50] The stay out decision covers the case where $v_1 > \frac{\pi}{m_2}$, which would otherwise result in Group 2 producing 0 violence.

The first-order condition is:

$$\frac{\sqrt{\pi m_2}}{2\sqrt{v_1}} - m_1 = 0$$

$$v_1 = \frac{\pi m_2}{4m_1^2}$$

Selecting this value induces Group 2 to choose a strictly positive quantity of violence if $m_1 > \frac{m_2}{2}$. If $m_1 < \frac{m_2}{2}$ instead, then Group 1 selects $\frac{(\sqrt{\pi} - \sqrt{c})^2}{m_2}$. (This is analogous to Lemma 6.4.)

Now for the $m_1 > \frac{m_2}{2}$ case. If Group 1 excludes Group 2, it earns $\pi - (m_1)\frac{(\sqrt{\pi} - \sqrt{c})^2}{m_2}$. If it produces the optimal competitive amount and Group 2 enters, Group 1's utility is the above objective function with $v_1 = \frac{\pi m_2}{4m_1^2}$. It therefore excludes Group 2 if:

$$\pi - (m_1)\frac{(\sqrt{\pi} - \sqrt{c})^2}{m_2} > \frac{\frac{\pi m_2}{4m_1^2}}{\frac{\pi m_2}{4m_1^2} + \sqrt{\frac{(\pi)\frac{\pi m_2}{4m_1^2}}{m_2} - \frac{\pi m_2}{4m_1^2}}}(\pi) - m_1\frac{\pi m_2}{4m_1^2}$$

$$\pi < \pi^* \equiv \frac{c}{\left(1 - \sqrt{\frac{m_2}{m_1} - \frac{m_2^2}{4m_1^2}}\right)^2}$$

By analogous argument, Group 1 induces entry if $\pi > \pi^*$ and is indifferent when $\pi = \pi^*$.[51]

Violence at the cutpoint. As with the other extensions, the quantity of violence near the cutpoint drives the state's decision. As π approaches π^* from the left, Group 1 corners and produces $\frac{(\sqrt{\pi} - \sqrt{c})^2}{m_2}$ in violence. As π approaches π^* from the right, the parties compete; Group 1 produces $\frac{\pi m_2}{4m_1^2}$ and Group 2 produces $\sqrt{\frac{\pi\left(\frac{\pi m_2}{4m_1^2}\right)}{m_2}} - \frac{\pi m_2}{4m_1^2}$. Substituting $\pi = \pi^*$, violence in the cornering case is greater than the sum of violence in the competitive case if:

---

[51] As with the baseline model, this covers the case where the optimal amount from the first-order condition exceeds the minimum necessary amount to force out Group 2; if this were the case, the utility on the right-hand side would produce less than π from the contest and at a greater cost than the left-hand side, even though the left-hand side gives the full π to Group 1.

$$\frac{\left(\sqrt{\dfrac{c}{\left(1-\sqrt{\frac{m_2}{m_1}-\frac{m_2^2}{4m_1^2}}\right)^2}}-\sqrt{c}\right)^2}{m_2} > \frac{\left(\dfrac{c}{\left(1-\sqrt{\frac{m_2}{m_1}-\frac{m_2^2}{4m_1^2}}\right)^2}\right)^2 m_2}{4m_1^2}+$$

$$\sqrt{\frac{\left(\dfrac{c}{\left(1-\sqrt{\frac{m_2}{m_1}-\frac{m_2^2}{4m_1^2}}\right)^2}\right)\left(\left(\dfrac{c}{\left(1-\sqrt{\frac{m_2}{m_1}-\frac{m_2^2}{4m_1^2}}\right)^2}\right)^2 m_2 \middle/ 4m_1^2\right)}{m_2}} - \frac{\left(\dfrac{c}{\left(1-\sqrt{\frac{m_2}{m_1}-\frac{m_2^2}{4m_1^2}}\right)^2}\right)^2 m_2}{4m_1^2}$$

This reduces to $m_1 > \frac{m_2}{2}$. This must be true at the cutpoint, otherwise Group 1 would have a strict preference to corner.

The State's grievance decision. We are now ready for the main proposition of this extension:

Proposition 6.5 Let $\pi^{**} = \frac{c}{(1-\alpha m_2)^2}$. *The following four cases describe the state's unique equilibrium action:*

1. If $\alpha > \frac{1}{2m_1}$ and $\pi^{**} < \pi^*$, the state chooses $\pi = 1$ if $\alpha - \frac{1}{2m_1} > \alpha\pi^{**} - \frac{(\sqrt{\pi^{**}}-\sqrt{c})^2}{m_2}$ and π^{**} if $\alpha - \frac{1}{2m_1} < \alpha\pi^{**} - \frac{(\sqrt{\pi^{**}}-\sqrt{c})^2}{m_2}$.
2. If $\alpha > \frac{1}{2m_1}$ and $\pi^{**} > \pi^*$, the state chooses $\pi = 1$.
3. If $\alpha < \frac{1}{2m_1}$ and $\pi^{**} < \pi^*$, the state chooses $\pi = \pi^*$ if $\alpha\pi^* - \frac{\pi^*}{2m_1} > \alpha\pi^{**} - \frac{(\sqrt{\pi^{**}}-\sqrt{c})^2}{m_2}$ and $\pi = \pi^{**}$ if $\alpha\pi^* - \frac{\pi^*}{2m_1} < \alpha\pi^{**} - \frac{(\sqrt{\pi^{**}}-\sqrt{c})^2}{m_2}$.
4. If $\alpha < \frac{1}{2m_1}$ and $\pi^{**} > \pi^*$, the state chooses $\pi = \pi^*$.

Proof: The state's utility function for a chosen π depends on whether it is greater than or less than π^*. For values greater than π^*, that function is $\alpha\pi - \frac{\pi}{2m_1}$. The first derivative of this is:

$$\alpha - \frac{1}{2m_1}$$

Therefore, the state maximizes its utility on this region at $\pi = 1$ if $\alpha > \frac{1}{2m_1}$ and at $\pi = \pi^*$ if $\alpha < \frac{1}{2m_1}$.[52]

For values less than π^*, the state's utility function is $\alpha\pi - \frac{(\sqrt{\pi}-\sqrt{c})^2}{m_2}$. The first-order condition of this is:

$$\alpha - \frac{1 - \sqrt{\frac{c}{\pi}}}{m_2} = 0$$

$$\pi = \pi^{**} = \frac{c}{(1 - \alpha m_2)^2}$$

Therefore, the state maximizes its utility on this region at π^{**} if $\pi^{**} < \pi^*$ and at π^* if $\pi^{**} > \pi^*$.

Now consider the four cases. If $\alpha > \frac{1}{2m_1}$ and $\pi^{**} < \pi^*$, the state most prefers selecting $\pi = 1$ in the higher region and π^{**} in the lower region. It therefore chooses whichever produces the greater expected utility. That is, the state chooses $\pi = 1$ if $\alpha - \frac{1}{2m_1} > \alpha\pi^{**} - \frac{(\sqrt{\pi^{**}}-\sqrt{c})^2}{m_2}$ and π^{**} if $\alpha - \frac{1}{2m_1} < \alpha\pi^{**} - \frac{(\sqrt{\pi^{**}}-\sqrt{c})^2}{m_2}$.

If $\alpha > \frac{1}{2m_1}$ and $\pi^{**} < \pi^*$, the state still most prefers selecting $\pi = 1$ in the higher region but now prefers π^* in the lower region. Notice, however, that the state's expected utility for π^* for the cornered market is less than its expected utility at π^* in the competitive market. Furthermore, the state's utility strictly increases in π above π^*. This implies that the utility for $\pi = 1$ must be greater than the utility for π^* in a cornered market. Therefore, the state must select $\pi = 1$.

If $\alpha < \frac{1}{2m_1}$ and $\pi^{**} < \pi^*$, the state now most prefers selecting π^* from the higher region and π^{**} from the lower region. For simplicity, assume that Group 1 chooses a competitive market when indifferent between cornering and competing.[53] Then the state chooses whichever of the two produces the greater expected utility. That is, the state chooses $\pi = \pi^*$ if $\alpha\pi^* - \frac{\pi^*}{2m_1} > \alpha\pi^{**} - \frac{(\sqrt{\pi^{**}}-\sqrt{c})^2}{m_2}$ and $\pi = \pi^{**}$ if $\alpha\pi^* - \frac{\pi^*}{2m_1} < \alpha\pi^{**} - \frac{(\sqrt{\pi^{**}}-\sqrt{c})^2}{m_2}$.

Finally, if $\alpha < \frac{1}{2m_1}$ and $\pi^{**} > \pi^*$, the state still most prefers selecting π^* from the higher region and now also prefers selecting π^* from

---

[52] There is no interior solution because the mapping of π to violence is affine in this region.

[53] This assumption is actually a necessary condition for equilibria for similar reasons as before. If Group 1 cornered with positive probability when $\pi = \pi^*$, the state could profitably deviate to some slightly larger amount.

the lower region. It therefore must select π^*. Following this, as an equilibrium condition, Group 1 must select a competitive market.[54]

Endogenous Barriers to Entry

Now consider a variant where the state begins by choosing $c \in [\underline{c}, \infty)$ and the remaining game is the standard model of entry. Here, Group 2's cost to enter equals c. The state's payoff equals $-(v_1 + v_2) - \alpha(c - \underline{c})$. The value $\alpha > 0$ once again captures how much the state cares about violence, this time weighed against the effort necessary to increase c. Note that the cost paid is based on the difference between Group 2's realized cost and the minimum.

Proposition 6.6 *Let* $c^{**} \equiv \frac{1}{(\alpha m_2 - 1)^2}$. *If* $m_1 < \frac{m_2}{2}$, *the state chooses* $max\{\underline{c}, c^{**}\}$. *If* $m_1 > \frac{m_2}{2}$, *the following four cases describe the state's unique equilibrium action:*

1. *If* $\underline{c} > c^*$ *and* $\underline{c} > c^{**}$, *the state chooses* $\underline{c}$.
2. *If* $\underline{c} > c^*$ *and* $\underline{c} < c^{**}$, *the state chooses* c^{**}.
3. *If* $\underline{c} < c^*$ *and* $c^{**} > c^*$, *the state chooses* $\underline{c}$.
4. *If* $\underline{c} < c^*$ *and* $c^{**} < c^*$, *the state chooses* c^{**} *if* $-\frac{(1-\sqrt{c^{**}})^2}{m_2} - \alpha(c^{**} - \underline{c}) > -\frac{1}{2m_1}$ *and* $\underline{c}$ *if* $-\frac{(1-\sqrt{c^{**}})^2}{m_2} - \alpha(c^{**} - \underline{c}) < -\frac{1}{2m_1}$.

Proof: Recall that the state's objective function is $-(v_1 + v_2) - \alpha c$. From Propositions 6.3 and 6.4, Group 1 produces $v_1 = \frac{m_2}{4m_1^2}$ if $c < c^*$. Group 2 enters and produces v_2^*, generating a total of $\frac{1}{2m_1}$ in violence. If $c \geq c^*$, Group 1 produces $v_1^* = \frac{(1-\sqrt{c})^2}{m_2}$ violence to force out Group 2.

Note that increasing the cost of entry does not affect equilibrium levels of violence if the chosen cost is low enough to fall into the competitive case. If the state wishes to push the cost of entry into the greater case, it must maximize:

$$-\frac{(1 - \sqrt{c})^2}{m_2} - \alpha(c - \underline{c})$$

[54] Again, this is because the state could profitably deviate to a slightly greater amount otherwise.

The first-order condition is:

$$-\frac{\left(1 - \frac{1}{\sqrt{c}}\right)}{m_2} - \alpha = 0$$

$$c = c^{**} = \frac{1}{(\alpha m_2 - 1)^2}$$

Now to the cases. First, suppose $\underline{c} > c^*$ and $\underline{c} > c^{**}$. This means that the minimum cost of entry is greater than both the highest possible cost for a competitive equilibrium and the state's optimal cost in the cornering equilibrium. Since the first-order condition shows that increasing c any further leads to a lower utility, the state optimally picks $\underline{c}$.

Second, suppose $\underline{c} > c^*$ and $\underline{c} < c^{**}$. The minimum cost of entry remains greater than the highest possible cost for a competitive equilibrium but is less than the state's optimal cost in the cornering equilibrium. The first-order condition showed that selecting c^{**} is optimal here.

Third, suppose $\underline{c} < c^*$ and $c^{**} > c^*$. The minimum cost of entry is less than the highest possible cost for a competitive equilibrium but is now greater than the state's optimal cost in the cornering equilibrium. The optimal cost for maintaining the competitive equilibrium remains $\underline{c}$ because anything greater needlessly exerts effort. Its payoff for choosing that amount equals $-\frac{1}{2m_1}$. The optimal cost to shift into the cornering equilibrium switches to c^* because the first-order condition showed that the state's payoff is decreasing going away from c^{**}. Its payoff for choosing that amount equals $-\frac{(1-\sqrt{c^*})^2}{m_2} - \alpha(c^* - \underline{c})$. The state therefore chooses $\underline{c}$ if

$$-\frac{1}{2m_1} > -\frac{(1 - \sqrt{c^*})^2}{m_2} - \alpha(c^* - \underline{c})$$

We can show this holds by instead demonstrating

$$-\frac{1}{2m_1} > -\frac{(1 - \sqrt{c^*})^2}{m_2}$$

Substitution and substantial algebraic manipulation yields $m_1 > \frac{1}{2m_1}$, which holds. So the state chooses $\underline{c}$.

Finally, suppose $\underline{c} < c^*$ and $c^{**} < c^*$. Now the minimum cost of entry is less than the highest possible cost for a competitive equilibrium and is also less than the state's optimal cost in the cornering equilibrium. Thus, the state can manipulate whether Group 1 induces Group 2 to enter. If the state wishes to deter entry, the first-order condition showed the optimal cost for doing so is c^{**}. This generates a payoff of $-\frac{(1-\sqrt{c^{**}})^2}{m_2} - \alpha(c^{**} - \underline{c})$. Alternatively, the state can maintain the competitive equilibrium; the optimal cost to do this is $\underline{c}$ because any additional cost lowers the state's payoff without manipulating the remainder of the game. The state earns $-\frac{1}{2m_1}$ for this. Thus, it prefers selecting c^{**} if $-\frac{(1-\sqrt{c^{**}})^2}{m_2} - \alpha(c^{**} - \underline{c}) > -\frac{1}{2m_1}$ and prefers selecting $\underline{c}$ if $-\frac{(1-\sqrt{c^{**}})^2}{m_2} - \alpha(c^{**} - \underline{c}) < -\frac{1}{2m_1}$.

Endogenous Marginal Costs of Violence for the Lead Group

Now the game begins with the state choosing $m_1 \in [\underline{m}_1, \infty)$. Afterward, the groups play the standard entry subgame, with Group 1's marginal cost of violence m_1 based on the state's decision. The state's payoff equals $-(v_1 + v_2) - \alpha(m_1 - \underline{m}_1)$. The modeling of the loss function is analogous to the previous case.

Proposition 6.7 *Let* $m_1^* \equiv \frac{m_2 + m_2\sqrt{2\sqrt{c}-c}}{2(1-\sqrt{c})^2}$ *and* $m_1^{**} \equiv \frac{1}{\sqrt{2\alpha}}$. *The following five cases describe the state's unique equilibrium action:*

1. *If $\underline{m}_1 > m_1^*$ and $\underline{m}_1 > m_1^{**}$, the state chooses $\underline{m}_1$.*
2. *If $\underline{m}_1 > m_1^*$ and $\underline{m}_1 < m_1^{**}$, the state chooses m_1^{**}.*
3. *If $\underline{m}_1 < m_1^*$ and $\underline{m}_1 > m_1^{**}$, the state chooses $\underline{m}_1$ if $-\frac{(1-\sqrt{c})^2}{m_2} > -\frac{1}{2m_1^*} - \alpha(m_1^* - \underline{m}_1)$ and m_1^* if $-\frac{(1-\sqrt{c})^2}{m_2} < -\frac{1}{2m_1^*} - \alpha(m_1^* - \underline{m}_1)$.*
4. *If $\underline{m}_1 < m_1^*$, $\underline{m}_1 < m_1^{**}$, and $m_1^{**} < m_1^*$, the state chooses according to the rule in (3).*
5. *If $\underline{m}_1 < m_1^*$, $\underline{m}_1 < m_1^{**}$, and $m_1^{**} > m_1^*$, the state chooses $\underline{m}_1$ if $-\frac{(1-\sqrt{c})^2}{m_2} < -\frac{1}{2m_1^{**}} - \alpha(m_1^{**} - \underline{m}_1)$ and m_1^{**} if $-\frac{(1-\sqrt{c})^2}{m_2} > -\frac{1}{2m_1^{**}} - \alpha(m_1^{**} - \underline{m}_1)$.*

Proof: To begin, we must restate Proposition 6.3 in terms of m_1. Recall from the proof that Group 1 prefers inducing entry if:

$$\frac{m_2}{4m_1} > 1 - m_1\frac{(1-\sqrt{c})^2}{m_2}$$

Analogously, Group 1 prefers cornering the market if the inequality is flipped and is indifferent when those two values are equal.

We can rewrite this inequality as:

$$4(1 - \sqrt{c})^2 m_1^2 - 4m_2 m_1 + m_2^2 > 0$$

Applying the quadratic formula yields the following roots:

$$\frac{m_2 \pm \sqrt{(4m_2)^2 - 4[4(1 - \sqrt{c})^2](m_2^2)}}{2[4(1 - \sqrt{c})]}$$

$$\frac{m_2 \pm m_2\sqrt{2\sqrt{c} - c}}{2(1 - \sqrt{c})^2}$$

Because the coefficient on the lead term of the polynomial is negative, Group 1 induces entry if $m_1 < \frac{m_2 - m_2\sqrt{2\sqrt{c}-c}}{2(1-\sqrt{c})^2}$. However, recall that Proposition 6.3 only applies if $m_1 > \frac{m_2}{2}$. The smaller root is therefore irrelevant if:

$$\frac{m_2 - m_2\sqrt{2\sqrt{c} - c}}{2(1 - \sqrt{c})^2} < \frac{m_2}{2}$$

$$c < 1$$

This is true. Thus, Group 1 corners the market up until m_1^* and induces competition afterward. As such, the state's choice is whether to keep m_1 small and allow for Group 1 to corner or force Group 1 to compete with Group 2 by raising m_1^*. In the cornered market case, equilibrium violence equals $\frac{(1-\sqrt{c})^2}{m_2}$. In the competitive market case, equilibrium violence equals $\frac{1}{2m_1}$. In this second case, the state's utility equals $-\frac{1}{2m_1} - \alpha(m_1 - \underline{m}_1)$. Thus, the first-order condition is:

$$\frac{1}{2m_1^2} - \alpha = 0 \quad m_1^{**} = \frac{1}{\sqrt{2\alpha}}$$

Without constraints, this is the best marginal cost the state can create if Group 1 induces competition.[55]

Now to the cases. First, suppose $\underline{m}_1 > m_1^*$ and $\underline{m}_1 > m_1^{**}$. This means that the minimum marginal cost is greater than the highest possible cost for the cornered market outcome and also higher than the state's optimal marginal cost within the competitive outcome. Consequently, the state can only induce a competitive equilibrium and any additional marginal costs only push the state further from its optimal m_1. In turn, the state chooses $\underline{m}_1$.

---

[55] It is a maximum because the second-order condition equals $-\frac{1}{m_1^3}$.

Second, suppose $\underline{m}_1 > m_1^*$ and $\underline{m}_1 > m_1^{**}$. The minimum marginal cost is still greater than the highest possible cost for the cornered market outcome but is now less than the state's optimal marginal cost within the competitive outcome. The first-order condition above showed that m_1^{**} is the state's optimal choice here.

Third, suppose $\underline{m}_1 < m_1^*$ and $\underline{m}_1 > m_1^{**}$. Now the minimum marginal cost is less than the highest possible cost for the cornered market outcome but is greater than the optimal marginal cost for a competitive outcome. Increasing m_1 within the cornered range cannot be optimal because it increases the state's effort without changing the total violence. Increasing past m_1^* cannot be optimal either because the state's utility for a competitive equilibrium strictly decreases past m_1^{**}. Therefore, the possible equilibrium amounts are $\underline{m}_1$ and m_1^*.

Although m_1^* is past the state's optimal competitive market marginal cost, it may still yet be optimal. This is because there is a discontinuous dropoff between violence in the cornered market case and in the competitive case. It is what guarantees that increasing m_1 leads to a decrease in violence even though it may switch the outcome from a cornered to a competitive market. Since Group 1 is indifferent between cornering the market and the competitive outcome at m_1^*, assume that it opts for the competitive market with probability 1 in this case.[56] In turn, the state prefers keeping the marginal cost at $\underline{m}_1$ if

$$-\frac{(1 - \sqrt{c})^2}{m_2} > -\frac{1}{2m_1^*} - \alpha(m_1^* - \underline{m}_1)$$

Analogously, the state shifts the marginal cost to m_1^* if the inequality is reversed.

Fourth, suppose $\underline{m}_1 < m_1^*$, $\underline{m}_1 < m_1^{**}$, and $m_1^{**} < m_1^*$. The minimum marginal cost remains less than the highest possible cost for the cornered market, but it is now less than the optimal marginal cost for a competitive outcome. Further, the optimal marginal cost for a competitive outcome falls in the region where Group 1 would corner the market. The state again has no incentive to change the marginal cost within the cornered market region. If it were to push to the competitive outcome, it would not want to increase the marginal cost past the cutpoint m_1^* because this is already beyond the optimal competitive marginal cost. Thus, the optimization problem is identical to the third case.

---

[56] In fact, for the same reasons as before, Group 1 must induce entry when indifferent in equilibrium.

Finally, suppose $\underline{m}_1 < m_1^*$, $\underline{m}_1 < m_1^{**}$, and $m_1^{**} > m_1^*$. This is the same as the fourth, except now the optimal competitive marginal cost is greater than the cutpoint that separates the outcomes. Thus, if the state wished to increase the marginal cost to induce a competitive market, it would select m_1^{**}. Keeping it at $\underline{m}_1$ is optimal if

$$-\frac{(1 - \sqrt{c})^2}{m_2} < -\frac{1}{2m_1^{**}} - \alpha(m_1^{**} - \underline{m}_1)$$

Analogously, the state shifts the marginal cost to m_1^{**} if the inequality is reversed.

Endogenous Defense

Finally, suppose that the state begins by choosing $\gamma \in [0, 1]$. The groups then play the same entry subgame except that only γ portion of each group's output is successful. This time, we model the state's cost of effort as any function that is continuous, differentiable everywhere, strictly decreasing in γ, and strictly convex. Let the state's objective function be $-\gamma(v_1 + v_2) - g(\gamma)$, where $g(1) = 0$, $g'(\gamma) > 0$ and $g''(\gamma) > 0$ for $\gamma \in [0, 1]$. Substantively, this means that defensive measures are not costly when none are taken ($\gamma = 1$), less defense is cheaper than more, and that each defensive measure is more expensive to implement than the previous one.

Proposition 6.8 *Let $V^* = v_1 + v_2$, where v_1 and v_2 equal the equilibrium violence levels given by Propositions 6.3 and 6.4. The following three cases describe the state's unique equilibrium action:*

1. *If $g'(\gamma) = -V^*$ for some $\gamma \in [0, 1]$, choose the γ that solves the equation. (The solution is unique.)*
2. *If $g'(\gamma) > -V^*$ for all $\gamma \in [0, 1]$, choose $\gamma = 1$.*
3. *If $g'(\gamma) < -V^*$ for all $\gamma \in [0, 1]$, choose $\gamma = 0$.*

If $\gamma > 0$, Groups 1 and 2 then play strategies according to Lemmas 6.3 and 6.4, which are not a function of γ. If $\gamma = 0$, the groups produce no violence.

The main text showed that the decisions from Groups 1 and 2 are not a function of γ. (The value of γ cancels out in the contest function.) The only exception is when $\gamma = 0$, as this creates a divide by 0 issue. The utilities for each group depend on how one defines the results of the contest when all effort equals 0, but this is inconsequential for the state's decision.

Because $v_1 + v_2$ is not a function of γ (unless $\gamma = 0$), we can rewrite $g(\gamma)$ as $V^* > 0$. The first-order condition is:

$$-V^* - g'(\gamma) = 0$$

If $g'(\gamma) = -V^*$ for some $\gamma \in [0, 1]$, the state picks this value. It must be unique because $-g'(\gamma)$ is strictly decreasing, and it is a maximum because the second derivative is $-g''(\gamma)$, which is negative.

If $g'(\gamma) > -V^*$ for all $\gamma \in [0, 1]$, then the solution for the optimization problem lies beyond $\gamma = 1$, and the state's utility is strictly increasing on the interval. It therefore chooses the maximum of that interval, $\gamma = 1$.

If $g'(\gamma) < -V^*$ for all $\gamma \in [0, 1]$, then the solution for the optimization problem lies before $\gamma = 0$, and the state's utility is strictly decreasing on the interval. It therefore chooses the minimum of that interval, $\gamma = 0$.

7

Conclusion

How does competition affect militant groups' decisions to use political violence? Existing research has explored how the presence of multiple groups forces each to exert effort and commit attacks, lest one of their rivals attract all of the attention. What this research has missed are some of the subtleties of competition. The gaps range from a clear articulation of whether the extra competition causes more violence at the individual or aggregate level to how government interventions affect the competition. Our book has sought to remedy those problems and has uncovered many interesting new results in the process.

In this concluding chapter, we tie together our narrative in a few ways. We begin with a review of the main results. Half of the results concern competition in isolation and the other half integrate the role of the target government and the broader population. Now operating in hindsight, the focus turns to how these results build together into a more comprehensive outbidding framework. With this new appreciation for competition, we then discuss avenues for future research and some primary takeaways for policymakers who wish to apply our findings.

COMPETITION PROMOTES POLITICAL VIOLENCE

Our first major contribution to the literature on outbidding was to build microfoundations for the theory. We started by making some sensible assumptions about group competition. Groups are strategic in their allocations of violence. Their primary objective is to maintain operational capacity, and this means acquiring what they can from a pool of limited resources. They pull in those resources – funds, recruits, and labor – by using violent attacks as a form of advertisement. More violence means greater brand awareness but also has diminishing marginal returns. In addition, one group's violence output hurts another group's ability to obtain resources. Competition is not winner-takes-all, but rather, the market can support many groups simultaneously, albeit at different levels. The drawback to violence is that it is costly and groups cannot recover those costs once paid.

These features of militant group competition gave us a clear path toward formalizing the incentives. Contest models from economics and political science capture all of these key features. This is fitting. After all, contest models originally analyzed how firms use advertisements to capture marketshare in traditional business environments. Outbidding theory has always treated militant organizations as oligarchs competing in the realm of violence. As such, the contest structure is a natural way to analyze outbidding incentives.

The contest model revealed two interesting properties of militant competition. First, total violence increases as the number of groups increases. This is a reassuring result for the existing outbidding literature. Outbidding theory has long held that additional groups inspire competition and force groups to output violence to distinguish themselves from the competition. Our model confirms this incentive, at least to some degree. Formalizing the incentives clarifies how groups compete over rents in the form of donations and labor sympathetic to the cause. In classic oligopoly theory, free from fully competitive markets, a handful of firms can cut production, cause an increase in prices, and enjoy the corresponding rents.

The same logic applies in our model. With only a couple of competitors, total violence stays low. The two groups therefore benefit from the relatively low total production and the relatively large share of the goods they split. Although each group can produce more violence and acquire more resources, the marginal additional gain is small because the group is already capturing so much. However, adding many competitors raises overall violence outputs. But this is to the detriment of the groups, as all the extra effort funnels those profits out of the market.

Despite the presence of existing outbidding theory's central expectation, the model also produces a new insight. Violence increases overall, but this is not the consequence of each group producing more violence when another competitor hits the market. Each group instead adjusts its violence output downward with the debut of a new group. However, consistent with the fact that more competition drives down profits, the new group more than covers the lost quantity of violence. As such, we observe the outbidding effect at the *aggregate* level, not the individual level.

We found evidence of both of these predictions in the data. In Chapter 3, we presented evidence that as the number of terrorist organizations increases in a country, that country will experience greater amounts of terrorist attacks. We then examined the process by estimating the average group behavior. The results demonstrated that increasing group numbers are significantly associated with decreasing average numbers of attacks. This effect is evident whether analyzing terrorist organizations or rebel organizations. We also noted that the empirical analysis is inherently biased against our hypothesis and, therefore, the results reported are likely conservative estimates of the actual relationship.

INTERVENTIONS REQUIRE CAREFUL THOUGHT

The second major contribution to the literature on outbidding was to consider how interventions by governments and international organizations impact competition. Existing research on terrorism sees governments and the various policy levers they can use as key determinants of the quantity of violence actually produced. However, the outbidding literature has mostly been quiet on this subject thus far. Building a baseline model of competition allowed us to extend the conversation on a variety of fronts. The key takeaway is that governments can influence the outbidding process, but they must exercise caution: the wrong intervention can be unhelpful or even counterproductive.

As a first cut, we looked into government enforcement. Militant groups use outbidding violence as a recruitment tool to secure funds and labor. If the government can exert effort to intercept that money and those people, it ought to temper each group's desire to pay costs to attract a fleetingly small quantity of resources. In fact, we discovered that such enforcement is a *triple* whammy to competition. As a first-order effect, enforcement stops some portion of the prize from reaching its beneficiaries. As a second-order effect, marginal contributors believe their donations are not worth the risk and therefore pull them altogether. Finally, as a third-order effect, groups recognize that the first two effects will reduce the pool of resources and correspondingly limit their violence production. All told, we predict that outbidding is conditional. The incentives for total violence increase but do so at a reduced rate in states with a strong ability to enforce laws. Measuring the ease of enforcement through bureaucratic quality, political reach, and regime durability, we presented evidence of this conditional effect in Chapter 4. The addition of new terrorist groups can dramatically increase the expected amount of terrorism a state experiences when the costs of state enforcement are high.

We also investigated how governments can influence political violence by making concessions to the disaffected parties. An audience's willingness to support violence depends on their anger at the target of that violence. If a state acts in a conciliatory manner and quells that anger, citizens have little reason to pay money or volunteer their time to assist a cause they no longer agree with. But a state that ignores those concerns can find itself facing a large pool of willing contributors. We verified that the state's decision impacts the outbidding process. Greater policy demands indeed cause groups to commit more violence. But this relationship yielded an unexpected finding. Because more groups implies more competition and more violence, greater competition has a deterrent effect. Recognizing that making expansive demands would trigger a painful backlash, the state moderates its policy choice. Due to the well of support drying up, we observe little violence in those cases despite the *potential* for massive violence. In turn, the empirical expectation for outbidding may not be as straightforward as the classic theory predicts.

The final series of interventions we considered occurred in an environment where an incumbent group considers whether to keep a rival from entering the market. In that framework, the incumbent sometimes overproduces violence to deter entry. After all, paying the startup costs to join the fray looks less attractive if it is near-impossible to put a dent in the industry leader. But this overproduction hurts the target of that violence and leads to some counterintuitive implications for how to solve the problem. Markets are easier to corner when the pool of resources is small and the costs of entry are large. As such, interventions to reduce grievances or increase the costs of entry can backfire and cause violence to rise. The target state can hammer the incumbent group's ability to produce violence to stop the overproduction. But a half-measure still causes the incumbent to maintain the same level of violence, and any effective intervention *must* cause another group to rise from the ashes. Balanced defensive measures absorb some of the punishment. Nevertheless, coordinating defensive efforts to stop attacks from would-be challengers again incentivizes the predatory cornering behavior. Increasing security against vectors preferred by the incumbent group can work but also requires substantial investments to see any effect. It must also result in the challenger stepping in to commit some attacks.

IMPLICATIONS FOR FUTURE RESEARCH

We view the results presented here as a first step in formalizing, quantifying, and appreciating some of the more subtle nuances that outbidding theory has to offer. Indeed, Chapters 2 and 3 were meant to introduce a basic structure of strategic competition between groups. The chapters afterward expanded our understanding by exploring some deeper challenges that both governments and militant groups must face.

Even with this approach in mind, our study has not completely modeled all the strategic considerations that these actors face. Fortunately, the framework we have developed generates a useful starting point for thinking about some of the deeper issues. We therefore describe a few promising avenues for future research below.

Group elimination. Although Chapter 6 focused on how an existing group might deter a new group from forming, we have not given full thought to what happens when existing groups disappear. A naïve interpretation of Chapter 2's main comparative static on the number of groups would indicate a clear benefit from the government's perspective. After all, one fewer group means a little less competition and therefore lower violence overall. Matching this, the Assad regime has made the elimination of as many groups as possible a central goal (Arsu, 2013). But this is a claim based on a static game without deeper considerations. The later chapters of this book suggest caution in thinking about how those incentives work once we move past one of the model's assumptions.

Indeed, the Syrian Civil War helps illustrate a dynamic about group removal that our models do not explain. By one count, within two years of the initial protests in Daraa, there were more than 1,000 non-state organizations waging political violence ("Guide to the Syrian rebels," 2013). The vast majority of these groups, of course, barely measured on the Richter scale. Very few of them gained any kind of notoriety and it was a foregone conclusion that many of these groups would not survive. As in the traditional marketplace, startups are less likely to survive, particularly when they are entering an already-crowded field (Bates, 1995). And also like the marketplace, organizations are more likely to fail as one or two competitors consolidate the field (McGee and Shook, 2000).

This is precisely what happened in Syria. The myriad of non-state organizations quickly shrank as power was consolidated by a few key actors, namely ISIS and Jabhat al-Nusra (JN). And yet the peak of violence in the conflict occurred not during the rapid proliferation of groups in 2013, but during later phases of the conflict when a smaller number of groups had monopolized the market. More than 75,000 deaths – up to 20 percent of all deaths in the conflict through 2018 – occurred in a single year according to one estimate ("76021 people killed in Syria in 2014," 2015). And as we discussed in the introduction to the book, much of the violence during this time can be classified as competitive violence, with JN, ISIS, and their affiliates attacking each other and their supporters in an effort to establish dominance over the other groups. But the elimination of groups allowed the major players to consolidate their power even more quickly. This runs contrary to both Chapter 2's central comparative static and the Assad regime's hope.

One limitation of our research that may help explain the disconnect is our focus on group numbers and competitive dynamics. This, of course, was an intentional feature of our research design, so we could focus on competition's theoretical and empirical implications. But it was not a declaration that competition is the only effect of an increased number of groups. Indeed, having multiple groups could also mean an inefficient division of capital, an inefficient division of labor, more effort spent on fighting within the groups, and a greater focus on short-term planning at the expense of long-term goals. All of these could reasonably cause a decline in aggregate violence if their net effect exceeds competition's sway on violence dynamics. Future research ought to consider these mechanisms with greater theoretical and empirical analysis and also consider how outbidding interplays with them.

Cooperation among groups. Our research has investigated how terrorist groups compete with one another over limited resources. But a clear implication we have not yet investigated is how the potential for competition incentivizes cooperation. After all, from the groups' perspective, effort is inefficient. All parties would improve their payoffs if they reduced their violence outputs by some percentage, allowing them to capture the same portion of the goods but exert less effort to do so. However, at least one actor would want to take advantage of the situation, increase their output, and acquire more than it otherwise should.

Given that these incentives form a prisoner's dilemma with n players, a clear solution presents itself. The shadow of the future could sustain cooperative behavior today and into the future (Axelrod, 1984). Future research could investigate why we do not observe more cooperation among groups.[1]

---

[1] Alternatively, future research could show that this premise is incorrect. Perhaps militant groups cooperate a great deal and our relative baseline is just skewed.

In a pure prisoner's dilemma framework, two obstacles seem to stand in the way of cooperation. First, cooperation requires actors to have long time horizons; otherwise, they prefer defecting to take the short-term temptation payoff and suffering the consequences later to the long-term cooperative payoff every period. Outside pressures create a barrier here. The possibility that a target state may eradicate any number of terrorist groups in short order forces those groups to value the short term over the long term. Beyond that, the inherent structure of resource allocations may make the temptation payoff too irresistible. Suppose capturing a disproportionate segment of the audience today eliminates any possibility that other groups can make up the difference in a later period of time. Then no groups would want to sustain cooperation; each would look to defect at a moment's notice.

A second problem with cooperation in the prisoner's dilemma framework is a matter of scope. Prisoner's dilemma situations are easier to manage with only a couple of actors. In contrast, as we discussed earlier, some outbidding cases involve dozens of actors. Even under less extreme circumstances, a handful of competing groups is common. A similar problem exists in interstate relations. However, countries can form international organizations to resolve those problems (Keohane, 1984). Because militant groups exist outside the law, they do not have the same luxury. In turn, they must rely on spontaneous monitoring and enforcement mechanisms, neither of which would seem to be effective in this domain.

Instead of traditional prisoner's dilemma cooperation, groups seem to have more luck with alliance relationships. Indeed, alliances between otherwise competing groups is commonplace. During the Ethiopian Civil War, for instance, a number of groups with disparate ideologies formed alliances with one another. Very different groups like the Oromo Liberation Front and the Tigrayan People's Liberation Front cooperated with one another and some of the groups even merged into larger umbrella organizations.

Future research could explore why groups choose to align themselves in this manner. Our core argument suggests one answer. The more groups that exist, the fewer rents the groups can collectively share. Removing one group from the fold collectively moves the remaining groups closer to a monopoly and the rent-seeking capability that comes with it. Another answer, hinted at in the discussion of group elimination, is that merging allows the new group to perform better on some dimension than its constituent parts could have done on their own. In effect, an alliance between two groups may just shore up each other's weaknesses.

Violence as a rent-seeking activity. By standard models of conflict, violence is inefficient. Rather than fight, the key players could divide the good they would expect to receive through that process but by peaceful means. Because conflict is costly, all would be better off as a result (Fearon, 1995).

Our model sympathizes with this idea to some degree but also breaks from the traditional framework in a key way. On one hand, conflict among the groups is inefficient. As just described, it is a prisoner's dilemma with n groups, all of whom would fare better if they could each proportionally cut their violence outputs. But competition between groups occurs in the shadow of some broader conflict with a third party that drives the audience to want to support one of the groups in the first place. From that perspective, violence is a rent-seeking activity. Militant groups act as businesses, wishing to turn a profit on their investments in violence. The greater the conflict with the third party, the more profits they can gain.

This has a nice analogue in the crisis bargaining literature. Expanding outside the unitary actor assumption, leaders may fight or prolong wars for their own personal benefit (Chiozza and Goemans, 2004; Goemans, 2000). Creating conflict against a third party allows the leaders of militant groups to enjoy similar sorts of benefits. This suggests the need for further research into how the leadership structure within terrorist groups operates, how they divide the spoils internally, and under what conditions leaders can secure more of the rents. Understanding these questions could yield new testable implications. It may also yield useful recommendations for policymakers who might want to sabotage the process.

Expanding the market. Given that outbidding violence is a rent-seeking activity, it would seem that the actors have an incentive to expand the marketplace. In fact, many of our formal results corroborate this. Each group's utility is proportional to the size of the market. As the pool of resources expands, so does each party's payoff. So too, of course, does the quantity of violence and therefore the costs paid to do that damage. But even accounting for those payments, the groups are still happier with a larger potential audience.

Chapters 4, 5, and 6 explored how adjusting the size of the market changes the interaction. But they all came from the perspective of the government or international organizations. That is, the government could tweak enforcement or alter grievances to expand or minimize the number of people wishing to support an organization. But the government does not have a monopoly on adjusting that market. In fact, militant groups exert effort to do the same. One way to do this is through propaganda that portrays the target in a negative light. Another option is provocation, seeking to bait the target into taking actions that only swell the ranks of the supporters (Crenshaw, 1981; Kydd and Walter, 2006; Spaniel, 2019). Researchers have investigated both competition and expansion in separate contexts, but future work ought to consider integrating these components together.

Indeed, although expansion appears to be a useful tool, competition creates a clear hurdle. Building larger markets is a public goods problem. Any organization that invests in growing the market expands the pie for itself but also for everyone else. Knowing this, a group will only invest in expanding the market until its own marginal benefit equals its marginal cost. From the militant groups' perspectives, this is socially inefficient: each would be better off allocating more to expanding the public good. This means that the target benefits from competition to some degree, as competition breeds an underprovision in the audience for political violence.

Thinking about the size of the pie from a group's perspective also suggests another reason that terrorist groups might consider merging. When competition would be most fierce, targets become reticent to take actions that swell the ranks of supporters. As such, removing a single group can convince the target to go from taking a completely conservative approach to capturing all of a controversial policy. Every militant group's utility increases here because the pie goes from nothing to something substantial. In turn, future research ought to think about the second-order consequences of group removal on other actors' decisions.

Measurement. Capturing the strategic environment means accounting for competition dynamics in our empirical models. As such, our discussion throughout the book has frequently focused on measurement challenges. We have identified limitations in previous measurement schemes, we have proposed new measurements, and we have speculated on possibilities when measures are not currently available. Large-n quantitative analysis of militant group competition focused initially on measuring state-level factors. The centerpiece of the analysis by Chenoweth (2010) – one of the pioneering quantitative studies on the subject – used political institutions as a proxy for the competitive environment among non-state actors. As with many subjects of interest to the social sciences, measurement has continually improved over time. Some of the subsequent innovations included counting the number of active groups, an approach that we rely on in this book. Nemeth (2014), on the other hand, takes the measurement a step further by creating estimates of "market share" based on the number of active groups within a particular ideological category.

Yet even these relatively newer studies do not capture specific, observable competition between militant groups. These measures all assume that if there are more active groups – within a state or within an ideological field – then more competition is occurring. And yet many groups form alliances and work together, demonstrating little if any active competition. Fortunately, a new series of studies and data collection efforts has begun capturing observable instances of rivalry and competitive behavior between groups (Conrad, Greene, and Phillips, 2018, 2019). While the data are still in the early development stage, such projects will allow researchers to create measures of *actual* competition, rather than *potential* competition. We therefore consider these efforts to be an important indicator of progress in the study of militant group competition, and of competition in general.

But our analysis has also yielded insights regarding the measurement of concepts beyond rivalry and competition. Our work has suggested that there are other areas that scholars may wish to focus on with respect to improving measurement quality. One common implication that has emerged from our models (and, indeed, from previous analysis on terrorism) is the heterogeneous nature of the civilian population that is the ostensible audience for terrorist violence (and counterterrorism responses). Some populations may be more receptive to the competitive violence perpetrated by terrorist organizations. As such, empirically capturing the full range of strategic actors also means capturing *variations* among the same category of actor.

The importance of modeling this kind of variation was demonstrated most clearly in Chapter 5. In that discussion, we demonstrated that a population's overall sensitivity to government encroachment may vary depending on the societal context. The resulting decisions of the terrorist organizations and the government, then, may depend on this initial level of receptiveness. In our model, we denoted this characteristic of the population with the parameter λ and concluded that the parameter needs to be sufficiently large to produce the hypothesized effect of competition on political violence. But this insight also extends to future empirical analysis of competitive behavior. Allowing the population's decision-making process to vary theoretically also means that we should allow this process to vary empirically. Future analysis could focus on how to operationalize λ, an issue beyond the scope of this book. Once an acceptable measure of λ is selected, empirical analysis of the strategic dynamics can be refined even further. For instance, scholars might limit their analysis only to those cases where λ is sufficiently large, or, alternatively, they may address research questions in cases where it is *not* large enough. While the basic outbidding expectations may not hold in such cases, we may see other observable forms of competition and violence.

Some scholars have empirically modeled a similar concept – the level of acceptance of political violence among a population. Like the population's sensitivity to government repression, its acceptance of violence can vary from one context to another. These studies measure the concept by creating an index involving a number of existing measures such as crime rates (Mullins and Young, 2012; Nemeth, 2014). But this better proxies overall receptiveness, not receptiveness as a function of government policies. As an alternative, we have suggested that the concept might be usefully captured through traditional survey mechanisms.

Of course, every measurement decision involves tradeoffs. Although surveys may be the most direct way of measuring a society's acceptance of violence, *dynamic* survey measurements are often difficult to come by and difficult to implement. For instance, it would be interesting and useful to examine temporal variation in the acceptance of violence from the beginning of the Syrian Civil War until today. But doing so would involve more than just asking respondents whether they think political violence is acceptable. It would also ideally involve asking respondents whether they would begin/stop/continue supporting groups like Jabhat al-Nusra if the Assad government changed its policies. Although this kind of questioning would be the "right" way to measure the concept of interest, it potentially creates new problems because it involves the problematic use of counterfactuals. Ultimately, the best empirical analysis should closely resemble the best theoretical models of competitive violence. It should account for both the *preferences* and *behavior* of the militant groups themselves, the target audience, and the government. Only with all of these aspects incorporated into the analysis can we approach a complete understanding of political violence.

Measurement in all of these respects will also likely benefit from an increased focus on microfoundations. As we have discussed previously, measurement thus far has relied heavily on macro-level information, typically collected at the country level. But the concept of societal acceptance of violence is a good example of why such measures may not be appropriate for many of the research questions that we want to address. A society's acceptance of violence, its support for terrorist groups, the grievances behind this support, the population's perception of the government, and many other key concepts are, at their root, micro-level processes. As such, they should be measured at the individual level where possible. In general, we conclude that whenever our empirical analysis can avoid the problem of overaggregation we will have more confidence in the results. Overaggregation, in fact, may be the central explanation for the mixed findings in past literature. Again, some ongoing data collection efforts are seeking to address this issue directly by collecting more information at the appropriate level of analysis. And yet, despite increased awareness of the problem and a concerted effort by some scholars to improve measurement and research design, such efforts are always easier said than done.

Interdisciplinary avenues. The need to examine competition and political violence from a more micro-level perspective suggests one important area of opportunity for such research. Insomuch as other disciplines beyond political science have a grasp on such processes, interdisciplinary research may assist with the completion of the puzzle. As we discussed in the introduction to this book, other fields have made much more significant advancements in the understanding of human competition. Those who study the effect of competition on political violence have lagged behind these other fields (and even other subfields within political science) in understanding competition and its correlates. Other disciplines such as psychology, economics, and business have produced a much greater depth and breadth of research on the subject of competition in various aspects of human life. Given that many of these fields examine individual- and organization-level behavior, they have also produced plenty of insights about the research design process. Political scientists, and scholars of political violence in particular, would likely benefit from increased collaboration across disciplinary boundaries.

To wit, a recent experiment-based study in *Psychological Science* demonstrates the surprising relevance of such an approach. The study links the negative individual-level effects of broad political and economic inequality (such as interpersonal conflict and risk-taking behavior) to local patterns of competition. The study concludes that the effect of inequality on individual-level behavior is most acute among neighbors, who may be seen as direct competitors (Krupp and Cook, 2018). An interesting implication of this argument is that it may explain the aggregate decline in crime over the last few decades. The author concludes that globalization has distributed economic inequality *globally*, so that people are now more likely to compete with someone on the other side of the world rather than their own neighbors. This, in turn, reduces individual incentives to engage in crime. Since proximity moderates the influence of competition, "offshoring" competition reduces such incentives. This is exactly the kind of research that could be useful to political scientists – microfoundational but with clear implications for state and even international-level policies.

IMPLICATIONS FOR POLICYMAKERS

Although our work primarily aims to make an impact among researchers of political violence, it also has important implications for policymakers. After all, terrorism and political violence have been at the forefront of both foreign and domestic policies within the West and the Middle East since the September 11 attacks. Competition has played an integral role on many of these fronts, including the rivalry between al-Qaeda and ISIS during the latter's formative years and the incredible number of militant groups in Syria that followed. Understanding how these groups compete is the first step in understanding how to manipulate their incentives.

We have correspondingly included ample discussion of policy implications throughout the book. This included Chapter 2's discussion of how removing each additional group brings increasingly higher rewards to the target government. The discussion extended into Chapter 4, with a conversation on the first-order, second-order, and third-order benefits of greater enforcement capabilities. Chapter 5 worked toward this by noting that governments need to consider how their substantive policies create the marketplace for terrorism. And Chapter 6 had the policy discussion center stage in understanding how a variety of policy levers alter competitive dynamics in market entry decisions.

Nevertheless, referring back to the previous six chapters and thinking through the lessons as a whole provides new perspective on what policymakers can gain from our study of outbidding. We cover three such topics below.

There is no silver bullet solution to terrorism. In a more convenient world, we would provide some straightforward recommendations on how to counter terrorism and recruitment into extremist organizations.

Policymakers would then implement those solutions and reap the benefits. The only difficult decision would be calculating how much to invest before the marginal returns would no longer justify the marginal expense. Unfortunately, many of our results urge caution in suggesting clear cut responses to terrorism. In some cases, certain policy levers may work effectively. But in other cases they may be a waste of resources or even backfire.

The results on grievances provide the clearest example of the problem. When the number of competing groups is static, our models in Chapter 2 and Chapter 5 provided an unambiguous recommendation. Greater grievances imply larger pies to fight over. Holding fixed policy demands, this in turn causes violence to rise proportionally. But Chapter 6 showed that such a recommendation is not universal. When an incumbent group wants to deter another from entering the market, decreasing the potential contributions has a perverse effect. With the market smaller, it becomes easier for the incumbent group to corner the market by inflating its own violence output. Thus, haphazard changes to grievances can backfire.

Unexpected implications like this give us greater pause on some of the other implications. The positive results regarding enforcement in Chapter 4 do not generalize either. After all, enforcement is just a reduction of the pie, which would incentivize cornering the market to deter new groups from entering. Even the most positive finding in this book – that balanced defensive measures cleanly mitigate violence – requires a closer look. As the previous section noted, we have only investigated a few of the incentives the outbidding could provide. We should be cautious that another set of circumstances, still yet unexplored, would produce contrary implications.

In short, there is no substitute for qualitative considerations of any particular case at hand. Policymakers need to understand which scope conditions are most prominent before applying any of the lessons of this book. This includes whether competitive outbidding is at issue at all. If it is, they also need to think about whether other concerns from outside the book's scope are prominent and work through how manipulations to the marketplace might interact with those incentives.

Good solutions do not imply good results. Even if a particular case matches the scope conditions of one of our models, the policy recommendations we gave do not guarantee success. Indeed, we assumed frictionless implementation of any of these solutions. This was for good reason. From a theoretical perspective, we want to know whether certain policy levers have the intended effect. Answering that question requires a vacuum and we obtained that vacuum with some clean-cut models. This has a substantial advantage over cases of actual implementation because we can rule out any deleterious effects as a consequence of shoddy implementation (Myerson, 1999, 1069).

However, taking that step demands that we think twice before using any of those policy levers. We already noted in Chapter 6 that offensive measures can hamstring existing organizations and lead to less violence, at least as long as the state implements those measures with enough force. But existing research on blowback and provocation indicates that reckless implementation of such operations can lure more individuals to support an organization. Imperfections like this do not doom the strategies that states may adopt. But states should nevertheless exercise caution in how they implement solutions, at least insofar as such oversight is possible and economically feasible.

The beginning of the Syrian Civil War helps illustrate the problem with implementation. In the very early days – before the situation had turned into full-blown civil conflict – Kurdish opposition leader Mashaal Tammo was killed. Although responsibility for Tammo's death was unclear – he was killed by masked assailants in his own apartment – regime forces were widely suspected to be behind the killing. As a result, when his funeral was held in the city of Qamlishi, the event attracted more than 50,000 people. The funeral proceedings quickly evolved into a large-scale anti-regime protest, which drew the attention of security forces. At least two people were killed by soldiers who fired on the procession (Karouny, 2011). The attack followed a similar incident that occurred just one day earlier in which security forces opened fire on a funeral procession in the Damascus suburb of Douma. As is typical in these kinds of situations, the violence used against protesters was frequently depicted by the government as spontaneous and not reflecting a strategic, top-down decision. Whether spontaneous or not, the Assad regime was clearly interested in addressing dissent wherever it might pop up. The first few months of the crisis, then, saw the regime trying a variety of repressive tactics to clamp down on the growing unrest in the country.

But the proliferation of violence against opposition activists and protesters led to unintended consequences. Particularly harsh responses, such as an alleged massacre of at least 350 civilians by regime forces in Daraya only fueled the dissent ("Assad slams anti-Syria 'conspiracy' after massacre claims," 2012). Further, these kinds of heavy-handed responses were becoming increasingly visible to both domestic and international audiences, delivering publicity victories for the anti-regime forces. As a result, the number of people (both Syrians and foreigners) willing to join the fight against the Assad government grew rapidly as 2012 came to a close. The increase in the number of people wishing to participate, in turn, led to a dramatic proliferation in the number of formal organizations opposed to the regime.

Another warning – and one that bleeds into suggestions for future research – is that all of our models have operated under complete information. That is, all actors knew each other's beliefs, capabilities, and intentions throughout each interaction. This is a strong assumption but a sensible one given the Myerson (1999) research design strategy. It has told us that the counterintuitive effects we observe are not the result of some rational miscalculation by the players. In practice, however, both militant groups and governments might not know key pieces of information that determine the best course of action. For example, a government might believe that tweaking its military strategy would result in higher marginal costs of violence for groups at a low grievance tradeoff. But such an action might miscalculate the public's general affinity to contribute, resulting in an offsetting gain in the overall pie. Policymakers need to take into account their uncertainties in formulating counterterrorism strategies, and future research could consider such informational asymmetries in an outbidding framework.

Exercise caution in analyzing cases of political violence. Lucas (1976) warns against using empirical data to make policy adjustments without an underlying theoretical model to understand the data-generating process. For example, while we have envisioned political violence as a strategic decision by a group's leadership, some attacks may be generated via alternative processes, such as principal–agency problems. Such organizational dynamics may explain why so many terrorist attacks are unclaimed (Abrahms and Conrad, 2017). The two explanations, however, are not mutually exclusive and so it is important for policymakers to understand a full range of conditions before prescribing a solution. We further caution policymakers in two respects. First, the central empirical result in our work and many prior analyses of outbidding is that areas with more active groups see more overall violence. However, Chapter 5 showed that the data-generating processes behind some cases can be misleading. It might be tempting to point to cases where groups are numerous and yet little violence occurs as evidence that competition concerns are overblown. This might be the evidence that convinces policymakers to test the waters on similar fronts. Alternatively, the trends may persuade an actor to believe that destroying a group can only depress violence rates. But Chapter 5's model noted that the *potential* for violence can cause it to never arise. Indeed, that potential is precisely why the would-be target takes actions to mitigate the damage. This plays into a similar lesson from before: it is unwise to make policy decisions without a full appreciation of the incentives at play in any given case.

Chapter 6 provided a series of results that further demonstrated the need to understand data-generating processes. Strategic states think through the incentives at play and do not take actions that cause active harm. Decreasing grievances, increasing barriers of entry, and erecting better defenses against the attack vectors of a would-be entrant can all backfire. In addition, increasing an existing group's marginal cost of violence or implementing defensive measures against that existing group can also have no effect. But we would not expect to observe widespread evidence of these measures backfiring or being ineffective – in cases where they would be, the state simply chooses to maintain the status quo. From a quantitative perspective, this means we should exercise caution in interpreting empirical results that suggest universal effectiveness. For example, just because there is large-n evidence that reducing grievances reduces terrorism does not imply that states should recklessly implement that strategy.

A FINAL WORD

Ultimately, we agree with the assessment that competition is one of the central motivators of human behavior. We have demonstrated that it is an important ingredient in understanding why political violence happens, who commits it, and how it can be managed. Given the tragic consequences of such violence, academics and policymakers should devote more energy and resources to understanding it.

Bibliography

"4 killed in National Socialist Council of Nagaland factional clash." 2012. *Times of India*, June 10.

"76021 people killed in Syria in 2014." 2015. Syrian Observatory for Human Rights, January 1.

Abeyratne, Sirimal. 2004. "Economic roots of political conflict: The case of Sri Lanka." *The World Economy* 27(8): 1295–1314.

Abrahms, Max. 2006. "Why terrorism does not work." *International Security* 31(2): 42–78.

Abrahms, Max. 2020. "Denying to win: How image-savvy militant leaders respond when operatives harm civilians." *Journal of Strategic Studies* 43(1): 47–73.

Abrahms, Max and Justin Conrad. 2017. "The strategic logic of credit claiming: A new theory for anonymous terrorist attacks." *Security Studies* 26(2): 279–304.

Ahanthem, Chitra. 2014. "The road to peace in Manipur." *Institute of Peace and Conflict Studies Special Report* 156: 111–133.

Alesina, Alberto, Arnaud Devleeschauwer, William Easterly, Sergio Kurlat, and Romain Wacziarg. 2003. "Fractionalization." *Journal of Economic Growth* 8: 155–194.

Allansson, Marie, Erik Melander, and Lotta Themnér. 2017. "Organized violence, 1989–2016." *Journal of Peace Research* 54(4): 574–587.

Al-Zawahiri, Ayman. 2013. "Untitled statement." *Al-Fajr Media*, May 23.

Amabile, Teresa M. 1982. "Children's artistic creativity: Detrimental effects of competition in a field setting." *Personality and Social Psychology Bulletin* 8(3): 573–578.

Amegashie, J. Atsu. 2006. "A contest success function with a tractable noise parameter." *Public Choice* 126(1): 135–144.

"ANVC(B) ask GNLA to surrender 'before time runs out'." 2012. *Meghalaya Times*, April 13.

"ANVC(B) boldly claims of attacking GNLA camp." 2013. *Meghalaya Times*, November 13.

"ANVC(B)'s irrational taxes taking toll on bus fares: Sohan." 2012. *Meghalaya Times*, June 10.

Araj, Bader. 2008. "Harsh state repression as a cause of suicide bombing: The case of the Palestinian–Israeli conflict." *Studies in Conflict & Terrorism* 31(4): 284–303.

Arce, Daniel G. and Todd Sandler. 2005. "Counterterrorism: A game-theoretic analysis." *Journal of Conflict Resolution* 49(2): 183–200.

Arjona, Ana. 2016. *Rebelocracy*. New York: Cambridge University Press.

Arsu, Sebnem. 2013. "Assad says he may seek re-election." *New York Times*, October 5.

Asal, Victor, Justin Conrad, and Peter White. 2014. "Going abroad: Transnational solicitation and contention by ethnopolitical organizations." *International Organization* 68(4): 945–978.

Asal, Victor and R. Karl Rethemeyer. 2008. "The nature of the beast: Organizational structures and the lethality of terrorist attacks." *Journal of Politics* 70(2): 437–449.

"Assad says de-escalation zones chance for rebels to 'reconcile'." 2017. *Reuters*, May 11.

"Assad slams anti-Syria 'conspiracy' after massacre claims." 2012. *Express Tribune*, August 27.

Axelrod, Robert. 1984. *The Evolution of Cooperation*. New York: Basic Books.

Azam, Jean-Paul. 2005. "Suicide-bombing as inter-generational investment." *Public Choice* 122(1–2): 177–198.

Azam, Jean-Paul and Véronique Thelen. 2008. "The roles of foreign aid and education in the war on terror." *Public Choice* 135(3–4): 375–397.

Bacon, Tricia. 2018. *Why Terrorist Groups Form International Alliances*. Philadelphia: University of Pennsylvania Press.

Baik, Kyung Hwan. 1998. "Difference-form contest success functions and effort levels in contests." *European Journal of Political Economy* 14(4): 685–701.

Bakke, Kristin M., Kathleen Gallagher Cunningham, and Lee J. M. Seymour. 2012. "A plague of initials: Fragmentation, cohesion, and infighting in civil wars." *Perspectives on Politics* 10(2): 265–283.

"Bashar al-Assad: Everything on table in Astana talks." 2017. *Reuters*, January 9.

Basit, Abdul. 2016. "Iran–Taliban cooperation: New dimension in Afghan conflict?" *RSIS Commentary* 1(132).

Bates, Timothy. 1995. "Analysis of survival rates among franchise and independent small business startups." *Journal of Small Business Management* 33(2): 26.

Bengtsson, Maria and Sören Kock. 1999. "Cooperation and competition in relationships between competitors in business networks." *Journal of Business & Industrial Marketing* 14(3): 178–194.

Benmelech, Efraim, Claude Berrebi, and Esteban F. Klor. 2014. "Counter-suicide-terrorism: Evidence from house demolitions." *Journal of Politics* 77(1): 27–43.

Berger, J. M. 2017. "Countering Islamic State messaging through linkage-based analysis." *The International Centre for Counter-Terrorism – The Hague* 8(2): 1–24.

Berman, Eli and David Laitin. 2005. "Hard targets: Theory and evidence on suicide attacks." Technical report, National Bureau of Economic Research.

Berman, Eli and David D. Laitin. 2008. "Religion, terrorism and public goods: Testing the club model." *Journal of Public Economics* 92(10–11): 1942–1967.

Bils, Peter and William Spaniel. 2017. "Policy bargaining and militarized conflict." *Journal of Theoretical Politics* 29(4): 647–678.

bin Laden, Osama. 1996. "Declaration of war against the Americans occupying the Land of the Two Holy Places," www.libraryofsocialscience .com/assets/pdf/Bin-Laden-1996-declaration-of-war-against-the-americans.pdf.

Blankenship, Brian. 2016. "When do states take the bait? State capacity and the provocation logic of terrorism." *Journal of Conflict Resolution* 62(2): 381-409.

Blomberg, S. Brock, Gregory D. Hess, and Akila Weerapana. 2004. "Economic conditions and terrorism." *European Journal of Political Economy* 20(2): 463–478.

Blomberg, S. Brock, Khusrav Gaibulloev, and Todd Sandler. 2011. "Terrorist group survival: Ideology, tactics, and base of operations." *Public Choice* 149(3–4): 441–463.

Bloom, Mia M. 2004. "Palestinian suicide bombing: Public support, market share, and outbidding." *Political Science Quarterly* 119(1): 61–88.

Bloom, Mia. 2005. *Dying to Kill: The Allure of Suicide Bombing*. New York: Columbia University Press.

Brambor, Thomas, William Clark, and Matt Golder. 2006. "Understanding interaction models: Improving empirical analyses." *Political Analysis* 14(1): 63–82.

Brancati, Dawn. 2006. "Decentralization: Fueling the fire or dampening the flames of ethnic conflict and secessionism?" *International Organization* 60(3): 651–685.

"Brawl among Naga militants kills 6." 2012. *Meghalaya Times*, June 21.

Brym, Robert J. and Bader Araj. 2006. "Suicide bombing as strategy and interaction: The case of the Second Intifada." *Social Forces* 84(4): 1969–1986.

Bueno de Mesquita, Ethan. 2005a. "Conciliation, counterterrorism, and patterns of terrorist violence." *International Organization* 59(1): 145–176.

Bueno de Mesquita, Ethan. 2005b. "The quality of terror." *American Journal of Political Science* 49(3): 515–530.

Bueno de Mesquita, Ethan and Eric S. Dickson. 2007. "The propaganda of the deed: Terrorism, counterterrorism, and mobilization." *American Journal of Political Science* 51(2): 364–381.

Burgoon, Brian. 2006. "On welfare and terror: Social welfare policies and political-economic roots of terrorism." *Journal of Conflict Resolution* 50(2): 176–203.

Bush, George W. 2002. "Remarks by the president at the United Nations Financing for Development Conference." *White House Press Release*, March 22.

Byman, Daniel. 2006. "Do targeted killings work?" *Foreign Affairs* 85(2): 95–111.

Campbell, Blake and Amanda Murdie. 2018. "Keep the informants talking: The pursuit and use of CBRN weapons by terrorist organizations." *Studies in Conflict & Terrorism* 1–20, doi.org/10.1080/1057610X.2018.1531517.

Carter, Chelsea J. 2014. "Video shows ISIS beheading U.S. journalist James Foley." *CNN*, August 20.

Carter, David B. 2016. "Provocation and the strategy of terrorist and guerrilla attacks." *International Organization* 70(1): 133–173.

Catignani, Sergio. 2012. "Israeli counterinsurgency: The never-ending 'whack-a-mole'." In Paul B. Rich and Isabelle Duyvesteyn (eds.) *The Routledge Handbook of Insurgency and Counterinsurgency*. New York: Routledge, pp. 263–276.

Caves, Richard E. and Michael E. Porter. 1977. "From entry barriers to mobility barriers: Conjectural decisions and contrived deterrence to new competition." *The Quarterly Journal of Economics* 91(2): 241–261.

"Centre unlikely to accede to Garoland, says G K Pillai." 2012. *Meghalaya Times*, February 14.

Chai, Sun-Ki. 1993. "An organizational economics theory of antigovernment violence." *Comparative Politics* 26(1): 99–110.

Chenoweth, Erica. 2010. "Democratic competition and terrorist activity." *Journal of Politics* 72(1): 16–30.

Chenoweth, Erica. 2013. "Terrorism and democracy." *Annual Review of Political Science* 16: 355–378.

Chenoweth, Erica and Maria J. Stephan. 2011. *Why Civil Resistance Works: The Strategic Logic of Nonviolent Conflict*. New York: Columbia University Press.

Cheon, Andrew, Johannes Urpelainen, and Maureen Lackner. 2013. "Why do governments subsidize gasoline consumption? An empirical analysis of global gasoline prices, 2002–2009." *Energy Policy* 56: 382–390.

Chiozza, Giacomo and Hein E Goemans. 2004. "International conflict and the tenure of leaders: Is war still ex post inefficient?" *American Journal of Political Science* 48(3): 604–619.

Christia, Fotini. 2012. *Alliance Formation in Civil Wars*. Cambridge: Cambridge University Press.

Chyba, Christopher F. 2001. "Biological terrorism and public health." *Survival* 43(1): 93–106.

Cingranelli, David L. and David L. Richards. 2010. "The Cingranelli and Richards (CIRI) Human Rights Data Project." *Human Rights Quarterly* 32(2): 401–424.

Clark, Derek J. and Christian Riis. 1998. "Contest success functions: An extension." *Economic Theory* 11(1): 201–204.

Conrad, Justin. 2017. *Gambling and War: Risk, Reward and Chance in International Conflict*. Annapolis, MD: Naval Institute Press.

Conrad, Justin and Kevin Greene. 2015. "Competition, differentiation, and the severity of terrorist attacks." *Journal of Politics* 77(2): 546–561.

Conrad, Justin, Kevin T. Greene, and Brian Phillips. 2018. "Militant group competition and civilian victimization. In Annual meeting of the Midwest Political Science Association, Chicago, Illinois, USA, April 5–8.

Conrad, Justin, Kevin T. Greene, and Brian Phillips. 2019. "Government responses to militant group competition." In Annual Meeting of the Southern Political Science Association, Austin, Texas, USA, January 17–19.

Cordesman, Anothony H. 2017. *The Patterns in Global Terrorism: 1970–2016*. Washington, DC: Center for Strategic & International Studies.

Crelinsten, Ronald D. and Alex P. Schmid. 1992. "Western responses to terrorism: A twenty-five year balance sheet." *Terrorism and Political Violence* 4(4): 307–340.

Crenshaw, Martha. 1981. "The causes of terrorism." *Comparative Politics* 13(4): 379–399.

Crenshaw, Martha. 1985. "An organizational approach to the analysis of political terrorism." *Orbis* 29(3): 465–489.

Crenshaw, Martha. 1987. "Theories of terrorism: Instrumental and organizational approaches." *Journal of Strategic Studies* 10(4): 13–31.

Cronin, Audrey Kurth. 2006. "How al-Qaida ends: The decline and demise of terrorist groups." *International Security* 31(1): 7–48.

Cronin, Audrey Kurth. 2009. *How Terrorism Ends: Understanding the Decline and Demise of Terrorist Campaigns*. Princeton, NJ: Princeton University Press.

Cunningham, Kathleen Gallagher. 2011. "Divide and conquer or divide and concede: How do states respond to internally divided separatists?" *American Political Science Review* 105(2): 275–297.

Dasgupta, Ani and Kofi O. Nti. 1998. "Designing an optimal contest." *European Journal of Political Economy* 14(4): 587–603.

Deci, Edward L., Gregory Betley, James Kahle, Linda Abrams, and Joseph Porac. 1981. "When trying to win: Competition and intrinsic motivation." *Personality and Social Psychology Bulletin* 7(1): 79–83.

"Declaring GNLA as terrorist outfit is for namesake, formality: Conrad." 2012. *Meghalaya Times*, February 22.

Della Porta, Donatella and Sidney Tarrow. 1986. "Unwanted children: Political violence and the cycle of protest in Italy, 1966–1973." *European Journal of Political Research* 14(5–6): 607–632.

Dettke, Dieter. 2009. *Germany Says "No": The Iraq War and the Future of German Foreign and Security Policy*. Baltimore, MD: Johns Hopkins University Press.

Diamond, Larry. 1994. "Toward democratic consolidation." *Journal of Democracy* 5(3): 4–17.

Diehl, Paul F. and Gary Goertz. 2001. *War and Peace in International Rivalry*. Ann Arbor: University of Michigan Press.

Dixit, Avinash. 1980. "The role of investment in entry-deterrence." *The Economic Journal* 90(357): 95–106.

Downs, Anthony. 1957. "An economic theory of political action in a democracy." *Journal of Political Economy* 65(2): 135–150.

Drakos, Konstantino and Andreas Gofas. 2006. "The devil you know but are afraid to face: Underreporting bias and its distorting effects on the study of terrorism." *Journal of Conflict Resolution* 50(5): 714–735.

Drezner, Daniel W. 2003. "The hidden hand of economic coercion." *International Organization* 57(3): 643–659.

Dugan, Laura. 2012. "The making of the Global Terrorism Database and its applicability to studying the life cycles of terrorist organizations." In David Gadd, Susanne Karstedt, and Steven F. Messner (eds.) The *SAGE Handbook of Criminology Research Methods*. Newbury Park, CA: Sage, 175–198.

Dugan, Laura and Erica Chenoweth. 2012. "Moving beyond deterrence: The effectiveness of raising the expected utility of abstaining from terrorism in Israel." *American Sociological Review* 77(4): 597–624.

"Dynamics of ethnic conflicts in Manipur." 2012. *Imphal Free Press*, July 3.

Elster, Jon. 2005. "Motivations and beliefs in suicide missions." In Diego Gambetta (ed.) *Making Sense of Suicide Missions*. Oxford: Oxford University Press pp. 233–258.

Enders, Walter and Todd Sandler. 1993. "The effectiveness of antiterrorism policies: A vector-autoregression-intervention analysis." *American Political Science Review* 87(4): 829–844.

Enders, Walter and Todd Sandler. 2002. "Patterns of transnational terrorism, 1970–1999: Alternative time-series estimates." *International Studies Quarterly* 46(2): 145–165.

Enders, Walter and Todd Sandler. 2006. *The Political Economy of Terrorism*. New York: Cambridge University Press.

Ensor, Josie. 2016. "Assad vows to retake whole of Syria ahead of ceasefire." *The Telegraph*. September 12.

Eyerman, Joe and Robert A. Hart Jr. 1996. "An empirical test of the audience cost proposition." *Journal of Conflict Resolution* 40(4): 597–616.

Eyerman, Joseph. 1998. "Terrorism and democratic states: Soft targets or accessible systems?" *International Interactions* 24(2): 151–170.

"Factbox: Syria's rebel groups." 2014. *Reuters*, January 9.

Fearon, James D. 1995. "Rationalist explanations for war." *International Organization* 49(3): 379–414.

Fearon, James D. 2002. "Selection effects and deterrence." *International Interactions* 28(1): 5–29.

Fearon, James and David Laitin. 2003. "Ethnicity, insurgency and civil war." *American Political Science Review* 97(1): 75–90.

Ferguson, Neil T. N. 2017. "Just the two of us? Civil conflicts, pro-state militants, and the violence premium." *Terrorism and Political violence* 29(2): 296–322.

Fey, Mark and Kristopher W. Ramsay. 2011. "Uncertainty and incentives in crisis bargaining: Game-free analysis of international conflict." *American Journal of Political Science* 55(1): 149–169.

Filkins, Dexter. 2009. *The Forever War*. New York: Random House Digital, Inc.

Findley, Michael G. and Joseph K. Young. 2012. "More combatant groups, more terror? Empirical tests of an outbidding logic." *Terrorism and Political Violence* 24(5): 706–721.

Findley, Michael G. and Joseph K. Young. 2015. "Terrorism, spoiling, and the resolution of civil wars." *Journal of Politics* 77(4): 1115–1128.

"Five killed by rebel gunmen at polling station near Imphal." 2012. *The National*, January 29.

Fjelde, Hanne and Desirée Nilsson. 2012. "Rebels against rebels: Explaining violence between rebel groups." *Journal of Conflict Resolution* 56(4): 604–628.

Fleck, Robert K. and Christopher Kilby. 2010. "Changing aid regimes? US foreign aid from the Cold War to the War on Terror." *Journal of Development Economics* 91(2): 185–197.

Fortna, Virginia Page. 2015. "Do terrorists win? Rebels' use of terrorism and civil war outcomes." *International Organization* 69(3): 519–556.

Fowler, Anthony and B. Pablo Montagnes. 2015. "College football, elections, and false-positive results in observational research." *Proceedings of the National Academy of Sciences* 112(45): 13800–13804.

Franke, Jörg, Christian Kanzow, Wolfgang Leininger, and Alexandra Schwartz. 2013. "Effort maximization in asymmetric contest games with heterogeneous contestants." *Economic Theory* 52(2): 589–630.

Frey, Bruno S. and Simon Luechinger. 2003. "How to fight terrorism: Alternatives to deterrence." *Defence and Peace Economics* 14(4): 237–249.

Freytag, Andreas, Jens J. Krüger, Daniel Meierrieks, and Friedrich Schneider. 2011. "The origins of terrorism: Cross-country estimates of socio-economic determinants of terrorism." *European Journal of Political Economy* 27(1): 5–16.

Friedman, Lawrence. 1958. "Game-theory models in the allocation of advertising expenditures." *Operations Research* 6(5): 699–709.

Friis, Simone Molin. 2015. "'Beyond anything we have ever seen': Beheading videos and the visibility of violence in the war against ISIS." *International Affairs* 91(4): 725–746.

Gade, Emily Kalah, Mohammed M. Hafez, and Michael Gabbay. 2019. "Fratricide in rebel movements: A network analysis of Syrian militant infighting." *Journal of Peace Research* 56(3): 321–335.

Galula, David. 2006. *Counterinsurgency Warfare: Theory and Practice.* Santa Barbara, CA: Greenwood Publishing Group.

"Garo Hills on high alert following GNLA ambush." 2012. *Times of India*, February 25.

Gladney, Dru C. 1990. "The ethnogenesis of the Uighur." *Central Asian Survey* 9(1): 1–28.

Gleditsch, Nils Petter, Peter Wallensteen, Mikael Eriksson, Margareta Sollenberg, and Håvard Strand. 2002. "Armed conflict 1946–2001: A new dataset." *Journal of Peace Research* 39(5): 615–637.

"GNLA dares Legislator with death sentence: Is Meghalaya really safe." 2013. *Meghalaya Times*, May 21.

"GNLA declared 'terrorist organization', police dept jovial." 2012. *Meghalaya Times*, February 1.

"GNLA declares war on Meghalaya police." 2012. *Meghalaya Times*, April 9.

"GNLA denies role in IED blast, Salgro Arengh's group claims responsibility." 2014. *Meghalaya Times*, November 19.

"GNLA justifies demand for Garoland, firm about dialogue." 2014. *Meghalaya Times*, March 15.

"GNLA labels victims informers." 2012. *The Telegraph (India)*, February 6.

"GNLA to support Congress in Garo Hills: Champion." 2012. *Meghalaya Times*, September 20.

"GNLA to take its demands directly to Centre, UN." 2012. *Meghalaya Times*, February 7.

"GNLA vents ire on bus, says 'this is against Govt'." 2013. *Meghalaya Times*, June 5.

Goemans, Hein E. 2000. *War and Punishment: The Causes of War Termination and the First World War*. Princeton, NJ: Princeton University Press.

Goldman, Russell. 2015. "What we know and don't know about the terrorist attack in Mali." *New York Times*, November 20.

Goodhand, Jonathan, David Hulme, and Nick Lewer. 2000. "Social capital and the political economy of violence: A case study of Sri Lanka." *Disasters* 24(4): 390–406.

Goodwin, Jeff. 2001. *No Other Way Out: States and Revolutionary Movements, 1945–1991*. New York: Cambridge University Press.

Gowa, Joanne and Kristopher W. Ramsay. 2017. "Gulliver untied: Entry deterrence under unipolarity." *International Organization* 71(3): 459–490.

Greenhill, Kelly M. and Solomon Major. 2007. "The perils of profiling: Civil war spoilers and the collapse of intrastate peace accords." *International Security* 31(3): 7–40.

"Guide to the Syrian rebels." 2013. *BBC*, December 13, www.bbc.com/news/world-middle-east-24403003.

Gurr, Ted. 1970. *Why Men Rebel*. Princeton, NJ: Princeton University Press.

Hafez, Mohammed M. 2000. "Armed Islamist movements and political violence in Algeria." *The Middle East Journal* 54(4): 572–591.

Hafez, Mohammed M. 2007. *Suicide Bombers in Iraq: The Strategy and Ideology of Martyrdom*. Washington, DC: US Institute of Peace Press.

Hafez, Mohammed M. 2020. "Fratricidal rebels: Ideological extremity and warring factionalism in civil wars." *Terrorism and Political Violence* 32(3): 604–629.

Hamming, Tore Refslund. 2020. "The Al Qaeda–Islamic State rivalry: Competition yes, but no competitive escalation." *Terrorism and Political Violence* 32(1): 20–37.

Harbom, Lotta, Erik Melander, and Peter Wallensteen. 2008. "Dyadic dimensions of armed conflict, 1946–2007." *Journal of Peace Research* 45(5): 697–710.

Harrigan, Kathryn Rudie. 1985. "An application of clustering for strategic group analysis." *Strategic Management Journal* 6(1): 55–73.

Hassan, Nasra. 2001. "An arsenal of believers." *The New Yorker*, November 19, pp. 36–41.

Hegre, Håvard, Tanja Ellingsen, Scott Gates, and Nils Peter Gleditsch. 2001. "Toward a democratic civil peace? Democracy, political change and civil war, 1916–1992." *American Political Science Review* 95: 33–48.

Hendrix, Cullen S. 2010. "Measuring state capacity: Theoretical and empirical implications for the study of civil conflict." *Journal of Peace Research* 47(3): 273–285.

Hendrix, Cullen S. and Joseph K. Young. 2014. "State capacity and terrorism: A two-dimensional approach." *Security Studies* 23(2): 329–363.

Hennessey, Beth A. 2003. "The social psychology of creativity." *Scandinavian Journal of Educational Research* 47(3): 253–271.

Hillyard, Paddy and Janie Percy-Smith. 1984. "Converting terrorists: The use of supergrasses in Northern Ireland." *Journal of Law and Society* 11(3): 335–355.

Hirshleifer, Jack. 1989. "Conflict and rent-seeking success functions: Ratio vs. difference models of relative success." *Public Choice* 63(2): 101–112.

Hoffman, Bruce. 2018. *Al-Qaeda's resurrection* New York: Council on Foreign Relations, March.

Howell, Llewellyn D. 2011. *International Country Risk Guide Methodology*. East Syracuse, NY: PRS Group.

Hoyt, Timothy D. 2015. "Pakistan: A tale of two allies." In Gale Mattox and Stephen Grenier (eds.) *Coalition Challenges in Afghanistan: The Politics of Alliance*. Stanford, CA: Stanford University Press.

Hutchinson, Martha Crenshaw. 1972. "The concept of revolutionary terrorism." *Journal of Conflict Resolution* 16(3): 383–396.

Iannaccone, Laurence R. and Eli Berman. 2006. "Religious extremism: The good, the bad, and the deadly." *Public Choice* 128(1–2): 109–129.

"Incidents and Statements Garo National Liberation Army (GNLA): 2010-2012." 2012. South Asia Terrorim Portal, www.satp.org/satporgtp/countries/india/states/meghalaya/terrorist_outfits/GNLA_tl.htm

"Incidents and Statements Involving NSCN-IM: 1992–2012." 2012. South Asia Terrorism Portal, www.satp.org/satporgtp/countries/india/states/nagaland/terrorist_outfits/NSCN$_I$M$_t$l.htm

"Indian government panel says northeast group harbouring rebels." 2012. BBC Monitoring South Asia – Political, July 4.

International Monetary Fund. 2015. World Economic Outlook Database. Washington, DC: IMF.

"ISIS' American recruitment on decline, FBI director says." 2016. *CBS News*, May 11.

"Jabhat al Nusra and ISIS: Sources of strength." 2016. *Express Tribune*, February 11.

"Joint combing operation for GNLA, ULFA rebels." 2012. *The Times of India*, March 3.

Kalyvas, Stathis N. and Matthew Adam Kocher. 2007. "How 'free' is free riding in civil wars? Violence, insurgency, and the Collective Action Problem." *World Politics* 59(2): 177–216.

Kaplan, Eben. 2006. "Tracking down terrorist financing." Council on Foreign Relations, April 4. www.cfr.org/backgrounder/tracking-down-terrorist-financing#chapter-title-0-5.

Kaplan, Morgan. 2015. "How civilian perceptions affect patterns of violence and competition in multi-party insurgencies." Unpublished Manuscript, University of Chicago.

Karouny, Mariam. 2011. "Syrian forces fire on Kurdish funeral: At least two killed after service turns into anti-Assad protest." *Ottawa Citizen*, October 9.

Kearns, Erin M. 2019. "When to take credit for terrorism? A cross-national examination of claims and attributions." *Terrorism and Political Violence* 33(1): 1–30.

Kearns, Erin M., Brendan Conlon, and Joseph K. Young. 2014. "Lying about terrorism." *Studies in Conflict & Terrorism* 37(5): 422–439.

Keohane, Robert O. 1984. *After Hegemony: Cooperation and Discord in the World Political Economy*. Princeton, NJ: Princeton University Press.

Kipgen, Nehginpao. 2013. "Politics of ethnic conflict in Manipur." *South Asia Research* 33(1): 21–38.

Kirk, Richard M. 1983. "Political terrorism and the size of government: A positive institutional analysis of violent political activity." *Public Choice* 40(1): 41–52.

Kondrashov, Sergei. 2000. *Nationalism and the Drive for Sovereignty in Tatarstan 1988–1992: Origins and Development*. New York: St Martin's Press.

Konrad, Kai A. 2009. *Strategy and Dynamics in Contests*. Oxford: Oxford University Press.

Kotler, Philip and Friedhelm Bliemel. 2009. *Marketing Management*. Stuttgart: Schäffer-Poeschel.

Krupp, D. B. and Thomas R. Cook. 2018. "Local competition amplifies the corrosive effects of inequality." *Psychological Science* 29(5): 824–833.

Kugler, Jacek and Ronald L. Tammen. 2012. *The Performance of Nations*. New York: Rowman & Littlefield Publishers.

"Kuki-Naga ethno-centrism in Manipur." 2013. *Assam Tribune*, February 10.

Kuperman, Alan J. 2008. "The moral hazard of humanitarian intervention: Lessons from the Balkans." *International Studies Quarterly* 52(1): 49–80.

Kupperman, Robert H., Debra Van Opstal, and David Williamson. 1982. "Terror, the strategic tool: Response and control." *The Annals of the American Academy of Political and Social Science* 463(1): 24–38.

Kurrild-Klitgaard, Peter, Mogens K. Justesen, and Robert Klemmensen. 2006. "The political economy of freedom, democracy and transnational terrorism." *Public Choice* 128(1–2): 289–315.

Kydd, Andrew H. and Barbara F. Walter. 2002. "Sabotaging the peace: The politics of extremist violence." *International Organization* 56(2): 263–296.

Kydd, Andrew H. and Barbara F. Walter. 2006. "The strategies of terrorism." *International Security* 31(1): 49–80.

LaFree, Gary, Laura Dugan, and Erin Miller. 2014. *Putting Terrorism in Context: Lessons from the Global Terrorism Database*. New York: Routledge.

Lai, Brian. 2007. "'Draining the swamp': An empirical examination of the production of international terrorism, 1968–1998." *Conflict Management and Peace Science* 24(4): 297–310.

Landes, William M. 1978. "An economic study of US aircraft hijacking, 1961–1976." *Journal of Law and Economics* 21(1): 1–31.

Lewis, Jeffrey. 2012. *The Business of Martyrdom: A History of Suicide Bombing*. Annapolis, MD: Naval Institute Press.

Lichbach, Mark. 1987. "Deterrence or escalation? The puzzle of aggregate studies of repression and dissent." *Journal of Conflict Resolution* 31(2): 266–297.

Lichbach, Mark. 1995. *The Rebel's Dilemma*. Ann Arbor: University of Michigan Press.

Lichbach, Mark and Ted Gurr. 1981. "The conflict process: A formal model." *Journal of Conflict Resolution* 25(1): 3–29.

Lieven, Anatol. 2011. *Pakistan: A Hard Country*. New York: Public Affairs.

Linz, Juan J. and Alfred Stepan. 1996. *Problems of Democratic Transition and Consolidation: Southern Europe, South America, and Post-Communist Europe*. Baltimore, MD: Johns Hopkins University Press.

Long, Austin. 2014. "Whack-a-mole or coup de grace? Institutionalization and leadership targeting in Iraq and Afghanistan." *Security Studies* 23(3): 471–512.

Lucas, Jr., Robert E. 1976. "Econometric policy evaluation: A critique." In Karl Brunner and Allan H. Meltzer (eds.) *The Phillips Curve and Labor Markets*. Amsterdam: North Holland/Elsevier.

Lum, Cynthia, Leslie W. Kennedy, and Alison Sherley. 2006. "Are counter-terrorism strategies effective? The results of the Campbell systematic review on counter-terrorism evaluation research." *Journal of Experimental Criminology* 2(4): 489–516.

Lyngdoh, Andrew W. 2012. "Arrest iterates GNLA threat." *The Telegraph* (India), November 27.

Mallaby, Sebastian. 2002. "The reluctant imperialist: Terrorism, failed states, and the case for American empire." *Foreign Affairs*, March/April, pp. 2–7.

"Manipur: All-party delegation to meet Centre on militancy." 2012. *DNA*, December 29.

"Maoist recruit Assamese youths." 2012. *Meghalaya Times*, July 11.

Marshall, Monty G. and Keith Jaggers. 2006. *Polity IV Project, Political Regime Characteristics and Transitions, 1800–2004*. Center for International Development and Conflict Management, University of Maryland, College Park, Maryland, USA.

Marshall, Monty, Ted Robert Gurr, Christian Davenport, and Keith Jaggers. 2002. "Polity IV, 1800–1999: Comments on Munck and Verkuilen." *Comparative Political Studies* 35(1): 40–45.

Martinez, Luis. 2000. *The Algerian Civil War, 1990–1998*. New York: Columbia University Press.

Mason, T. David and Dale A. Krane. 1989. "The political economy of death squads: Toward a theory of the impact of state-sanctioned terror." *International Studies Quarterly* 33(2): 175–198.

McCants, William. 2013. "How Zawahiri lost al qaeda." *Foreign Affairs*, November 19.

McCarthy, John D. and Mayer N. Zald. 1977. "Resource mobilization and social movements: A partial theory." *American Journal of Sociology* 82(6): 1212–1241.

McCauley, Clark R. and Mary E. Segal. 1987. "Social psychology of terrorist groups." *Review of Personality and Social Psychology* 9: 231–256.

McGee, Jeffery E. and Christopher L. Shook. 2000. "Responding to industry consolidation in fragmented industries: The role of capabilities in small business survival." *Journal of Small Business Strategy* 11(2): 21–32.

McLauchlin, Theodore and Wendy Pearlman. 2012. "Out-group conflict, in-group unity? Exploring the effect of repression on intramovement cooperation." *Journal of Conflict Resolution* 56(1): 41–66.

Medvedev, Dmitry. 2011. "Open address to the World Economic Forum in Davos." Moscow: Kremlin Press Release.

"Meghalaya Assessment-2009." 2009. South Asia Terrorism Portal, www.satp .org/satporgtp/countries/india/states/Meghalaya/2009.htm.

"Meghalaya Assessment-2014." 2014. South Asia Terrorim Portal, www.satp .org/satporgtp/countries/india/states/Meghalaya/2014.htm.

"Meghalaya: Renewed terror." 2013. *South Asia Intelligence ReviewIBNS*, October 15.

"Meghalaya: The hills run red." 2013. *South Asia Intelligence ReviewIBNS*, November 19.

Mendelsohn, Barak. 2019. "The battle for Algeria: Explaining fratricide among armed nonstate actors." *Studies in Conflict & Terrorism*, pp. 1–23, DOI: 10.1080/1057610X.2019.1580419.

Mills, Harland D. 1961. "A study in promotional competition." In Frank M. Bass (ed.) *Mathematical Models and Methods in Marketing*. Homewood, IL: R. D. Irwin, 245–301.

Milton, Daniel and Bryan Price. 2020. "Too central to fail? Terror networks and leadership decapitation." *International Interactions* 46(3): 309–333.

Moghadam, Assaf. 2017. *Nexus of Global Jihad: Understanding Cooperation among Terrorist Actors*. New York: Columbia University Press.

Moneyhon, Matthew D. 2002. "China's great western development project in Xinjiang: Economic palliative, or political trojan horse." *Denver Journal of International Law & Policy* 31: 491.

Mukherjee, Kunal. 2014. "The conflict in the Indian northeast." *Defence Studies* 14(2): 111–133.

Muller, Edward N. and Erich Weede. 1990. "Cross-ational variation in political violence: A rational action approach." *Journal of Conflict Resolution* 34(4): 624–651.

Mullins, Christopher W. and Joseph K. Young. 2012. "Cultures of violence and acts of terror: Applying a legitimation–habituation model to terrorism." *Crime & Delinquency* 58(1): 28–56.

Musgrave, Paul and Daniel H. Nexon. 2018. "Defending hierarchy from the Moon to the Indian Ocean: Symbolic capital and political dominance in early modern China and the Cold War." *International Organization* 72(3): 591–626.

"My Arab Spring: Syria's Revolution Betrayed." 2016. *Al Jazeera*, March 16.

Myerson, Roger B. 1999. "Nash equilibrium and the history of economic theory." *Journal of Economic Literature* 37(3): 1067–1082.

"Landscape architecture and the site security design process." In *National Institute of Building Sciences Whole Building Design Guide*. 2016. Security Design and the Landscape Architect. Washington, DC: National Institute of

Building Sciences. www.wbdg.org/resources/landscape-architecture-and-site-security-design-process.

"National Socialist Council of Nagaland – Isak-Muivah, Centre discuss ceasefire violations." 2012. *Times of India*, May 13.

Nemeth, Stephen. 2014. "The effect of competition on terrorist group operations." *Journal of Conflict Resolution* 58(2): 336–362.

Nesser, Petter. 2006. "Jihadism in Western Europe after the invasion of Iraq: Tracing motivational influences from the Iraq war on Jihadist terrorism in Western Europe." *Studies in Conflict & Terrorism* 29(4): 323–342.

"NSCN-IM deny allegation of contractor's abduction." 2012. *Meghalaya Times*, July 12.

Nti, Kofi O. 2004. "Maximum efforts in contests with asymmetric valuations." *European Journal of Political Economy* 20(4): 1059–1066.

Ogutcu-Fu, Sema Hande, Seden Akcinaroglu, Efe Tokdemir, Evgeny Sedashov, Jeremy Berkowitz, and Carlos Moreno Leon. 2019. "Rebel rivalry and the strategic nature of rebel group ideology and demands." Annual Meeting of the American Political Science Association, Washington, DC, August 29–September 1.

Olson, Mancur. 1982. *The Rise and Decline of Nations: Economic Growth, Stagnation, and Social Rigidities*. New Haven, CT: Yale University Press.

Oots, Kent Layne. 1989. "Organizational perspectives on the formation and disintegration of terrorist groups." *Studies in Conflict & Terrorism* 12(3): 139–152.

Paine, Jack and Scott A. Tyson. 2020. "Uses and abuses of formal models in political science." In Dirk Berg-Schlosser, Bertrand Badie, and Leonardo Morlino (eds.) *The SAGE Handbook of Political Science*. Oxford: Oxford University Press, pp. 188–202.

Pape, Robert A. 2003. "The strategic logic of suicide terrorism." *American Political Science Review* 97(3): 343–361.

Pape, Robert A. 2005. *Dying to Win: The Strategic Logic of Suicide Terrorism*. New York: Random House.

Parmentier, Guillaume. 2008. "French-American relations after the Iraq War: How to redefine the relationship." In Mairi MacLean and Joseph Szarka (eds.) *France on the World Stage: Nation State Strategies in the Global Era*. New York: Palgrave, pp. 20–36.

Pauly, Jr., Robert J. 2013. "French security agenda in the post-9/11 world." In Tom Lansford and Blagovest Tashev (eds.) *Old Europe, New Europe, and the U.S.: Renegotiating Transatlantic Security in the Post 9/11 E*. Burlington, VT: Ashgate, pp. 1–18.

Pearlman, Wendy. 2009. "Spoiling inside and out: Internal political contestation and the Middle East peace process." *International Security* 33(3): 79–109.

Pedahzur, Ami, William Eubank, and Leonard Weinberg. 2002. "The war on terrorism and the decline of terrorist group formation: A research note." *Terrorism and Political Violence* 14(3): 141–147.

Perkins, Richard and Eric Neumayer. 2007. "Do membership benefits buy regulatory compliance? An empirical analysis of EU Directives 1978–99." *European Union Politics* 8(2): 180–206.

Perliger, Arie, Ami Pedahzur, and Yair Zalmanovitch. 2005. "The defensive dimension of the battle against terrorism – an analysis of management of terror incidents in Jerusalem." *Journal of Contingencies and Crisis Management* 13(2): 79–91.

Phillips, Brian J. 2014. "Terrorist group cooperation and longevity." *International Studies Quarterly* 58(2): 336–347.

Phillips, Brian J. 2015. "Enemies with benefits? Violent rivalry and terrorist group longevity." *Journal of Peace Research* 52(1): 62–75.

Phillips, Brian J. 2017. "Deadlier in the US? On lone wolves, terrorist groups, and attack lethality." *Terrorism and Political Violence* 29(3): 533–549.

Piazza, James A. 2008. "Incubators of terror: Do failed and failing states promote transnational terrorism?" *International Studies Quarterly* 52(3): 469–488.

Piazza, James A. 2009. "Economic development, poorly managed political conflict and terrorism in India." *Studies in Conflict & Terrorism* 32(5): 406–419.

Piazza, James A. 2011. "Poverty, minority economic discrimination, and domestic terrorism." *Journal of Peace Research* 48(3): 339–353.

Piazza, James A. 2013. "Regime age and terrorism: Are new democracies prone to terrorism?" *International Interactions* 39(2): 246–263.

Pillar, Paul R. 2001. *Terrorism and U.S. Foreign Policy*. Washington, DC: Brookings.

Pischedda, Costantino. 2020. *Conflict among Rebels: Why Insurgent Groups Fight Each Other*. New York: Columbia University Press.

Pockrass, Robert M. 1987. "Terroristic murder in Northern Ireland: Who is killed and why?" *Studies in Conflict & Terrorism* 9(4): 341–359.

Porter, Michael E. 1979. "How competitive forces shape strategy." *Harvard Business Review* 57(2): 137–145.

Powell, Colin L. and Joseph E. Persico. 1996. *My American Journey*. New York: Random House.

Powell, Robert D. 1999. *In the Shadow of Power: States and Strategies in International Politics*. Princeton, NJ: Princeton University Press.

Powell, Robert D. 2007. "Defending against terrorist attacks with limited resources." *American Political Science Review* 101(3): 527–541.

Quanrud, Pamela. 2018. "The global coalition to defeat ISIS: A success story." *The Foreign Service Journal Association*, January/February, www.afsa.org/global-coalition-defeat-isis-success-story.

Rashid, Ahmed. 2008. *Descent into Chaos: The US and the Failure of Nation Building in Pakistan, Afghanistan, and Central Asia*. New York: Penguin.

Rasler, Karen. 1996. "Concessions, repression, and political protest." *American Sociological Review* 61(1): 132–152.

Ricolfi, Luca. 2005. Palestinians, 1981–2003. In Diego Gambetta (ed.) *Making Sense of Suicide Missions*. Oxford: Oxford University Press, pp. 77–130.

Rose, William, Rysia Murphy, and Max Abrahms. 2007. "Does terrorism ever work? The 2004 Madrid train bombings." *International Security* 32(1): 185–192.

Rosendorff, B. Peter and Todd Sandler. 2004. "Too much of a good thing? The proactive response dilemma." *Journal of Conflict Resolution* 48(5): 657–671.

Rosendorff, B. Peter and Todd Sandler. 2010. "Suicide terrorism and the backlash effect." *Defence and Peace Economics* 21(5–6): 443–457.

Routray, Bibhu Prasad. 2015. "Insurgencies in India's north-east." In Harsh V. Pant (ed.) *Handbook of Indian Defence Policy: Themes, Structures and Doctrines*. New Dehli: Routledge, p. 304.

Rummel, Rudolph J. 1985. "Libertarian propositions on violence within and between nations: A test against published research results." *Journal of Conflict Resolution* 29(3): 419–455.

"Saleng seeks security cover." 2013. *Meghalaya Times*, January 24.

Sarma, Kiran. 2005. "Informers and the battle against republican terrorism: A review of 30 years of conflict." *Police Practice and Research* 6(2): 165–180.

Savun, Burcu and Brian J. Phillips. 2009. "Democracy, foreign policy, and terrorism." *Journal of Conflict Resolution* 53(6): 878–904.

Sawyer, John Paul. 2008. "A spiral of peace: Competition, monopoly and diversification in the market for political violence in Northern Ireland." *Quest* 6: 20–53.

"SBI manager kidnapped in Meghalaya." 2012. *Times of India*, February 25.

Schmalensee, Richard. 1976. "A model of promotional competition in oligopoly." *The Review of Economic Studies* 43(3): 493–507.

Schultz, Kenneth A. and Henk E. Goemans. 2019. "Aims, claims, and the bargaining model of war." *International Theory* 11(3): 344–374.

Schweitzer, Yoram. 2000. "Suicide terrorism: Development and characteristics." International Policy Institute for Counter-Terrorism: Online Article Series 21. Herzliya, Israel: International Policy Institute for Counter-Terrorism.

Scott, James C. 1998. *Seeing Like a State: How Certain Schemes to Improve the Human Condition Have Failed*. New Haven, CT: Yale University Press.

"Security forces foil ULFA–GNLA terror plan." 2012. *The Times of India*, March 3.

Shapiro, Jacob N. 2013. *The Terrorist's Dilemma: Managing Violent Covert Organizations*. Princeton, NJ: Princeton University Press.

Shapiro, Jacob N. and David A. Siegel. 2007. "Underfunding in terrorist organizations." *International Studies Quarterly* 51(2): 405–429.

Singer, J. David, Stuart Bremer, and John Stuckey. 1972. "Capability distribution, uncertainty, and major power war, 1820–1965." In Bruce M. Russett (ed.) *Peace, War, and Numbers*. Beverly Hills, CA: Sage, pp. 19–48.

Skaperdas, Stergios. 1996. "Contest success functions." *Economic Theory* 7(2): 283–290.

Skaperdas, Stergios and Samarth Vaidya. 2012. "Persuasion as a contest." *Economic Theory* 51(2): 465–486.

Spaniel, William. 2018a. "Only here to help? Bargaining and the perverse incentives of international institutions." *International Studies Quarterly* 62(1): 14–22.

Spaniel, William. 2018b. "Terrorism, wealth, and delegation." *Quarterly Journal of Political Science* 13(2): 147–172.

Spaniel, William. 2019. "Rational overreaction to terrorism." *Journal of Conflict Resolution* 63(3): 786–810.

Spaniel, William and Peter Bils. 2018. "Slow to learn: Bargaining, uncertainty, and the calculus of conquest." *Journal of Conflict Resolution* 62(4): 774–796.

Staniland, Paul. 2012. "Between a rock and a hard place: Insurgent fratricide, ethnic defection, and the rise of pro-state paramilitaries." *Journal of Conflict Resolution* 56(1): 16–40.

Stanton, Jessica A. 2013. "Terrorism in the context of civil war." *Journal of Politics* 75(4): 1009–1022.

START. 2016. "Global Terrorism Database" [Data file]. National Consortium for the Study of Terrorism and Responses to Terrorism, www.start.umd.edu/gtd.

Stedman, Stephen John. 1997. "Spoiler problems in peace processes." *International Security* 22(2): 5–53.

Steinbuch, Yaron. 2016. "Virginia stabbing possibly ISIS-inspired beheading attempt." *New York Post*, August 23, http://nypost.com/2016/08/23/virginia-stabbing-possibly-isis-inspired-beheading-attempt.

Stern, Jessica and J. M. Berger. 2015. "Thugs wanted – bring your own boots: How ISIS attracts foreign fighters to its twisted utopia." *Guardian*, March 9, www.theguardian.com/world/2015/mar/09/how-isis-attracts-foreign-fighters-the-state-of-terror-book.

Stokes, Donald E. 1963. "Spatial models of party competition." *American Political Science Review* 57(2): 368–377.

"Surrenders bring hope for peace." 2015. *Assam Tribune*, January 4.

Svolik, Milan. 2009. "Power sharing and leadership dynamics in authoritarian regimes." *American Journal of Political Science* 53(3): 477–494.

"Syria protests: Rights group warns of 'Deraa Massacre'." 2011. *BBC News*, May 5.

Takeyh, Ray and Nikolas Gvosdev. 2002. "Do terrorist networks need a home?" *Washington Quarterly* 25(3): 97–108.

Tarrow, Sidney. 1994. *Power in Movement: Social Movements, Collective Action and Politics*. Cambridge: Cambridge University Press.

"The chilling Chokpot killing." 2014. *Meghalaya Times*, December 30.

Themnér, Lotta. 2013. "UCDP Dyadic Dataset Codebook, v 1-2013." Uppsala Conflict Data Program (UCDP), Department of Peace and Conflict Research, Uppsala University.

Themnér, Lotta and Peter Wallensteen. 2013. "Armed conflicts, 1946–2012." *Journal of Peace Research* 50(4): 509–521.

Themnér, Lotta and Peter Wallensteen. 2014. "Armed conflicts, 1946–2013." *Journal of Peace Research* 51(4): 541–554.

Thomas, Howard and Niloufer Venkatraman. 1988. "Research on strategic groups: Progress and prognosis." *Journal of Management Studies* 25(6): 537–555.

Thomas, Jakana. 2014. "Rewarding bad behavior: How governments respond to terrorism in civil war." *American Journal of Political Science* 58(4): 804–818.

Trebbi, Franceso, Eric Weese, Austin L. Wright, and Andrew Shaver. 2017. "Insurgent learning." manuscript, University of British Columbia.

Tullock, Gordon. 1980. "Efficient rent seeking." In James M. Buchanan, Robert D. Tollison, and Gordon Tullock (eds.) *Toward a Theory of the Rent-Seeking Society*. College Station, TX: A&M University Press.

"UN agencies welcome green light for Rohingya projects in northern Myanmar; urge 'more effective access'." 2018. *UN News*, December 17, https://news.un.org/en/story/2018/12/1028731.

U Department of State. 2017. *The Global Coalition – Working to Defeat ISIS. FY 2017 Department of State Agency Financial Report*. Washington, DC: Department of State.

U Department of State. 2019. *The Global Coalition – Working to Defeat ISIS. Office of the Spokesperson*. Washington, DC: Department of State.

Vittori, Jodi. 2011. *Terrorist Financing and Resourcing*. New York: Springer.

Walsh, James I. and James A. Piazza. 2010. "Why respecting physical integrity rights reduces terrorism." *Comparative Political Studies* 43(5): 551–577.

Walter, Barbara F. 2006. "Building reputation: Why governments fight some separatists but not others." *American Journal of Political Science* 50(2): 313–330.

Waltz, Kenneth N. 1979. *Theory of International Politics*. Boston, MA: McGraw-Hill.

Whitney, Craig. 1997. "98 die in one of Algerian civil war's worst massacres." *New York Times*. August 30.

"Why Al-Qaeda Kicked Out Its Deadly Syria Franchise." 2014. *Time*. February 3.

Wilson, James Q. 1995. *Political Organizations*. Princeton, NJ: Princeton University Press.

Winer, Jonathan M. 2008. "Countering terrorist finance: A work, mostly in progress." *The Annals of the American Academy of Political and Social Science* 618(1): 112–132.

Wintrobe, Ronald. 2006. *Rational Extremism: The Political Economy of Radicalism*. Cambridge: Cambridge University Press.

Wood, Reed M. and Mark P. Gibney. 2010. "The Political Terror Scale (PTS): A re-introduction and comparison to the CIRI Human Rights Database." *Human Rights Quarterly* 32(2): 367–400.

World Bank, The. 2015. *World Bank Development Indicators*. Washington, DC: The World Bank.

World Peace Foundation. 2015. "Algeria: Civil War." *Mass Atrocities Endings*. August 7, http://sites.tufts.edu/atrocityendings/2015/08/07/72/#_ednref13)

Wright, Lawrence. 2006. *The Looming Tower: Al-Qaeda and the Road to 9/11*. New York: Knopf.

Young, Joseph K. and Laura Dugan. 2014. "Survival of the fittest: Why terrorist groups endure." *Perspectives on Terrorism* 8(2): 2–23.

Zakaria, Fareed. 2016. "Obama's Whac-A-Mole strategy." *Washington Post*, July 14.

Index

9/11 attacks, 59, 175, 198

Abazid, Naief, 125
Abu Ghraib scandal, 187
Achik National Volunteer Council
    (ANVC), 78, 79
advertisements, 8, 9, 37
    cost, 32
    through violence, 8, 20, 25, 37
Afghan National Security Forces, 119
Afghanistan, 132, 170, 172
airport security, 167
AIS policing, 94
al-Assad, Bashar, 125, 173
al-Baghdadi, Abu Bakr, 1, 173
al-Gama'a al-Islamiyya, 44
al-Qaeda, 1, 46, 164, 175, 198, 234
    Bamako hotel attack, 2
    ISIS rivalry, 1–3
    monopolization of the jihadist
        movement, 30
    Syria, in, 1
    violence, 2, 3
al-Qaeda in Iraq (AQI), 1
al-Shabaab, 2
al-Zarqawi, Abu Musab, 1
al-Zarqawi, Ayman, indiscriminate tactics,
    1
al-Zawahiri, Ayman, 1
Algeria, 91
    conflict in, 90

Algerian Civil War, 90, 93
altruism, 132
amputations, 2
Anbar Awakening, 44
anti-IED technology, 186
anti-terrorism conventions, 170
anti-terrorism laws, 170
Armed Islamic Group (GIA), 90
Assam, India, 75, 76
assassinations of leadership, 171
asymmetric audience preferences, 46, 51
asymmetric defensive measures, 175
asymmetric group capabilities, 47, 54, 64
attacks on state sponsors, 171
audience resources, 178

backlash, 31
Bali bombings, 30
barriers to entry, 165
Big Allied and Dangerous dataset, 74
bin Laden, Osama, 1, 24, 198
biological attacks, 173
black market commerce, 171
Black, William, 95, 98
bomb blast
    2002 Bali bombings, 30
    2004 Madrid train bombings, 151
    camps and convoys, 171
    Tura, Meghalaya, 78
    USS Cole bombing, Yemen, 24
brotherhoodness, 80

bureaucratic quality, 108–111, 113, 116, 117
Bush, George W., 170

centralization, 163
Chokpot killing, Meghalaya, 84
citizen decisions, 137
civil conflict, 66, 72
competition, 21, 23, 106
  across subfields, 8
  effect, 43, 126, 141
  game, 21
  incentives of, 25
  increase in, 58, 72, 79
  indirect, 86
  LTTE, 162
  mechanism, 40
  militant groups, 3, 4, 6, 8, 10, 19, 90, 97, 107, 113, 137, 141
  non-state actors, between, 12
  organizations, between, 1, 3
  outbidding, 155
  political, 12, 88
  political violence and, 11, 16, 20, 21
  second-order effect, 150
  Stackelberg, 168
  states, between, 8
  subgame, 179
  subtleties, 222
  suicide attacks, 58
  supporters, 7
  violence, 57, 138, 162
  violent, 91
  zero-sum, 9
competitive violence, 16, 18, 20, 66, 92–94, 96, 127, 142, 143, 163, 183
  advertisement, 9
  incentives of, 128
  political violence, 222
  strategic context, 11
contest models, 31, 35
context models, 21
control variables, 110
cornering-the-market logic, 165
cost of attacks, 41
counterinsurgency, 9, 13, 19, 192
counterintuitive relationships, 72, 126, 154, 165, 166, 187, 204
counteroffensives, 3
counterpropaganda, 175, 202

counterterrorism, 7, 9, 13, 19, 20, 28, 93, 118, 119, 162, 165, 167–169, 174, 192, 195, 231, 237
  funds, 174
  market manipulation, 185
  microfoundations of policies, 168
  modeling entry, 177
  offensive, 172
  optimal levels of violence, 179
  recruitment, 234
  tactics, 186
country-level violence, 107
crisis bargaining, 152
crucifixions of non-combatants, 2
cumulative distribution function, 135

Dabiq, 176
Damascus, 236
de-escalation zones, 126
Declaration of War against the Americans Occupying the Land of the Two Holy Places, 24
defensive measures, 200
defensive strategies, 167
democracy–autocracy scale, 109
Department of Homeland Security, 173
Dima Jagi Nyso Army (DJNA), 75
disutility, 136
domestic attacks, 107
domestic political movements, 130
domestic terrorism, 130
dropoff, 140, 141

economic crisis, 125
economic inequalities, 169
empirical analysis, 111
endogenous barriers to entry, 215
endogenous defense, 220
endogenous grievances, 210
Endogenous Group Destruction, 45
endogenous marginal costs of violence, 217
enforcement, 102
  costs, 106, 107
equilibrium
  analysis, 31
  repeated game, 33
  violence, 43, 45, 105, 106, 139, 145, 157
  violence quantity, 36, 106
Ethiopian Civil War, 228
ethnic fractionalization, 66

ethnic minorities, discrimination against, 130
extremism, 132

Farooqi, Wasil, 26, 27
financial assets, seizing, 171
first principles approach, 20
first-order effect, 224
Foley, James, 27, 28
folk theorem, 33
fragmented groups, 163
friendly groups, 23

game theory, 22
Gandhi, Rajiv, assassination, 163
Garo Hills, 79, 81
Garo National Liberation Army (GNLA), 17, 58, 75–79, 82, 172
   militants of, 80
   violent campaign, 2012, 79
Garoland, 77
global jihadist movement, 3
Global Terrorism Database (GTD), 4, 17, 44, 59–61, 75, 107
GNLA-ULFA camp, 84
governmental bureaucracy, 98
Great Western Development Drive, 131
grievances, 125, 126, 169, 235, 238
   endogenous, 210
   microfoundations of, 129
   modeling endogenous, 133
   reduction, 165, 166, 168
   resolving, 187
gross domestic product (GDP), 110
group competition, 149
group elimination, 226
group recruitment processes, 90, 96
group-level violence, 72
guerrilla war, 162

Hagel, Chuck, 27
Hamas, 10, 26, 148
Han cultural assimilation, 131
happiness, 132
Hezb-e Islami Gulbuddin, 172
Hezbollah, 75
Hui, 131
Hutus, 65
Hynniewtrep National Liberation Council (HNLC), 78
hyperviolent individuals, 26

ideological positioning, 43
incentive compatibility issues, 148
incentives, 15, 227
Indian terrorist groups, 75
indiscriminate violence, 93
individual violence, 39
individual-level incentives, 58
inequality, 125, 233
insurgency in Northeast India, 74
interdisciplinary avenues, 233
intergroup competition, 3, 4, 13, 90, 93, 96
intergroup cooperation, 9
intergroup violence, 24, 93
international attacks, 107
International Civil Aviation Organization (ICAO), 177
International Country Risk Guide (ICRG), 108
International Monetary Fund, 66
international organizations, 129
   competition, 224
international organizations and group elimination, 152
International Security Assistance Force (ISAF), 119
   Afghanistan, 173
internationalized intrastate conflict, 66
interstate war, 152
intra/inter-group conflict, 60
intrastate conflict, 66
Iraq, 170
   Afghanistan, war termination, 152
   militant attacks, 65
   military force, withdrawing, 151
Iraq War, 151
Irish National Liberation Army, 91
Isak-Muivah faction (NSCN-IM), 85
Islamic Movement of Uzbekistan, 172
Islamic Salvation Army (AIS), 90
Islamic State in Iraq and al-Sham (ISIS), 1, 175, 226, 234
   beheadings of abductees, 25, 27
   brutality, 2
   Foley kidnapping, 27
   Foley's beheading, 28
   Mosul and Raqqa defeat, 3
   oil with, 171
   Paris attacks, 2
   recruitment, ability to, 175
   Sotloff beheading, 28
   violence, style of, 26

Islamic State violence, 26
Islamist guerrillas, 91
Islamists, 65

Jabhat al-Nusra (JN), 1, 173, 226, 232
Jemaah Islamiyah, 30
jihadis, 172

Karbi National Liberation Army, 75
Kassig, Peter, 28
Kazakhs, 131
Khaplang faction (NSCN-K), 85
Khasi tribe, 78
Khorasan Province, 173
Kirghiz, 131
Kuki National Front (KNF), 87
Kuki National Organization (KNO), 87

large-n quantitative analysis, 230
Lebanese Civil War, 75
Lebanon, 132
legitimization, 163
Liberation Tigers of Tamil Eelam (LTTE),
    162
Luxor massacre, 44

Madrid train bombings, 151
Manipur authorities, 87
mass beheadings, 2
Medvedev, Dmitry, 170
Meghalaya, India, 75–77
    Chokpot killing, 84
    Tura bomb blast, 78
Meiteis, 86, 87
microfoundations, 232
militant groups, 4
    competition, 3, 4, 6, 8, 10, 14, 19, 29,
        137, 141
    defensive measures, 165
    goals, 23
    offensive measures, 165
    political organization, 24
    violence, 5, 6
militant Tamil youth movements, 162
modeling endogenous grievances, 133
Mountbatten, assassination of, 91, 94
Mujahideen, 132
multi-dimensional insurgency, 17
multi-faceted insurgencies, 88
Mumin, mujahidin, Abdiqadir, 2
Muttahida Qaumi Movement, 131

Naga and Kuki groups, 77
Naga Rengma Hills Protection Force
    (NRHPF), 75
Nagaland, India, 76
Nagas, 86, 87
Nash equilibrium, 181
National Socialist Council of Nagaland
    (NSCN), 17, 58, 85
negative binomial approach, 67, 111
negative payoff, 99
NexisUni media database of stories, 28
nonomotonicity of violence, 160
Northern Ireland, 91

Obama, Barack, 171, 172
offensive military operations, 31
offensive operations, 171
operational security, 30
operationalization, 111
operationalizations of outbidding, 146
opiates in Afghanistan, 171
Optimal Political Violence, 103
optimal violence level, 179
organization's welfare, 149
Oromo Liberation Front, 228
outbidding, 9–11, 14, 15, 17, 20, 21, 38,
    40, 49, 88, 97, 117, 127, 129,
    145–147, 162, 223
    competition, 155
    contest models, 21
    empirical analysis, 97
    hypothesis, 58, 59, 63, 71
    incentives, 49, 187
    literature, 105
    operationalizations, 146
    political violence, 22
    violence, 154, 229
outbidding-as-deterrence, 145
outbidding–terrorism link, 59
overaggregation, 233

Pakistan, 131
Palestine, 147
Palestinian Islamic Jihad (PIJ), 10
Palestinian statehood, 10
Paris attacks, 2
partial equilibrium analysis, 185
payoff utility function, 33
payoffs, 98–100, 134
peace processes, 12
People's Liberation Army (PLA), 85

per-group violence, 15, 40
physical integrity rights, 66, 69, 72, 114, 169
plane hijacking, 174
political competition, 8
political protest, 26
political violence, 4, 6, 10, 12, 18, 20–22, 26, 31, 32, 35, 111, 130, 147, 156, 222, 232
  audience for, 230
  competition, 20, 222, 233
  entrepreneurs, 20, 170
  marketplace, 162
  model, 31
  offensive measures, 171
  organizations, 92, 117
  waging, 226
poverty, 125
power distributions, 24, 135
principal–agent problems, 187
prisoner's dilemma situations, 37, 228
probability density function, 99
probability distribution, 135
psychological science, 233
public backlash, 44

Qamlishi, 236
quantitative empirics, 57

radicalization, 144
rebel groups, 69
reconciliation, 126
recruitment by militant groups, 95
regime durability, 109–111, 113, 116, 117
regime quality, 116
regional autonomy, 132
relative political reach, 109, 111, 113, 114, 116, 117
religious fractionalization, 66
repression, 134
resources
  acquisition, 25
  pool of, 23
revenue, 37
risk-neutral actors, 98
rivals, 23
robustness, 116
robustness tests, 74
Rohingya-dominated areas in Malaysia, 169
Royal Ulster Constabulary (RUC), 95

Rummel's conception, 130

San Bernardino attack, 152
Sangma, Champion, 77, 81, 82
Sangma, Conrad, 79
Sangma, Josbina, 84
Sangma, Mukul, 78
Sangma, Pakchara, 77
Second Intifada in Israel, 26
second-order effect, 224
security measures, 175
self-preservation, 9
Sharia law, 93
Shira, Sohan, 77, 79, 81, 83
Sinjar massacre, 2
sister states, India, 77
social services, 130
social solidarity, 132
Sohan, Sirhan, 80
Somalia, 163
Sotloff, Steven, 28
South Asia Terrorism Portal, 76
Sri Lanka, 162, 163
Stackelberg competition, 168
standard contest model, 49
state capacity, 66
state enforcement, 93
  costs, 113
state enforcement capacities, 106, 107
state's equilibrium effort, 100
strategic groups, 22
structural equation model (SEM), 117
students, 65
subgame perfect equilibria, 100, 103
suicide attacks, 26, 162
suicide bombers, 30
suicide terrorism, 162
Sunningdale Agreement, 1973, 94
Surviving, 25
Syria
  prewar repression, 126
  rivalry in, 2
Syrian Civil War, 1, 27, 28, 61, 125, 126, 176, 226, 236

Taliban, 119, 128, 131, 172
Tamil Tigers, 46
Tammo, Mashaal, assassination, 236
tax revenue, 114
terrorism
  coercion and, 148

disincentivize, 204
effectiveness of, 128, 148, 149
price of, 129
socioeconomic roots, 170
terrorism-as-public-goods, 131
terrorist
incentives, 174
terrorist attacks, 7, 31, 59, 75, 128
cost, 30
GIA involved in, 90
terrorist competition, 97, 111, 113
terrorist groups, 15, 61, 68, 69, 107, 162
terrorist organizations, 1, 106, 107, 113, 169
terrorist violence, 106, 113
theories of interstate rivalry, 8
third-order effect, 224
threat of violence, 134
Tigrayan People's Liberation Front, 228
total tax revenue, 110
tradeoffs, 15, 142, 154, 197, 232
transnational terrorists, 130, 170
Tullock model, 34, 35

US counterterrorism policy, 172
US National Strategy for Combating Terrorism, 130, 170
US–Afghanistan War, 172
UN Refugee Agency (UNHCR), 169
UN's Office of Counter-Terrorism, 176
United Achik Liberation Army (UALA), 82, 84
United Committee of Manipur (UCM), 86
United Dimasa Kachari Liberation Front, 75
United Karbi People's Front, 75
United Liberation Front of Assam (ULFA), 80, 82
United Nations Development Programme (UNDP), 169
United Nations Security Council, 119
United Nations Security Council Resolution, 1373, 170
United People's Liberation Army, 75
United People's Liberation Front, 75
Unlawful Activities (Prevention) Act, 79
Uppsala Conflict Data Program (UCDP), 4, 63, 79
USS Cole bombing, 24
utility function, 33

van Gogh, Theo, 151
violence, 8, 9, 12, 13, 16, 28, 34, 149, 165, 184
advertisements, 20
allocation, 22, 32
audience's willingness to support, 225
citizen contributors, 150
competition and, 138
competitive, 93, 142
competitive incentives, 97
control variables, 110
corner/complete cutpoint, 210
cost, 30, 31, 33, 35, 136, 151
cutpoint, 212
decision, 36
decline in, 41, 81
disincentivize, 194
empirical analysis, 111
endogenous marginal cost, 217
enforcement capacity, 104
equilibrium, 145
financial resources, 33
groups, number of, 37, 139
increase in, 58, 223
incumbents, 166
junkies, 26
level, 165
market of, 29
marketplace of, 24
mitigation, 235
monotonic reduction in, 202
motivators of, 131
nonmonotonic, 48, 139
nonomotonicity of, 160
optimal levels, 179
outputs, 29
overproduction, 166, 182
Palestinian groups, 10
prevalence, 183
production, 29, 36, 224
public displays of, 31
rates, 132
recruitment tactics, 90
reduction, 137, 187
rent-seeking activity, 228
returns, 27
Taliban, 128
threat of, 134
utility of, 27
violence model, 97
mass citizens, 97

militant groups, 97
　optimal citizen contributions, 101
　optimal political violence, 103
　optimal state enforcement, 100
　state, 97
violence-as-advertisement, 22, 25
violent attacks, 57, 61
violent campaigns, 61
violent non-state actors, 177
vulnerability, 132

War on Terror, 167, 198
wars in Iraq and Syria, 29
Weinberger, Caspar, 132
Whac-a-Mole, 8, 167, 172, 173, 195, 198,
　199

Wirth, Tim, 172
World Trade Center bombing, 172

Xinjiang, China, 131
　economy, 131

Yazidi civilians massacre, 2

Zeliangrong United Front (ZUF), 86
zero attacks, 107
zero terrorist attacks, 70
zero terrorist groups, 111
zero-inflated negative binomial models, 71
zero-sum benefit, 23
zero-sum competition, 9
zero-sum game, 25

Printed in the United States
by Baker & Taylor Publisher Services